MW00576427

John Henry
A Biography
Faulk

— *Courtesy Alan Pogue*

The Making of a Liberated Mind

John Henry

A Biography

Faulk

By

Michael C. Burton

EAKIN PRESS ★ Austin, Texas

The language and descriptions used in quoted material in this book do not necessarily reflect the personal views or opinions of the author and are used for the purpose of authenticity.

FIRST EDITION

Copyright © 1993
By Michael C. Burton

Published in the United States of America
By Eakin Press
A Division of Sunbelt Media, Inc.
P.O. Drawer 90159 ★ Austin, TX 78709-0159

ISBN 0-89015-923-8

Library of Congress Cataloging-in-Publication Data

Burton, Michael C.
    John Henry Faulk : the making of a liberated mind / by Michael C. Burton –1st ed.
        p.   cm.
    Includes bibliographical references (p.) and index.
    ISBN 0-89015-923-8 : $19.95
    1. Faulk, John Henry. 2. Authors, American–20th century–Biography. 3. Blacklisting of entertainers–United States. 4. Blacklisting of authors–United States.
5. Entertainers–United States–Biography. 6. Trials (Libel)– New York (N.Y.)
I. Title.
PS3556.A92Z59   1993
818'.5409–dc20
[B]   93-30091
                                                                              CIP

This book is dedicated
to my mother and father,
who instilled in me
the value of a liberated mind.

Contents

Preface   vii

Acknowledgments   xi

Introduction   xv

1. Miss Mattie and Judge Faulk   1
2. Greener Pastures   11
3. Formation of a Raconteur   29
4. Professor Pancho and the Folklore Renaissance   40
5. The Struggle for Equality   56
6. Fighting Fascism   65
7. Johnny's Front Porch   78
8. CBS Personality   98
9. Blacklisting: Conform or Else!   111
10. Aware's Assault   133
11. The Public Pariah   150
12. John Henry's Legacy   171

Afterword   177

Appendix: Selected Letters by John Henry Faulk   185

Notes   191

Bibliography   201

Index   207

Preface

One afternoon, I was copying some photographs of John Henry Faulk I planned to use for this book. A man in his late thirties to early forties walked next to me to use the adjacent copier. Leaning over, he noticed the photo of John Henry with Edward R. Murrow. "I beg your pardon," he said. "What are these photographs? Who is this man?" He was pointing to Faulk.

"That's John Henry Faulk," I said, waiting to see any glimmer of recognition in the man's eyes, but none came.

"Who is he?"

I launched into my standard, brief description of what Faulk was known to the masses for: He was a *Hee Haw* fixture for years; he was a popular radio talk show host in New York in the 1950s; he was blacklisted. Before I could say anything more about how he stood up to his accusers by taking them to court, he interrupted me: "Why was he blacklisted? What did he do? Was he a communist?"

"He spoke his mind."

"But what was he mostly known for?" he asked.

I paused, disturbed that he had changed the subject.

"Storytelling," I said.

The man looked as if he were pacified by this sound-bite answer to his question. But before he wandered away, I told him to read Faulk's book, *Fear on Trial*, first published by Simon and Schuster in 1963.

Versions of this conversation occurred many times while I was working on this book. Some were with intelligent, politically aware people who had never heard of John Henry Faulk or didn't understand why artists were blacklisted in the 1940s and 50s. The incredible thing about their perception of blacklisting is that a person must have "done something" wrong to get blacklisted;

that he or she must have demonstrated unpatriotism in some way. The easiest thing to tell these people, who didn't know about the history of McCarthyism, was that people were blacklisted for holding unpopular views.

Less easy to answer, however, was the question "Who is John Henry Faulk?" That question was what led me to write this book. Raconteur? Humorist? Philosopher? Entertainer? Satirist? Writer? Political activist? First Amendment scholar? Not even John Henry, when I asked him what *he* thought of himself, could answer. "I don't know. What do you think of me as?" he asked. I guess that the answer lay in the person asking the question.

To many, John Henry was simply a fine storyteller, chronicling the stories of friends and relatives he met through the years. To others, he was an actor and impersonator, who could impeccably mimic the speech and mannerisms of people. Many saw him as a masterful satirist, one who used his cutting humor to expose the ultra-patriots and the ignorant racists for what they were. To others, he personified the meaning and intent of the First Amendment because he had the courage to speak his mind and dissent against the prevailing views of the day.

"He was a pioneer in protecting freedom of speech and expression," said the late Broadway producer Joseph Paap.

"A lot of people will remember him for his humor, wit and country boy charm," said humorist Steve Allen. "But when I think of him, I think of his courage."

"He makes agitation respectable," said actress Ruby Dee. "Like agitation in a washing machine — how else will the clothes get clean?"

In 1990, the last year of Faulk's life, such accolades were profusely heaped upon him. Although not undeserved, I wanted to look beyond the praises and examine his character, and what events and people had helped to shape that feisty character in his early years. To do so, I had to probe his roots: his relationship with his parents, sisters, and close friends; his development as a child; his motivations in his thinking and the way he perceived the world. I hope that another book can be written about the last third of Faulk's life, which was filled with political activism and stage acting. This book is not a collection of John Henry's stories or character sketches (much of which is detailed elsewhere). Instead, it is an exploration of the major influences on his life.

Such an exploration was not made without difficulty: many close to John Henry were extremely protective of him, even three years after his death. This is understandable, because I agree with writer Virginia Durr, who told me that "John Henry was the most endearing character I've ever known." Anyone who knew him for any length of time would find it difficult not to be pulled in by that "puckish charm," as Molly Ivins said — a charm that used such Southern colloquialisms as "honey" and "angel" as expressions of friendship. He was opinionated without being dogmatic; warm and caring without being maudlin; direct and honest without being insolent.

What I found interesting about John Henry was that his "country boy" demeanor belied a powerful intellect, phenomenal memory, and keen sense of human nature. He had an uncanny ability not only to mimic the personalities he'd known, but also the ability to strip the superfluous part of their personalities down to their essentials. Through his performances, one could see some of the more dynamic and forceful characters in his life, and come away with a deeper sense of the human condition. The regrettable aspect of this was that the majority of Americans were deprived of this talent after his career in the entertainment business was destroyed.

Through my research of John Henry's personal papers and letters he wrote to his mentors, J. Frank Dobie and Roy Bedichek, I came to understand John Henry the man (versus John Henry the folk myth) much better. Exhilarated by these men, John Henry strove to live his life fulfilling their shared ideal — the ideal of being a free and independent thinker, a person who could question traditional mores and ideas without fear of persecution. John Henry Faulk meant many things to many people, but to me, he meant the opposite of demagoguery: the ability to have an open mind in exploring new ideas and questioning traditional ways of thinking. As he once said to Dobie and Bedichek:

"My devoutest ambition is to retain a youthful, inquiring mind, as you gentlemen have, until I shuffle off this mortal coil. Then, regardless of what has befallen me in the material world, I shall have lived well."

John Henry Faulk lived well.

Acknowledgments

There are several people I wish to thank for their kind assistance in developing this book:

Dr. Frederick Williams, director at the University of Texas at Austin's Center for Research on Communication and Technology, who advised me on my book proposal.

Texas authors Mike Cox and Jim Haley, both who gave me much needed advice and encouragement in the initial development of the book.

Joe Froh, who gave me understanding and time to work on this.

Anne McAfee, John Henry's niece, who read the manuscript and provided invaluable help in checking historical facts.

Ken Oden, Travis County attorney, who aided in detailed research on "Judge" Henry Faulk.

Don Carleton, director of the Center for American History at the University of Texas at Austin, whom John Henry trusted and respected.

Mattie Sink, manuscript librarian at Mississippi State University's Mitchell Memorial Library, who developed the inventory of the Faulk Papers.

John Wheat and Ralph Elder, and the rest of the staff at the Center for American History.

John Pope, who wrote an excellent master's thesis on blacklisting at the University of Texas and gave me many leads and much insight into the period.

Max Nofziger, who supported the project in its infancy.

Charles Ward, a fellow journalist with much more experience!

Marge Hershey, who provided some valuable sources.

Dr. Doug Kellner, who provided videotapes of "Alternative Views."

Ed Eakin, a publisher who's committed to progressive writing and writers.

Melissa Sinclair Stevens, who saw this project through with me and provided much encouragement *and* valuable editorial criticism.

Other people I should thank for their input into this project are Alan Pogue, Don Gardner, Bob Rosenbaum, Michael Green, Steve Speir, Shannon Sedwick, John Williams, Cynthia Bock-Goodner, Steve Carr, and Saundra Shohen.

And many thanks go to John Henry's widow, Liz, and his family, without whom this book could not have been written.

"And little David started feeling something move in his arms and in his heart. Stole off down that tent where old King Saul sitting there holding his head in his hand. Little David walk in and say, 'King Saul, old King Saul,' he said, 'don't nobody else want to fight that giant man Goliath? Let me have a go at him. He might look like tall timber to you boys, but he look like brush to me. And I'll chop him off even with the ground this morning."

—John Henry Faulk,
from "Ten Negro Sermons"

Introduction

Texas political writer Molly Ivins, who owes much of her skill at satire and salty prose to John Henry Faulk, often introduced him to many Texas audiences. She has one favorite story about Faulk that illustrates a salient point.

"Many of you may not know," she said at a gathering of Texas journalists in 1989, "that this particular freedom fighter didn't hit just one lick in behalf of these principles, and has been fighting for what is good and right and just ever since, right here on the grounds, in Austin, Texas. I'll explain about the story I'm going to tell you.

"About two years ago, I got a call from someone in the Central Texas Office of the American Civil Liberties Union. [This person] was highly upset, and said she needed my help urgently, to save the First Amendment from the Austin City Planning Commission. I said, 'damn,' as we all know the First Amendment is under fairly steady fire in this state, but I had not previously counted the City Planning Commission among the forces of jackbooted fascism.

"But as some of you know, we have here in Austin, Texas, a fundamentalist divine, the Reverend Mark Weaver, who is hell-bent on driving sin out of Austin, Texas — he has his life's work cut out for him. Well, the Reverend Weaver was particularly upset that he formed the 'Citizens Against Pornography,' who march up and down dirty bookstores with signs saying 'honk if you hate pornography' (I always honk when I go by — I *hate* pornography).

"But, Weaver and the Citizens Against Pornography had come up with a zoning ordinance, a scheme of the provisions of which were you could not have the dirty bookstores or movie theatre within so many feet of a church or a school or a neighborhood. The upshot would be that it would drive all the dirty book-stores and movie theatres out of Austin, Texas — a terrible loss to the civic, cultural life, as we all realize.

"When [the ACLU people] said, 'Well, this is a First Amend-ment issue,' well, it's one thing being a feminist civil libertarian — and I do hate to defend dirty bookstores and pornography — but somebody has to do it. So I agreed that I would show up there. And, as you all know, the Central Texas chapter is not a mighty organization ... there were five of us from the Civil Liberties Union; there were 450 people with Citizens Against Pornography.

"So, we were all huddled, we civil libertarians, kind of like an island in the middle of this sea of Citizens Against. And I will tell you that there's nothing like sitting in the middle of this sea of Citizens Against Pornography to make you notice that your friends all look like perverts.

"And Reverend Weaver spoke first. For those of you all who had not had the pleasure of hearing him, he is a very fine preacher, and he started off right away. He had gotten a call the very day before from a lady who lived behind that dirty movie theatre on South Congress Avenue — 'I know it well, it is my neighborhood dirty movie theatre.' And, after the five o'clock show, a man came out of that theatre, went into an alley behind that theatre, which is also right behind that lady's house, and there ... masturbated. Four-hundred-and-fifty people simulta-neously went *'Uuugghhh!'* It made a very odd noise. And she said: 'Reverend Weaver, he masturbated behind my house!'

" 'Yes,' the Reverend Mark Weaver continued, 'that man *masturbated* right there in the alley, right behind that lady's house. And she has two little girls who might have seen it — if it weren't for the wooden fence around her yard." And with that, he was off and runnin'. He was on a tear, he was on a job; he was just chasin' sin around one side and the other. And by the time he got through, it looked bad for the First Amendment.

"So the guys on the Planning Commission were all standing up there looking mighty depressed at Reverend Weaver. So we huddled, and decided to send up as our first 'batter' the 'Rev-erend' Faulk, who went to the microphone, congenially and sweetly, doing his well-known impersonation of an elderly South-ern gentleman, and said:

" 'Ladies and gentlemen of the Planning Commission, Reverend Weaver, Citizens Against, ladies and gentlemen: my name is John Henry Faulk. I am seventy-four years old. I was born and raised in South Austin, Texas — not a quarter of a mile from where the dirty movie theatre stands on Congress Avenue. And I think you all should know, there was a *great deal* of masturbation in South Austin long before there was ever a dirty movie theatre there.' "

Ivins' story of Faulk's appearance before the Planning Commission was told and retold many times when she frequently introduced him before civic, cultural, and professional groups. Faulk returned to address the Austin City Council on the sticky question of pornography on September 4, 1986. In that meeting, he was nothing but serious in his defense of the First Amendment:

"Out in South Austin in 1927, as a member of the Methodist Church and the son of a very pious pillar in that church, I became alarmed as Brother Culpepper described to us the imminent choruses of Austin becoming Sodom and Gomorrah on the Colorado. The burden of his song was that the sins that were going on at the University of Texas — women were bobbing their hair and smearing their faces with lipstick and dancing the Charleston to all hours of the night — was resulting in a loss to the morality of Austin life that would very soon become chaotic.

"Then, to prove his point, he cited the instance of some little school boys — and I was one of them going home from Fulmore School down on Johanna Street — who discovered, under the Johanna Street Bridge off South First Street, several four-letter words chalked up. He said it has hit our youth and our youth is caving in (and the fact that you had to crawl down a barbed wire fence and slip down an embankment and wade the water to see those words didn't matter to Reverend Culpepper). He and others undertook to get my father, who was a lawyer, to draft an ordinance against this.

"Daddy examined their complaints — that you couldn't stop dancing at the University of Texas, which was what their aim was. It was just a cesspool of atheism and nastiness out there and they were determined to dance and there's nothing you could do about it, without doing violence to the First Amendment and to the Constitution.

"Daddy shared their concerns over the loss of morality in Austin, but felt that damaging the First Amendment of the Constitution in order to protect us against sin and ugliness, was like cutting a man's heart out to reduce his blood pressure. And that's what I wanted to speak to you about tonight because I'm very alarmed over this whole tendency in our society.

"We're celebrating the 200th anniversary of our Constitution — it was drawn up in September of 1787, and then there was a cry that it wouldn't be ratified because the people were jealous of their individual freedoms; that this Republic couldn't stand without them, and they would not accept a Constitution without a Bill of Rights.

"I saw a Gallup Poll that showed that eighty-five percent of Americans do not recognize the First Amendment — they didn't know whether it was a city ordinance or a state law or a federal law. That certainly alarmed me.

"The First Amendment was the prime jewel of the Crown of Liberty — the fuel that would carry this Republic down through history. James Madison said, 'I am writing this as a mandate,' because anything of lesser force cannot survive the up-tides of history. Crises will come up, like the crisis we see in Austin today, which is perceived by some to be a crisis of pornography and smut. This ordinance is not about pornography and smut; it is basically an assault on the First Amendment of the United States Constitution. Therein lies its danger.

"Thirty years ago we were told by Senator Joe McCarthy that this country was threatened by a conspiracy — a huge international communist conspiracy that took the form of running its long hand right up to the White House. We discovered that what it actually was was a means of shutting off the dialogue — the very life's breath of a self-governing democratic society such as ours.

"And when we do that, shut off the dialogue, we do violence to the First Amendment and to the children of this generation and the next generation, in far greater measure than any porno house or disgusting 'adult movie' theatre."

A tireless defender and supporter of the Bill of Rights, John Henry Faulk brought the meaning and relevance of the First

Amendment alive to thousands of people. He did so because he was involved in a long, life-and-death struggle that reinforced the crucial importance of those freedoms. Perhaps more than any single American, his fight brought an end to an ugly, repressive period in our history. But, as he would have reminded us, the same thing could happen again, if we don't fight to preserve those freedoms.

1.

MISS MATTIE
AND
JUDGE FAULK

I n 1870, after the Civil War had devastated much of the economy of the South, a roving tenant farmer named Henry Lafayette Faulk and his wife, Lucy Card Faulk, moved their family in a covered ox wagon from Clio, Alabama, to Henderson County, Texas. The Faulks, descended from the French Huguenot family who came to the United States to escape religious persecution, lived in several small Texas towns, farming and clearing other people's lands. One of the sons, born in 1868, was named Henry.

Lucy Card Faulk was twenty years old when Henry was born. In 1885, when Henry was seventeen, the Faulks moved to the West Texas town of Brownwood. The eldest of nine children, Henry bore a strong sense of responsibility for the rest of the family. To raise money, he worked all day on the farm and at night would go to a janitorial job at a hotel. The manual work was unpleasant: The hotel lacked a sewage system, and Henry's job was to collect all the slop jars from each room and empty them.

At the hotel, Henry met two old schoolteachers from an affluent ranching family in Coleman, Texas. They took an interest

1

in this bright, congenial boy and wanted to educate him. Henry, seeing that his father's effort to make a living as a migrant farmer would never lead them out of poverty, determined to succeed where his father had failed. He read every book the teachers gave him over the next six years. He dreamed of owning his own small farm.

The teacher discovered that an affluent state senator and lobbyist for the railroad interests, J. J. Faulk, was a distant cousin of Henry's father. They wrote the senator a letter soliciting his help to find work for Henry to enable him to attend college at the University of Texas at Austin. They offered to prepare Henry for college and buy him some decent clothes if J. J. Faulk would find him a job. The senator obligingly found Henry a job as a clerk at the university library.

In 1889 Henry moved to Austin and enrolled at the university three years later. About 25,000 people lived in the capital city. It was still a frontier town. Most residents had no indoor toilets, and most lived without electricity and running water. The only brick-paved streets in the city were on Congress Avenue and on one or two blocks of Sixth Street. Gamblers, horse traders, and Indians roamed the outskirts of the city, and ladies of the evening inhabited a large portion of downtown along Congress Avenue between First and Sixth streets known as "Guy Town." The chief forms of entertainment in the city were circuses, horse races, and medicine shows. That year also marked the construction of the new Texas Capitol.

The University of Texas had opened its Main Building in 1883. Henry saw the chance for a stable future with his schooling at the university. He became a member of the prestigious Rusk Literary Society, in which he debated social and political issues of the day. After a couple years of general courses, he entered the school's first law program in 1894, living above a livery stable while studying.

When Henry graduated from the university in 1896, less than 400 students were enrolled. He quickly passed his bar exam and soon became a very able trial lawyer. He had an innate ability to tell anecdotes and dramatize events. His bright wit and unique idioms from the sharecroppers' world appealed to both juries and audiences. This folksy talk and unique style of imitating the other parties involved in a case proved effective in swaying juries. As his name and face became known in Austin, it wasn't long before the sagacious Henry Faulk was encouraged to run for a political office. In 1900 he ran for Travis County attorney, defeating incumbent George C. Calhoun.[1]

At that time the Travis County attorney was the only prosecuting attorney in the county; there was no district attorney. Much of "Judge Faulk's" (as many called him) time as county attorney was spent amassing evidence against the Waters-Pierce Oil Company, a subsidiary of John D. Rockefeller's Standard Oil Company. At the turn of the century, Texas imported almost all of its oil from Appalachia and the Midwest. The company that controlled most of the state's supply was Waters-Pierce, selling over ninety percent of the oil in the entire Southwest in the 1880s and 1890s. Waters-Pierce maintained this monopoly in Texas through intimidating other competitors, selling below cost to run out other smaller oil companies, and exacting secret, illegal rebates from merchants that agreed to carry only Standard Oil products. Waters-Pierce officials maintained their company was not part of the Standard Oil conglomerate, although they purchased much of their petroleum from Standard Oil refineries. Standard Oil was already in trouble for violating the United States Congress' recently passed Sherman Anti-Trust Act. That law defined a "trust" as a combination or cartel that restrained trade, fixed prices, hampered competition, or entered into anti-competitive contracts.[2]

Texas had a proud heritage of being an anti-monopoly state, with anti-monopoly declarations written into its state constitution. In 1889 it had became the second state in the nation to enact its own legislation against monopoly. The state's legislators got this sense of proud tradition of independence from those who had fought at the Alamo and San Jacinto. Monopolies, according to state law, were "contrary to the genius of a free government, and shall never be allowed."

Henry Faulk also believed in this essential tenet about monopolies and large corporations. Cartels, he believed, were inherently anti-human, because they couldn't possibly consider the human factor – only the profit motive. In 1901 Henry found that the Waters-Pierce Oil Company officials, who had recently reorganized the company in order to do legal business in Texas, had never signed a required affidavit declaring compliance with the state's anti-trust law. What Henry and others did not know was that Standard Oil had a plan to thwart the anti-trust law by secretly retaining 2,748 shares of Waters-Pierce stock.

Henry went to Texas Attorney General Charles Bell, who, in conjunction with him, filed charges against Waters-Pierce. Henry tried to extract penalties from the company under the 1899 legislation, but a trial court acquitted the them. That was only the beginning of the Waters-Pierce controversy, which embroiled a popular and influential U.S. senator from Texas, Joe Bailey. Bailey had previously attested to Governor Joseph Sayers that Waters-Pierce was not controlled by Standard Oil, but neglected to mention that he took large "loans" from the company and ran interference for them with the Texas attorney general.

About this time, on a visit to Webberville, a small town about twelve miles east of Austin near Bastrop, Henry was invited to dinner at the home of Oscar and Janie Miner Downs. There he met Janie's younger sister, Martha. Called "Mattie," she was the fifth of six children born to Ashford Tannehill Miner and Medora Murrell Jones. The Tannehill family, like many of the early Central Texas pioneers, had settled in this land just east of Austin with a 4,400-acre land grant from the Mexican government.

Henry was immediately struck with Mattie's deep, black eyes and sensitive nature, calling her "the prettiest woman south of St. Louis." She, likewise, was attracted to this auburn-haired, blue-eyed lawyer from Austin. For the next few months, Henry made many more trips by horse and buggy to Webberville. During these several months of courting, the couple discovered they had much in common. Both were Democrats and both devout Methodists. Mattie shared Henry's penchant for education. She taught elementary school at Hornsby Bend near Webberville. She had lost her mother early in her life, and she and her five brothers and sisters had been reared by their maternal grandmother.[3] After many visits and romantic letters sent from Austin and Webberville, the two married on September 15, 1902. They bought a house near the university, on 20th and Oldham (where Red River is today). There they would live for thirteen years.

Shortly after the wedding, Henry lost his re-election bid for Travis County attorney. Running on the nonpartisan ticket against Democrat John Brady, Henry lost in part because he aroused the ire of prominent Austinites who indulged in illegal gambling and because he offended the local newspaper, the *Austin Daily Statesman*. He criticized the paper for plugging certain candidates in its news stories; in particular, he decried the paper's method of printing cards that included their written endorsements.

Henry campaigned in favor of women's right to vote. He also campaigned strongly against the town's red-light district. He took the position, still controversial today, that if Austin really wanted to wipe out its red-light district, then all it had to do was to apprise and pressure the city proprietors and state legislators who frequented there.

After losing the election, Henry resumed his private practice on a full-time basis, building a reputation as a trial lawyer. He also managed and published a daily newspaper, the *Austin Daily Tribune*, for two years (1906–1907). Austin sustained several fledgling daily newspapers around the turn of the century, including the *Austin American*, which would go through various names. *The Tribune*, established in 1898, carried cartoons, religious columns, and news of city politics, Texas history, and "affairs at the University of Texas." [4]

Henry's private law firm played an important role in the prosecution of Waters-Pierce and the other Standard Oil companies, which included Security Oil Company, Navarro Refining Company, and Union Tank Line Company. By mid-1906, both Standard Oil's control of Waters-Pierce and the illegal loans to Bailey were common knowledge. On September 10, 1906, Waters-Pierce President Henry Clay-Pierce took the stand in Missouri and publicly admitted that Standard Oil controlled his company. On September 20, 1906, Texas filed another suit against Waters-Pierce, demanding revocation of the company's business permit. The suit went to trial before a district court jury in Austin in May 1907. On June 30, 1907, the jury found the company guilty on eighteen counts. [5]

The company's assets were seized and it was prohibited from doing business in Texas. The fines totaled a whopping

$1.623 million, upheld by the U.S. Supreme Court (which broke up Standard Oil's monopoly in 1911, creating Exxon and other companies that thrive today). Henry received national publicity for his role in the case. He was among the state entourage (which included the bank officials, the district judge who tried the case, the county attorney, the state treasurer, other lawyers and elected officials) that paraded down Congress Avenue in August 1909 with an automobile full of $1.6 million in cash, escorted by a guard of mounted peace officers.[6]

Thanks to a provision in Texas anti-trust law that granted the prosecuting attorneys a twenty-five percent share of a judgment, Henry and his partner, J. M. Patterson, made a substantial sum when the money was received. With this notoriety in the community, Henry soon found himself invited to the Governor's Mansion and to various political functions.[7] This popularity made him somewhat uncomfortable, because by now he was beginning to adopt a different political philosophy from that of his fellow Democrats.

Henry Faulk found truth in the philosophy of democratic socialism. Before the Bolshevik Revolution launched communism, America was the home of active social reformers such as Eugene Debs (1855-1926), the founder of the American Socialist Party in 1901 and one of the great liberal orators in American history. With the advent of industrial capitalism in U.S. society, the relationship of the haves to the have-nots was becoming starkly apparent to Henry, and he became convinced that the exploitation of the huge majority of the American people was a result of an unjust economic system. He studied and became a student of Debs' philosophy of pacifism and industrial unionism. Debs believed in the transfer of power from the corporate elite, who controlled the means of production, to the working people, who produced society's wealth. At least seventeen socialist newspapers were published in Texas between 1912 and 1918,[8] and Henry read some of them. He subscribed to *The Social-Democratic Herald* and *The Appeal to Reason*. He came to know Debs by helping with one of his five U.S. presidential campaigns, and invited him to speak at the old Hancock Opera House in Austin. Debs accepted the invitation.[9]

By most accounts, Debs was an electrifying speaker, "a

compelling, commanding force." During his speeches, which lasted more than two hours, he often challenged the assumptions and perceptions of his audience, particularly on the issue of racial integration and prejudice. Unlike other Socialist Party leaders, who excluded blacks from the party, Debs broke the color barrier by speaking out for racial desegregation and an end to prejudice, which led to Henry's keen interest in his politics. In 1894 Debs forcefully insisted that the American Railway Union abolish the color line. In 1903 he argued that "there is no Negro problem apart from the general labor problem" and expressed hope that in the South racial prejudice would soon disappear. In 1904 he attacked Thomas Dixon's popular racist novel, *The Leopard's Spots*, for its assumption that "one race was created to be the bondsmen of another race." And in 1916 he condemned D. W. Griffith's racist movie, *Birth of a Nation*.[10]

Debs once told his audience that racism in America created "a false and pernicious civilization." If Christ were to return, he said, "the Galilean carpenter would . . . scorn and lash the pharisees who profess to be his followers while . . . they exercise their despotic and damnable (racial) domination."[11]

Twice, in 1912 and 1914, Henry ran for Texas attorney general on the socialist ticket. The last public office he ran for was for associate justice of the Texas Supreme Court in 1920, the same year Debs ran his last campaign for U.S. president. Henry's interest was mainly in political issues, not political campaigning. His daughter Mary remembered him saying, "If everybody who told you they were going to vote for you voted for you, you'd always be elected."[12]

Henry also led an Austin campaign to free labor leader Tom Mooney, a member of the International Workers of the World in California who was imprisoned in San Quentin for allegedly planting a bomb at San Francisco's Preparedness Day Parade in 1916. Although the evidence against him was weak at best (and may indeed have been a frame-up), he was convicted for life, and socialists around America rallied around the cause to release him. Henry displayed signs in his office that read "Free Tom Mooney" and wrote letters to government officials on behalf of the political prisoner. Mooney wasn't released until California

Governor Culbert Olsen fulfilled his campaign promise to the socialists in 1938.

Henry Faulk was never ostracized in the community for his radical views. Because he was a loyal member of the Methodist Church and an able and reputable lawyer, many just accepted his opinions as singularly eccentric or odd. He was never militant, but never hesitated to speak out against injustice. At many church gatherings and town meetings he would denounce the activities of the state's Ku Klux Klan.

In 1912 Henry acquired property in East Austin, which he leased to poor tenants who couldn't afford to live anywhere else. He began to become known as a friend to poor minorities by inviting them to his house or deferring rental payments on the houses he leased. When he rode his horse and buggy to collect his rent, he'd often stop at Mr. Wukasch's store downtown to buy boxes of apples, oranges, bacon, and stick candy to give to his tenants. "I'd see him come out of those houses with tears in his eyes," said daughter Mary, "and he'd say, 'Oh, those poor devils, those poor devils.' He really empathized with poverty, because he had certainly been brought up in it." [13]

Henry was one of the few strong supporters of the black community in Austin. Bob Eckhardt, former U.S. congressman who also grew up in Austin, remembers that Henry operated, to a large extent, "a free legal service establishment" for poor blacks. Many times he defended blacks in court at a time other white lawyers would not. Said Eckhardt: "They [Austin's blacks] had been cozened and brow-beaten in every conceivable way by loan sharks, shysters, land-grabbers, and funeral [home] operators. It was not unusual that the funeral cost swept away the deceased person's entire estate." [14]

In the last criminal case he took, Henry defended a white man accused of killing his mistress, Mollie Carrington. The defendant was Henry Brock, a handsome, red-haired, cigar-chewing owner of a saloon in Austin's nefarious Guy Town. The district contained many raucous saloons and more than a dozen houses of "ill repute." Respectable, self-righteous members of the community were strongly opposed to saloons and to the operators of the businesses in Guy Town. To further the cause of Prohibition they turned Brock into a scapegoat, an example of the dire consequences of demon liquor.

Henry didn't approve of the community acting like moral vigilantes, and he saw a strong element of hypocrisy in the citizens who sternly disapproved of Brock and other proprietors in Guy Town, but who looked the other way when the elite class (particularly members of the Texas legislature) frequented the brothels there. He also believed Brock may have acted in self-defense. Mollie had assaulted him with a knife in a jealous fit, and Brock had reacted by striking her with his gun handle, which went off and killed her. Yet the stubborn Brock refused to claim self-defense against a woman, and the jury found him guilty of first-degree murder.

In his plea for another trial, Henry wrote that the jury did not take into consideration several mitigating factors, including their failure to prove alleged threats Brock made to Mollie, or whether these threats "were not made while defendant was too drunk or intoxicated to have knowledge of having made such threats; and, if he made them, he did not intend to execute them; that if he made them they were made in a 'jocular or hurrah manner,' and were not made seriously and with any intention of taking the life of the deceased; that defendant and deceased were intimate friends and on the best of terms at the time of said threats." [15]

Although a teetotaler himself, Henry believed that if the state licensed you to drink, it should bear some responsibility for the consequences. Henry, who opposed the death penalty, believed that Brock was not an evil man but a victim of circumstance and alcoholism (which wasn't considered a disease at the time). He introduced a motion for retrial on the basis of "alcoholic insanity" (there was no manslaughter charge then, either). Doctors were brought in to testify on the effects of alcohol on the mind. The experts couldn't decide whether alcohol was a food or a poison. Henry argued that the exposure to drink and living in Guy Town made Brock "morally bankrupt and insane."

Henry lost the appeal that winter of 1912. Henry Brock was hanged on May 30, 1913, near the Governor's Mansion. It was the last public hanging in Texas.

This marked the first criminal case Henry Faulk lost. He never dreamed that the state would put Brock to death, since

Governor Oscar Colquitt himself granted three stays of execution and had personally told Henry that Brock would not hang for the crime. The hanging "made Daddy [physically] sick," said daughter Martha. "He had really felt sorry for that man. He had that kind of attitude and that kind of empathy for people who were victims." [16]

That summer, Guy Town was shut down. Shortly afterwards, on August 21, Mattie gave birth to their fourth child, John Henry Faulk.

2.

GREENER
PASTURES

I f he didn't take his horse and buggy, Henry usually walked to his law firm at 911 Congress, across from the Gammel Bookstore (the location of Austin's Sweetish Hill Bakery in 1993). Sometimes, he might be bold enough to pick up the streetcar that ran along the electrical lines on First Street. He never learned to drive because he had no patience for anything mechanical. But, in 1915, at Mattie's prodding, Henry went shopping for an automobile.

As Clyde Mayne from the Moon Car Agency was trying to sell Mr. Faulk a Studebaker, he told him about a large house for sale just south of town.[1] Henry Faulk had always dreamed of owning a country home where he could raise cattle and grow a garden, and Mayne told him this had twenty-three acres of arable land, secluded on 911 West Live Oak Street. The Victorian-style house was built in 1895 by the editor of the Firm Foundation, Dr. E. W. Herndon. Henry liked the description of the place, so he had Clyde drive him there in the new Studebaker. They drove over Austin's sole steel bridge across the Colorado River, down Congress Avenue, and then turned on the dusty, unpaved Live

11

Oak Street. Soon, they reached the cedar post gates in front of the solitary white house standing out against the green pastures. Henry fell in love with the place immediately. Beyond the ragweeds and Johnson grass, he envisioned the fulfillment of his boyhood dreams: a self-sufficient farm where he could live out his desire to be in touch with the earth.[2]

When Henry told Mattie about the house, she was less impressed. She was fond of her neighbors and enjoyed living in the heart of town, close to the First Methodist Church on 10th Street and to Winn School, where eleven-year-old Hamilton, her first-born child, was going to school. She wanted her newborn baby, Texana, three-year-old John Henry, and her daughters Martha (age eight) and Mary (five and a half) to go to school there as well. Henry's dream house wasn't even in the city limits. The rural community surrounding the house was peopled by poor whites and sundry blacks and Mexicans who eked out a meager living hauling cedar and burning charcoal. Her friends told her, "Oh, Mrs. Faulk, don't go over there — that's bootlegger's paradise."[3]

When Mattie first set eyes on the house, she knew instinctively that they'd be moving into it, despite her reservations. Her husband adored its Victorian-style exterior, as well as its cherry and walnut-finished interior walls and twelve-foot-high ceilings. As they crossed the oak threshold, they saw, directly in front of them, an impressive wooden stairway, its large banisters rising like guiding signposts to the upstairs. On the second floor, five bedrooms provided more than enough space for the children. The hall could hold day beds and cots, and to the west "The Boys Room" could lodge three in bunk beds. Next to that room was another narrower staircase that led directly to the downstairs kitchen. Each of the rooms upstairs had a fireplace.

So, in 1916, Henry traded his property near the university to move to the country. On the small, upstairs front porch rested a white stone bed where many guests slept amidst the overhanging oak trees and the cool summer-night breeze. One of the chief reasons Henry bought this house was so that he could provide housing for relatives who wanted to get an education at the university. He loved to see people go to school because he felt education would teach them *how* to think, not *what* to think. Henry placed his younger brother, James Monroe, into the university's School of Pharmacy. Other relatives came to live with the Faulks to go to high school, like Mattie's nephew, Ashford Miner. The Faulk home would become home to many relatives over the years, with the children sharing rooms and sleeping in the hallway when needed to make room for aunts, uncles, or cousins.[4]

For the children, it was "as if they'd died and gone to heaven." There was ample space inside to play, and several smaller structures surrounded the house: a barn for the cows; surrey house for their lone horse, Old Mac; a tin shed; a separator house that contained the heavy milk separator; an outhouse; and a house in the backyard for the maid, Mary Benford.

Thickets of cedar and oak trees grew behind the house, where young Johnny Faulk played with Jack Kellam and other friends, like Snooky Bates and Boots Cooper. Jack and Johnny would scope out the neighborhood, walking the iron lines of the Missouri, Kansas, and Texas railroad, pausing every so often to put an ear to the track for the expected rumbling of the *Katy Flyer*. They became two fearless explorers braving a haunted house. Everything in sight became part of the adventure: the outhouse was an imaginary airplane; the swing, a ship at sea; the woods, a jungle full of tigers and lions. With Snooky, one of his black playmates, he would play around his family's cow lot and barn; investigate hay stacks and cedar thickets; uncover bird nests in the fields; and climb live oak trees in the neighborhood. There wasn't a bend in the creek within ten miles of the house that Johnny and his playmates didn't explore.[5]

For the most part, the Faulk home, despite its looming exterior and ample space, remained a simple farm house until after the Second World War. The Faulks could not afford to lavishly decorate it. Upstairs floors were covered with linoleum carpets. A rudimentary electrical system was rigged to provide lighting in the house. Woodstoves and coal fireplaces remained the sources of heat in the winter. During the summer, cords were attached to the transom windows, so that they could be opened easily to admit the breeze. Because there was no indoor plumbing, clothes had to be washed in water heated from a kettle. For a long time, the only toilet was in the outhouse in the back. Since toilet paper was scarce then, Mattie would put out the Sears Roebuck catalog, sans the corset ads, lest they excite young Johnny and Hamilton.[6]

A wide front porch completely encircled the home, with a swing on the northeast side where family and friends would sit on the cowhide-laced rocking chairs or the porch swing, shelling peas and talking, bantering about every conceivable subject. When distraught clients came to attorney Faulk, he often suggested they "go out to my house. Sit on the porch, drink buttermilk, and eat good cooking. Miss Mattie will see you through your troubles."[7] A huge vegetable garden extended west of the house to where South Fifth Street is today. To the south of the house lay the cow pasture and barn; east of the barn was the large cornfield. Henry bought several cows and chickens. Soon, other animals were seen roaming the land, including guineas, dogs, and later, peacocks.

Mattie was a spirited, capable woman who held the family together. She answered the telephone, scheduled entertainment and social activities for the family, churned butter, gathered eggs, tended the garden in front and chickens out back. She believed that a chicken wasn't fit to eat unless she got out and wrung its neck just before dinner. On any weekend day, it was a common sight to see dozens of children running in and out of the Faulk home. And Mattie made sure they were all fed. "She was an excellent cook," recalled Lester Kitchens. "I can remember her hollerin', 'Dinner's ready,' and we'd smell those biscuits cooking and come running down those stairs. It didn't matter if there were forty kids; if she'd have lunch ready, all of them would be in by noon." Miss Mattie prepared all the food eaten by family and guests: hot raisin bread, ham from the smokehouse, homemade jelly and jam, and fruits and vegetables fresh from the garden.[8]

She had no time nor forbearance for those who engaged in self-pity. If something needed doing, she'd do it without fanfare and with a healthy dose of common sense. When the family had extra milk left over, Mattie would see to it that the needy in the neighborhood got some. Some of the milk was delivered by the Faulk children or friends through a circuitous route along the creek banks and railroad track in South Austin. During Christmas season, the Faulks would load up their buggy with food and sometimes toys for the poor children down the creek.

Miss Mattie often entertained church socials at one of the two parlor rooms downstairs, in front of the staircase. She was never idle; always sewing, mending, or canning vegetables. She had learned how to can food, picking fresh fruits and vegetables only when they were ripe. If the food were jams, preserves or pickles (which had enough sugar in them to prevent spoilage), she would cook several batches fifteen minutes apart so the canning would be continuous. Packing each sterilized jar one-half-inch from the top with boiling produce and liquid, she would then fill and seal a jar at a time. The tedious process took one hour for each jar.[9]

Late in her life, Mattie would receive a proclamation from Mayor Tom Miller and the City of Austin in 1956 as honorary "First Lady of South Austin." The proclamation recognized "the unselfish life of service which Martha Faulk lived, her strong convictions which have never interfered with her cheerful tolerance of differing views, and her habit through the years of offering a home to others who needed it despite the demands of her own family of five."[10]

Henry and Mattie were Methodists—not just religious Methodists, but social Methodists. During their life, the main form of entertainment and social life for families was the church. If you weren't a Methodist, you were either a Southern Baptist or a "Holy Roller," as the more fundamentalist group was called. When you weren't in church, you were at a church supper or a church picnic or a church social. Women in the church would manage rummage sales or serve dinners to judges working at the county precinct elections. When the circus came to town off the banks of Town Lake, the women went and sold homemade pies and other food to raise money for the church. Of the picnics, John Henry's sister Texana recalled: "We'd get on a big old wagon and go out into the country and have them at the creeks where Oak Hill is now, or down at Montopolis Bridge, along the river bank. It was a lot of fun."[11]

Both Henry and Mattie taught Sunday school at the South Austin Methodist Episcopal Church, only the second church to be established in South Austin after a brush revival meeting in 1897. The church became the Fred Allen Memorial Methodist Episcopal Church when it moved to 205 Monroe Street in 1916;

later it was called Grace United Methodist Church of Austin. Mattie taught Sunday school there for more than forty years. She faithfully attended the Methodists' Wednesday evening prayer meetings and Women's Quilting Circle meetings for twenty-seven years, never missing one Thursday of quilting. The money from the quilts that she and others sold helped pave the street in front of the church.[12]

Henry taught the Men's Adult Bible Class. But his religious views were more nontraditional than those of his wife, or any Methodist of the time. He believed more in the teachings of Jesus than in his divinity, valuing the social significance of Christ rather than his supernatural significance. His Adult Bible classes, in addition to the teachings of the Bible, were a strange mixture of Plato, Thoreau, and Emerson. Despite the difference in religious philosophies, the Faulk children cannot recall their parents ever getting into a serious argument, even when Henry's beliefs, particularly his firm opposition to World War I, led to a temporary estrangement from his Methodist minister. Because he was a congenial, affluent, and well-respected member of the community, most people shrugged off his ideas as those of a quirky or eccentric intellectual. As a successful lawyer, he held status that many, particularly in rural South Austin, did not have.[13]

When it came to sexual matters, however, the Faulks' attitudes mirrored the rigidly puritanical mores of the white society. Talking or thinking about sex was considered sinful, and children were strongly discouraged from touching their genitals. Mrs. Faulk would tell them that "nice people don't do that," or "respectable people don't behave like that." Yet such prudish sensibilities and mores didn't interfere with Johnny being able to associate with the poor blacks and Mexican-American children nearby. Henry Faulk believed that the children should feel free to play with all of their neighbors.[14]

Johnny's constant companions until he went to high school were those black children who lived behind the Faulk home in a wooded area known as "The Flat." Many of these children's parents were children of former slaves. They lived in primitive shacks along the creek, and their fathers made a living chopping cedar, selling willow furniture, plowing the fields, or burning charcoal. For some of these families, the only access to food was hunting in the woods and fishing in the nearby streams.

Arleatha Overton Williams, whose father owned a small farm just one-half mile from the Faulks, remembered that young Johnny spent many days playing with her and her brother, John Herman. "Each day we'd plan a picnic and bring eggs and sandwiches in this little thicket behind a grove of trees," she said.

In addition to playing at a small swimming hole nearby, the threesome would fly kites made from newspapers, or tissue paper, and sticks they found in the fields. "Our favorite game was to have two kites up in the air at the same time," Williams said. "We also enjoyed riding a horse, one in particular. John Henry was not such a good bare-backed rider, I recall, but this horse was very gentle, and would just stop and wait for you to get back on." She said Johnny was "always a comedian," but was very well-behaved and helped their family out with chores on the farm.[15]

Johnny found the Overton, Batts, Dallas, and Biles families (all black) a bit more down-to-earth and unpretentious than most of his fellow white children. These families weren't expected to live by the same rigid rules the whites did, and so they had a more relaxed way about them that appealed to Johnny—a way that discarded straight-laced inhibitions and embraced joy, laughter and pleasure. He also sensed a fierce pride and self-sufficiency in these families, despite their lack of material goods. And he was drawn to them because, through them, he was introduced to a fascinating and mysterious subject that was taboo with his parents—sex.

"By the time I was four or five years old," Faulk said, "I was a definitive authority on calf having and hen screwing and dog screwing. It was something that these other children never even thought of. They had been told, just as I had been told by my mother, that babies came from storks or were found in old logs and all kind of euphemistic stories. Anything that would deprive the child of knowing that there was any sexual connotation to the matter of reproduction. But this reached further than reproduction. All of the bodily functions were pretty much suppressed in the white Bible Belt mentality. To the black, this wasn't true."[16]

On occasion, Snooky would take him to his two-room house

only to find the parents copulating in the small room seen from a window. Faulk remembered this well, mimicking the high-pitched voice of Snooky's mother: "You two boys get away from that winda, now! And don't be comin' down thar no more!" [17]

The place that Johnny Faulk found out that white adults not only concealed the "facts of life" from children but would castigate them for revealing the truth was in Sunday school. His teacher, Elsie McKeller, considered an "old maid" because she was past thirty and unwed, told the class that the Mostellar children wouldn't be attending one Sunday because "the stork is flying round South Austin now, so Frank and Annie Lee have been sent up to Liberty Hill to stay with their grandparents until the old stork lands because he's planning to land at the Mostellar home and he's going to leave them a little bundle there, and next Sunday Frank and Annie Lee will come and tell us whether it was a little boy baby or a little girl baby that the stork left there."

Shortly after that announcement, Miss Elsie was called out of the Sunday school classroom and Johnny Faulk took his cue. "You know, she's crazy," he told the other five- or six-year-olds there. "She don't know what she's talking about. She's just making all that up about a stork coming. Mrs. Mostellar's knocked up. Did you see how her belly pooches way out like that? Well, there's a baby up in her belly, and it's going to come right out between her legs where she pee-pees — there's this hole it's going to come right out through, just like an old cow having a calf, or an old cat having kittens. That's what she was going to do."

As Johnny proceeded to explain how Mr. Mostellar had put "his peter" in Mrs. Mostellar, the other children sat wide-eyed, silent, when Miss Elsie stormed back in the room. She had been listening to the boy telling this story for minutes but had been too stunned to move at first. The look on Miss Elsie's face was one that John Henry Faulk would never forget — a contortion of white outrage, of a kind that struck a mixture of terror, fury, and almost pathetic disgust. He said it was "the darndest countenance I ever beheld at a two-foot distance."

She grabbed Johnny and said, "You dirty, disgusting little animal. You can't stay in here. How dare you." Then she lifted him up from his seat by his left ear and dragged him out of the room. Miss Elsie was so shocked and speechless by what Johnny had said that she couldn't even explain to his mother what had occurred. All she could do was say he couldn't come back to the class, and little Johnny pleaded ignorance when his mother questioned him about it.

Johnny would carry this experience with him as an example of how someone was so paralyzed by fear of nature and consumed by piousness that she would insist on misrepresenting a fact known by everyone.[18] Incidents like these drew Johnny closer to people who didn't hide behind a facade of propriety; those who "were not in the category of the 'respectable' people of those days." He started suspecting the authority of respectability and gravitated toward black children, whom he found very uninhibited, as opposed to the rigid, puritanical ways of the churchgoers. Instead of playing baseball with his schoolmates after school, he would much rather go ride on stick horses between Mama's back door and the cow lot with playmate Boots Cooper, "shooting" outlaws and cattle rustlers.

Yet it wasn't all fun and games for the five Faulk children: Hamilton, Mary, Martha, Johnny, and Texana. With more than thirty Jersey cows, an assortment of pigs, turkeys, and guinea hens, daily chores were a fact of life. Johnny and his older brother, Hamilton, woke up at the crack of dawn each day to milk the cows or carry in wood for the fireplace while their mother tended the chickens, then they would pull Johnson grass or clean the chicken house after school. The three girls helped their mother gather the eggs and can the vegetables.

"I loathed and detested the chores that I had to do," John Henry recalled, "splitting kindling, carrying wood in — because we had all wood-burning stoves and fireplaces in the house — and milking [cows] and pulling weeds. I had a thousand-and-one chores, and I was expected to do them, and I resisted them with all my might, and sometimes it was more trouble to get me to do them than it was to do them themselves, so Mama would pitch in and do it herself; and use a kind of shame technique on me."[19]

Johnny found much release with the Becketts, a farm family who lived on a ranch in South Austin about twelve miles away. "Grandma Beckett" wasn't related to Johnny, and neither were her daughters, "Aunt" Ollie and "Aunt" Mary, but they were as good as kin to Johnny. The boy eagerly looked forward to his trips to their farm, where he would hunt turkeys and help the family with chores. The Becketts would give Johnny spelling bees, show him the varieties of plants and animals that lived on the land, and let him ride their old deaf mule, Pete. Unlike his parents, the Becketts would encourage him to tell stories he had heard, no matter how bawdy, and Grandma Beckett would tell Johnny stories about life before the Civil War. With the Becketts, Johnny could not only share his enjoyment of the outdoors and of storytelling, but he didn't have to wash his feet before he spent a night there. [20]

Johnny found solace and comfort at the Becketts and with his neighbors, the Brodies. One of the more stalwart characters who affected Johnny from his elementary to his college years was John Brodie. A mule auctioneer with a bulbous nose and stern visage, Brodie had a big pot belly and chest hair that nearly always showed through his shirt, as his shirts never seemed to be quite shut. Johnny adored Brodie because the man treated him like an adult and listened to him. Of course, it helped that Brodie freely talked about sex and bodily functions, which the young Faulk was fervently curious about. This bawdy fellow enjoyed teasing the young five- or six-year-old.

Frequently, when Johnny went to visit the Brodies, he would be chased by the family's large gander, which acted as their watchdog. The gander would chase the terrified young boy up a tree or back him up on a post, then come at him with his neck curled out, hissing a warning. Consequently, Johnny learned never to come through the Brodies' front yard. One morning, however, when Mrs. Brodie asked him to go fetch a rake, he forgot the rule. He found himself face to face with the old gander, so he turned and quickly backtracked to the house.

Mrs. Brodie told him, "Oh, that pesky old gander! Johnny, just take this broom and if he gives you any trouble, you just swipe the daylights out of it. He's just bluffing you. He knows you're just scared of him and just walk right on by him and if even sticks his neck out at you, let him have it good and proper."

So Johnny walked around the corner of the house and the old gander came straight for him, screeching loudly. After the boy gave a couple of half-hearted sweeps at him, the gander spread his large wings and ran toward him. Johnny dropped the broom and ran.

John Brodie came around and said, "Johnny knows what that old gander's after—he's after his pecker. There ain't nothing that old gander loves like little boys' peckers. He can find one anywhere, he'd walk five miles to get at it and I don't blame old Johnny for running from him, neither. He's a pecker gander—a little boy's pecker's gander." [21]

Brodie's daughter, Marie, took after her father when it came to cursing. About five years older than Johnny, Marie would read to him by the hour passages from *Tom Sawyer* or *Huckleberry Finn*, or walk with him barefoot six miles to the Becketts. She had a very protective, maternal attitude toward Johnny, once helping him nurse a cotton-tail rabbit back to health. Marie was not considered a "nice girl" in the community because she cursed and had a number of boyfriends, but this never bothered Johnny (or Marie) in the least. They were attracted to each other because both felt alienated and ostracized. [22]

Even at a young age, Johnny felt the strictness and hypocrisy of severe religious attitudes. This "dedication to decency" that prevailed in his upbringing actually drove him to rebel—to use profanity, steal things, and associate with a different crowd. Often he would play hooky from school with his neighbors to go crawfishing in the creek or imaginary bear hunting in the thick woods (and later, real rabbit hunting). [23]

Fulmore Elementary School didn't admit blacks then, but they did allow Mexican-Americans. Johnny was friends with the Garcia children at Fulmore. He chose Alicia Garcia as his partner at the Maypole Dance in the first grade, ignoring the teasing and humiliating snickering of his fellow students. Johnny resented the slurs and unkindness to the Riggs and the Grumbles. Many of these kids slept in the same clothes they wore to school every day, with only pallets to sleep on at night. Most of them wet the bed, and the stench of urine on a winter's day in the schoolhouse was quite pungent. The other children would poke fun at them, saying "*Ooo, they smell like pee.*" [24]

Johnny would walk home with these children after school, barefoot through the woods. Although there wasn't anyone in South Austin who could be considered rich, the "respectable" children—sons and daughters of lawyers, bankers, shopkeepers, or car salesmen—wore shoes and stockings to school. As much as Mattie tried to get him to wear shoes, Johnny almost always walked barefoot.

Mattie had the responsibility of disciplining the children. She rarely used physical punishment, but if Johnny spouted too many vulgarities inside the home, she would wash his mouth out with soap. More often, however, she'd employ more subtle methods of discipline. For instance, if the children would repeat some unacceptable behavior, she'd scare them with the threat of giving them to "the sack man." The sack man was a wizened, haggard old man who took burlap sacks used for cattle feed and sold them back to the feed company for a small profit. He traveled through town on a fragile, dilapidated wagon with a decrepit horse, trying to solicit bran sacks from whomever he could. Children were terrified of him. "Mama would tell us," Texana said, "if you all don't behave, the sack man is going to come and get you and carry you off." [25]

When Johnny acted rowdy in "mixed company," Miss Mattie would say things like: "I'd love to buy Johnny for what he's worth, and sell him for what he thinks he's worth." Or "I wouldn't take a million dollars for Johnny, but you know, I wouldn't give you a dime for a dozen just like him." These gentle put-downs would keep Johnny from getting "too big for his britches" and teach him how to laugh at himself.

Still, Johnny did find himself in trouble for cursing one too many times. He'd learn from his black friends to say "I've got to go hookey" or "I've got to go shit," rather than saying "I've got to go do number 2 at Mrs. Jones" or "I've got to go visit Mrs. Jones" like the white children did. Usually, he'd know better than to talk this way in front of adults, but his sisters would often report it to their mother. This built Johnny up into kind of an outcast in the church, leading to his resentment of prudish attitudes. His sisters would sometimes say, "All right, Johnny, I'm going to tell Mama on you that you said that word."

Johnny's reply would often be: "I don't give a damn, god-damn old pea shit hockey on you." [26]

Such talk in a pious culture was not without consequences. One Easter, Johnny wasn't invited to the annual picnic with the other children because he'd done or said something nasty. He feigned disdain for the picnic, although he felt very rejected for not being invited: "That's the last thing in the world I want to do," Johnny told them, "is to go to a durn old crazy Easter egg hunt."

Instead, Johnny decided to saddle up his father's old deaf mule, Maude, and visit his Grandma Beckett and her two daughters, Aunt Ollie and Aunt Mary. He'd often ride Maude bareback with just a field bridle and rope reins on her so he could pull her hair. Since the mule was tender in that spot, she'd hump her back and pitch, with the main thrust from her bowels. She'd throw her tail up in the air and it would cause her to fart in the most bugle kind of *broooo, broooo, broooo, broooo.* Johnny could produce mule farts at will with the beast, and it gave him a sort of prideful distinction.

Johnny waited until the Easter egg hunt to ready Maude for the trip to Grandma Beckett's. When all the children, surrounded by their Easter egg baskets, saw Johnny round the corner with his mule, several of them ran up to him, taunting insults. One of the adult women, Mrs. Herring, looking tight-lipped, "like a rusty gut lizard looking over an oak limb," confronted Johnny. "You're not invited to this, young man. Don't you come over here to make no trouble," she said. Instead of dismounting and peeing in their Easter baskets or using one of his innumerable ways of getting even, Johnny pulled Maude's grey hair, causing her to fling her tail up and let out a "beautiful rising fart." Thus Johnny paid his compliments to the Easter egg crowd.

This typical response as a child – to deal with perceived injustice with a savage satire – gave Johnny so much joy that he would carry such behavior with him through adulthood.[27]

Although his mother did not mind Johnny playing with black children, she did begin to worry that he was spending too much time away from home, not returning until after dark on many instances. She began to try everything she could think of to break him of the habit of running away. In some cases, this resulted in her using a heavy-handed form of intimidation.

"It wasn't so much that she objected to him being there," said Johnny's sister Mary, "but she just wanted him home." One night, she became so distressed with his absences that she waited late for him to return. She was so exasperated with him that she got some black shoe polish while he was sleeping and painted part of his stomach with it. Johnny awoke, aghast at the black spots on his tummy, and heard his mother on the telephone, pretending to talk to the doctor about her son's "condition." When Johnny started to panic, she told him that his black spots would grow bigger: "See, you're starting to turn black!" At first he agreed never to go over to his friends' homes again, until he discovered that the black spots were indeed just shoe polish.[28]

Another time, his mother became so frustrated with Johnny running off that she told him she was trading him for some neighborhood black children. She enlisted Johnny's cousin Ashford to take him outside in a bogus gesture of wanting him out of the house.

Mattie told Mary, "I closed the deal today, I've got his clothes packed. Ashford, if you and Mary will take him up there, we'll just get this over with this afternoon." Johnny protested, but she told him, "Well, if you want to stay up there all the time, we'll just let you stay up there and live there."

After supper, Ashford, a tall, strong and imposing teenager, picked up Johnny and took him a short distance outside, with Mary following. Johnny started bucking and crying over Ashford's shoulder, going into hysterics until Ashford had to put him down on a fence. When Miss Mattie saw him in such a state, she said, "Well, Ashford, bring him back." She took the sobbing little Johnny in her arms and tried to soothe him: "Oh, darlin',' we wouldn't let anything happen to you. You're our little june bug."[29]

Sister Martha said that the seven-year-old Johnny was really traumatized by the event. "He was pitiful," she said. "It really horrified and hurt him at the time."[30]

Miss Mattie would often despair in finding suitable methods of punishment, not knowing how to deal with Johhny's misbehavior. When Johnny was ten years old, a friend named Lonnie Paul promised him a pair of white king pigeons if Johnny would steal Mrs. Kellam's diamond ring. So he snatched it when he was playing with Jack. When the ring turned up missing, Johnny denied he took it at first, then admitted it, telling his father that Lonnie Paul had it. Of course, the whole family was distraught because

Mrs. Kellam (Mrs. Faulk's best friend) was missing her diamond ring, and Johnny was made to feel the frustration and humiliation. "This was just a bit too much for a ten-year-old child," John Henry later said of the incident. "That fell in the felony class; it wasn't just stealing pennies out of your sister's tithing box."

Lonnie had turned the ring over to brother Hamilton, who brought it in the house. John Henry remembered his mother's reaction, pretending a faint. "Mama was not the swooning sort, so I've always figured that maybe this was some sort of punishment for me," he said. Sisters Martha and Mary dashed to fetch her some water, and Daddy said to Johnny, "Well, I hope you're happy, you've killed your mother!" This event was so traumatic in Johnny's life that he blocked it out of his mind entirely for several years.[31]

Yet, at about this age, Johnny learned to deal with some of these anxieties and feelings of rejection through the use of humor. One day his mother told him to clean out the yard and the chicken coop, as she was expecting visitors from the Women's Methodist Missionary Society. More than a group to discuss foreign missions through the Methodist Church, the Women's Missionary Society was a social get-together, with women serving pies and cakes at members' homes.

Johnny had been expecting some friends over to play cowboys and Indians, but canceled that plan with reluctance and got to work on the chicken pen. He stewed over the unfortunate turn of events when he got to the henhouse. While running the hens out, he forcibly caught one hen, held its feet with one hand, and grasped its neck with the other, squeezing its windpipe. As he let go of the pressure on the hen's neck, it let out a loud squawk. When he closed his hand on its neck, it was silenced. This discovery prompted Johnny to take the hen below the window of the kitchen, where his mother's church group had gathered. In his best imitation of a lady's voice, he said, "The Women's Missionary Society will please come to order. Sister Allen, will you please call the roll." Then, in a mocking of Sister Allen's creaky voice, he said, "Sisssster Brodie?" *Cwaaak.* "Sister Forbis?" *Cwaaak.* By squeezing and releasing the hen's neck, he went through the entire roll call of the society's members.

Because his mother usually chided him when he mocked religious institutions, he expected some form of retribution for his impulsive behavior. Instead, he saw that the women were in the kitchen, laughing uproariously. His mother, trying in vain to keep laughter out of her own voice, told Johnny, "Get yourself and that hen back out to the henhouse and get busy, young man, or I will make you wish you had."

Johnny used his knack of imitation again after this, especially in situations where he felt resentment and anger. Through mimicking others, he found he could express his feelings without fear of punishment.[32]

The Faulk family employed a black maid, Annie Mae Finnin, who also had an influence on the speech of young Johnny. She tried to instill in him a God-fearin' fear of "the Debil," so she would keep the young Faulk informed of all the church work at the Goodwill Baptist Church. She'd cook supper early on Wednesday nights so that she could go to her prayer meetings. On his own, Johnny would often go with her. He was surprised and pleased that the black Baptists seemed to have more fun in church, singing loudly and joyfully.[33] In addition to the black prayer meetings, Johnny and his sisters would go to many plays performed or weddings given at that church as a source of entertainment. But their mother would warn them never to laugh at the plays or at any of the people in the church. "Mama would tell us, 'You can go over there, but don't laugh at them if they do something funny, because it was very serious to them,'" recalled Mary.[34]

"I'd love their singing and all," said Texana. "John Henry was real good friends with Brother Pyburn, who was the minister for the Friendly Will Baptist Church. But I'll never forget the Sunday that Daddy was the attorney for Annie Mae in the church. They were trying her because she was an unwed mother (with two illegitimate children). She asked Daddy to go and represent her. They were going to 'church' her—that's what you call it when you get them out of church, you 'church' them—you don't come back in. So Daddy said, 'Now Annie Mae, are you aware . . . do you know who the man was, who, ah, got you pregnant?' And she said, 'Now, Mr. Faulk, you know as well as I do, that if you're thrown in a briar patch, you don't know which one of those briars stick you first."[35]

During his childhood, Johnny never heard anyone else but his father question segregation. Unlike most Americans, Henry Faulk did not accept segregation as a fact of life.

John Henry later wrote about his father: ". . . his profound concern and dedication to them [the black community] was wholly revolutionary. He would lecture the most indifferent and illiterate of them endlessly on the fact that they were victims of an unjust but changing society, pointing out that only with the advent of socialism could their lot be improved. They would yawn and doze without it having the least dampening effect on daddy, who would veer in my direction and continue unabated. When Mama raised a racket against some client who had abused his confidence by cheating or lying to him, daddy would point out that she should address herself to the society that had made it necessary for the client to do so. And then he would launch into a discourse on the vaster and more wicked crimes of Standard Oil and Mellon. Yet, he did not hold powerful persons in our society individually responsible. They, too, were victims of the system as far as daddy was concerned." [36]

To his son, Henry predicted that integration was inevitable. "It's one thing for us to think of the Negroes as second-class citizens," he told his Johhny, "but it's another to convince them they should think that way. When they insist on their full rights, they'll be voting; they'll be going to school, Johnny, in your lifetime, because that's the nature of our Republic." [37]

"Our father taught us to respect all people," said Texana. "When young John Henry was acting smart-aleck and all, saying 'Those old niggers, I'm just going to beat the devil out of 'em,' Daddy would say: 'You know, until you can look down past the color of a person's eyes, down into their soul, you don't know what they're like.' And I can remember that—he taught that we were all brothers and children of God. He had little time for fundamental religion." [38]

Although Johnny's father was kind and sensitive to the plight of others, he was somewhat detached in the lives of his own children, interested more in improving their minds than in acting as a personal companion. Instead of taking his sons hunting or fishing, like many other fathers did, he would take them to his office down on Congress Avenue. "I envied the other boys who went hunting with their fathers," Johnny said.[39]

"Our father was a man who didn't talk a whole lot to the family," said Mary. "It was always kind of brief one-liners of what to do and what not to do, like at the breakfast table . . . he was often preoccupied with ideas and didn't notice details; he was a lovable person, but not very demonstrative." [40]

Henry was the quintessential iconoclast, one who was profoundly concerned with social injustice wherever it occurred. He tried to give his children a healthy distaste for anyone who claimed to have the absolute answer and the absolute truth. He was reluctant to speak ill of any man or woman, and would scold the children if they engaged in "idle gossip" about others. He would only judge a person's ideas and opinions, not the individual personally. He would say, "I do not clearly understand all the things about myself, so how can I judge my neighbor?"

From their father, the Faulk children learned the love of books. While driving the cows in the barn, out tending the garden, or cleaning the table after supper, he read works of Plato, Aurelius, or Cato to Mattie or the children, and he encouraged the family to read on their own. He revered the words of such thinkers as Henry David Thoreau, Ralph Waldo Emerson, Thomas Jefferson, and James Madison. "My daddy would remark to me that James Madison was literally the genius of the First Amendment," Johnny said. "He conceived of it as the jewel of our crown of liberty, and one that contained all our great freedoms." [41] Little did young John Henry Faulk know how significant that message would be to him.

3.

FORMATION

OF A

RACONTEUR

D espite having many friends throughout elementary and high school, Johnny Faulk was still looking for his niche. His sister Texana once said that he felt uncomfortable with many injustices and prejudices in society, but "did not know how to overcome that, other than to do something that would be completely different; that would call attention to it or would appear to be negative. In reality it wasn't—he was just trying to find what he needed in life."[1] As a child, Johnny was known in the white community as "the Faulk boy." Even though his family was accepted, "that Faulk boy" was regarded as something of an anomaly or outsider to the church-going community, because he associated with the "wrong crowd." His sisters didn't share his propensity for telling bawdy stories, and they took stern exception when he started mimicking their talk.[2]

Hanging out with the neighboring black and Mexican-American children, Johnny picked up a great knack for mimicking people's speech. He observed how these families used mimicry as both a means of establishing discipline among their families and as an outlet for their hostility and frustration. When

Johnny encountered others who treated black people as something less than human, he automatically suspected they were covering up some insecurity and fear, and he would fight this attitude through his own wiles.

One day Johnny went with a friend, Jack Burnet, to Chum's Feed Store and spotted Max Sherman, a reputable white man who sold insurance, inside buying some chicken feed. Burnet said something to a black delivery boy who worked there. Johnny didn't hear his reply, but suddenly Sherman knocked the boy down and started kicking him, shouting, "Don't you ever speak to a white man like that, nigger, or I'll knock that wooly head off your shoulders." After the brutal attack, Sherman coolly walked to the store's faucet and washed his hands, telling the boy to "get up and get out of here." The boy, bruised and shaken, walked out.

After talking about the incident with his friend, Johnny decided to call Sherman on the telephone. Mimicking the voice of an indignant black woman, Johnny asked for him. He heard Sherman's son say, "Some nigger gal wants you, Dad." When Sherman came to the phone, Johnny let him have it in his best Negro dialect: "You old yellow-bellied egg-sucking Max Sherman."

"Who are you?" Sherman stuttered.

"You going to find out who I is when my husband come down there and kick your white butt up and down South Congress Avenue," Johnny screeched. "You ain't nothing but a yellow-bellied coward. You might pick on little colored boys, but you won't stand up to no real colored man. You too yellow."

For nearly twenty minutes, Johnny barraged Sherman with insults, enjoying the uneasiness he gave the man by simply talking to him over the telephone. Johnny was learning that humor was a weapon that could be used with precision.[3]

At Fulmore Elementary School in South Austin, where he attended from 1921 to 1929, Johnny was known as one of the class jokesters. Like his father, he could impart humor in conversation through witticisms and impersonations. "John Henry was always a cut-up," said schoolmate Lester Kitchens. "He always had that dry humor about him."[4] He used that dry humor in stories he told to gain attention from his classmates.

Johnny's parents sometimes held up the example of his

friend Jack Kellam as a boy who "didn't curse" and "always made good grades." Johnny's average to below-average grades at Fulmore Elementary were often compared with Kellam's very good marks. "Why can't you be more like Jack?" his mother would ask him. Throughout elementary and middle school, the great cry in the Faulk family was one of relieved joy when it was announced that Johnny had passed a course.[5]

However, Kellam was known to get into some trouble with Johnny during their adolescence. One time the two friends decided to brand the family's cows while the folks were away. With a tin can and some wire, they made the letter "F" for Faulk and tied down some of the cows and branded them on their hips. "It upset Daddy very much," Texana said, "because the cows wouldn't give him any milk for a while." Yet the elder Faulk, while scolding the boys, would leave the disciplining of the children to Miss Mattie.

Also as a youngster, Johnny helped his brother Hamilton make "home brew" beer during the Prohibition years. One day, while his mother was visiting her brother in Magnolia, near Houston, Johnny and Hamilton decided they'd make some "home brew" in the hayloft of the barn.

After making the beer with bran, yeast, sugar and water, the two boys put the jars up in the top corner of the barn to ferment, explained Texana. "Mama would have a habit of going in there and looking for eggs. She couldn't climb up to the loft, because she was afraid she'd fall through, but she could crawl up and look over the top and see the chicken nests. Usually one of the Boring boys went with her. This particular afternoon after she'd returned from her trip, she got one of them, Marvin, to go with her to look for eggs.

"Well, she got up high enough and said, 'Marvin, what's that up in that jar in the corner?' He got over there and opened the lid, and of course could smell the beer. He asked her what she wanted him to do with it and she said, 'Just put the lid back on it.' So she knew then that the boys had been up to making home brew. Marvin got the eggs and brought them down. The next day at lunch (or dinner as we called it), we were all sitting at the table, and she said, 'Oh, by the way, John Henry, I meant to tell you. Yesterday, while little Marvin and I were looking for eggs, he was up there in the loft, and there was a bucket of something over

there in the corner. And do you know he peedaddled in that?'
And she said, 'Would you please go and turn it over and pour it
out? Because if you don't, it's going to smell very bad.' Oh,
Hamilton and John Henry just looked at each other and gulped,
because they'd been out there the night before, drinking."[6]

By this time, after repeated warnings from his daddy,
Johnny had quit stealing. One night, when Johnny was twelve
years old, Henry sat him down and had a rather long talk about
stealing, convincing him that he was going to have to give it up or
he would wind up in the penitentiary, where it would be beyond
his capability to "redeem" him.[7]

That talk came on the heels of a situation he got into with a
boy named George Priest. One night, Johnny and George went to
a man's house on the corner of Live Oak and South First streets
to steal some of his pigeons while he was away. Johnny stood
guard next to the pigeon coop while Priest took them.

John Henry recalled: "I walked up and squatted there and
George slipped around to the pen while I went up to the front
door to find out whether he had gone off or not. Turned out he
had taken the babysitter home – he and his wife – and were gone
only a very short time. The lights on the front porch were on, and
he came driving in his car, with the lights thrown directly on the
pigeons. He came out and said: 'They're stealin' pigeons!' And
his wife screamed, 'But there's somebody on the front porch!' I
ran up Live Oak Street just like greased lightning."[8]

After that experience, Johnny became somewhat more disciplined, and his grades steadily improved at Austin High (where
the student population consisted of nearly all of the white students residing in Travis County). His teachers saw that he was a
bright boy, but that he only applied himself to those courses that
interested him. After his father upbraided him for not taking an
interest in any subject or school activity ("Why can't you do something like that, Johnny?" he said, pointing out another student
who was involved in writing), he got involved in the school newspaper.

In classes, Johnny was without peer at the school in making
both students and teachers laugh. Bob Eckhardt recalled Johnny
loudly reciting passages of Dickens in class: " 'The law is a ass, a
idiot', said Mr. Bumble." Eckhardt said Johnny was a "grand past

master of shooting folly where it flies." Often, Johnny would at-
tract a group of students in the hallway or outside as he started
telling stories about an old turkey gobbler or a dominecker hen.
"He was a perfect mimic," Eckhardt said, "and he could inhabit
his stories with real characters, black and white, from South Austin—just as Dickens did. But imagine the written story in his own
voice. I remember sitting on the floor in a little cupboard house,
without double walls, eating rolled roast, and hearing Johnny's
stories; and I laughed so hard, beating the wall, until I nearly
loosened the nails from the board-and-batten siding."[9]

John Henry fancied himself a writer, however, not an entertainer. He started writing for the school paper, the *Austin Maroon*, with Kellam, Eckhardt, and Alice Sutherland. He and
Kellam wrote humorous and feature pieces for the paper. Kellam
would take more of a serious interest in journalism, becoming
editor of the high school yearbook, *The Comet*.

In addition to writing, Johnny began to respect his father's
abilities in public speaking, so he tried out for the Calhoun Debate Club. He became president of that club in 1931. According
to school debate partner Creekmore Fath (who later became a
lawyer and a staff member in Franklin D. Roosevelt's administration during the war), Johnny had "the most unusual arguments
ever seen in debate," using his skills at humor and storytelling.
The debate team became one of the best in Texas, going to the
state meet in San Antonio in 1933 against the "Fabulous Baker
Boys," the state's premier high school debate club. [10] In spite of
the recognition, Johnny never considered himself much of a de-
bater. He wouldn't prepare for a debate with any motivation or
thoroughness. This lack of desire and drive carried through in
other endeavors in high school. Although one day he might write
a biting, satiric piece for the paper, he wouldn't write another for
months. The recognition that he yearned for from his father was
never really attained. "He took no active interest in the reality of
my life," John Henry said. "It was sort of taken for granted that
I'd be a lawyer, but we never had discussions about it. We had
discussions, but they were always on a philosophical level. We'd
have discourses while out milking cows, but they were mostly lectures given to me. Later on, when I was in high school and college, he'd take me to lectures and speeches." Until his death,

Henry Faulk remained a respected, but isolated, figure to Johnny; someone he never got to know on a personal, direct level.

Competitive sports never attracted Johnny at all, and proved difficult after he nearly lost his right eye at age sixteen. Swimming at Barton Springs, he picked up an old, dirty towel to wipe his face and suffered some pain in both eyes later in the day. The doctor diagnosed it as pink eye, but his mother knew better, since one eye was deteriorating faster than the other. She quickly covered up his good eye with a patch and irrigated the other one with saline solution. She took him to the doctor again, who now said the eyeball needed to be removed. His Aunt Pearl, who had been visiting the Faulks, insisted on taking him to an eye doctor in Dallas, who saved the right eye. Johnny had picked up a gonorrheal infection from that towel, and it had cost him the sight of one eye.

Gradually, Johnny regained eyesight in his good eye, but the event was very traumatic for him. Since he couldn't do some of the things he had done before, he turned to fantasizing through stories, books, and movies. He enjoyed the "picture shows" at Skinny's Theater, with "Hoot" Gibson, Tom Mix, Douglas Fairbanks, and Mary Pickford as his favorites.

But even movies, at five cents admission, were a form of entertainment that could only be enjoyed sparingly in the early 1930s. Although Austin fared better than most Southwestern towns during the Depression (partially due to Mayor Tom Miller's successful lobbying efforts for federal grants), times were lean for all. Many people relied on bartering for their needs, and Henry Faulk would occasionally represent a plumber or carpenter in court in return for their services.[11]

Fewer than half a dozen students at Austin High had automobiles, and although the Faulk family had one, Johnny rarely got to use it for pleasure. He had often ridden a donkey to elementary school, but in high school he walked the two-mile journey every day. He'd get stone bruises on the heels of his feet from these walks, and Mattie would put bacon-gel on them to pull the infection out.

Because few families could afford to buy new clothing, he, like many students, wore hand-me-down clothes.[12] At the time, it was the fashion for boys to wear sleeveless undershirts. Mattie would make these shirts out of a strong cotton bran sack. She'd put buttermilk on them and then hang them out on the clothesline so that they would bleach white. From these, she'd make the children some underwear or slips for the winter. Johnny wanted one of those knit undershirts to wear to school one day. By mistake he grabbed a girl's shimmy, which differed in that it had a string that was supposed to hold a dress in. He thought it looked just like a boy's undershirt, so he put it on. Schoolmate Barnes Fowler noticed the small string hanging down from Johnny's garment during P.E. class, and shouted to the other boys: "Johnny has on his mother's undershirt!" [13]

Although he was an attractive boy with an expressive face, square chin, and solid stature, Johnny didn't go out on a date with a girl until he was sixteen. His only exposure to sex up to then had been through the stories of people like Brodie and the Gartmans, who lived about 200 yards from the Faulks. Willie Gartman, an "indescribably homely" person, could tell the tallest sexual tale that a young boy could imagine. One of the many stories Faulk recalled from the Gartmans concerned Willie riding with a plumber friend who advertised his services on a sign on his pickup truck. Willie said: "Hell, we'd be ridin' out there and old [Governor] Dan Moody's wife come runnin' out in the middle of Lavaca Street standin' thar with her damn titties half bare, with kindofa komona thing on, wavin' at us. And she said to us: 'You all plumbers, well I got some plumbin' stopped up.' And we went in thar, and by God, she just threw that robe off and that thar thing she had on and didn't have nothin' but a pair of teddy bears under it. And her ol' tits — them big ol' nipples stickin' out thar on them — God durn, she said, 'Boy, you want to bite one of them, don't you?' And I said, 'No, ma'am, I don't, not in the Guvnah's Mansion. I ain't come up here to bite on no Guvnah's Mansion wife's titty.' "[14]

Although this type of "barnyard" education had little, if anything, to do with the reality of healthy sexual relationships, it was the only sexual education Johnny could find at the time. Throughout high school, he found it difficult to relate to girls because he both feared and awed them at the same time. Around a group of girls, Johnny could feel very comfortable and spout stories and witticisms, but he had difficulty relating to just one. It was something he didn't overcome for a long time.

"I had an almost dual personality back then," John Henry said. "Because I ran with the Gartmans and never went to church, and cursed . . . but I loved the Sunday school picnics. I enjoyed the social life [of the church]." Henry and Mattie would not forbid Johnny to see anyone, and Henry actually encouraged Johnny to explore other people's cultures and viewpoints. Where Johnny had to be discreet was in the presence of his mother's relatives, like Cousin Teck and Cousin Florence, who lived at the Faulk home for years. "They were both gentle women, Southern gentle women, and regarded themselves as such. They were the branch of the family that would take that kind of thing very seriously." [15]

As he developed as a teenager, Johnny left behind not only poor grades but also the close association he had with his young black friends. Part of the reason for that, of course, was that Austin High was a segregated school in the 1930s. Although blacks still lived behind the Faulk home, and some worked with his family, Johnny no longer left home to play with these old friends. He had a different peer group at school and at church — the white children who came from the Southern Bible-belt, puritanic, protestant community. "I began to not reject the blacks, but accept society's attitude of segregation," Johnny said. "I always had sympathy for the poor blacks I was growing up with, but it was mixed with a heavy dose of a patronizing feeling, although a warm one." [16]

Schoolmate Fath remembered when Johnny gave entire Shakespeare soliloquies in black dialect during his early high school years, which delighted fellow students as well as teachers. On one occasion, he portrayed a black character in a church play that had his audience cackling.

It didn't occur to Johnny until later, when he started reading and collecting black folklore at the University of Texas, that this pretending — and the black-painted faced comedians he saw at medicine shows on South First Street — actually dehumanized black culture and reinforced white stereotypes.[17] Still, his characterizations and impersonations, while crude, did hone his storytelling and dialect skills, and they were nothing like the real prejudice that permeated society at the time.

One of the most striking recollections of segregation and prejudice Johnny recalled was with his first job at age sixteen, as a water boy for the Travis County Courthouse. He'd get there at 8:00 A.M. and carry two buckets of water to the building for drinking, one marked for the "coloreds" and the other for the whites.

"I was supposed to empty the white one first," Johnny said, "but sometimes I wouldn't and would spill some of the water into the buckets for the whites. I remember some people would say, 'Don't give me that water where the niggers drink out of.' "[18]

Johnny's father encouraged him to work. He never paid his son an allowance, not even for his work collecting rents from tenants. Generous to a fault to others less fortunate, Henry emphasized the value of hard work on character to his children. "Work, learn to work hard," he would tell his son, "and good things will come to you." Henry would spend hours pulling Johnson grass on his farm after he'd get home from his law practice. Mattie would have to prod and push her husband to get him to take the children to a movie theater, because he considered that and other forms of "modern entertainment" a waste of time. He thought the same for ballgames and fishing and hunting. He'd rather see his children read a good book or pull some weeds on the farm: "Pull some weeds when you feel you need to go out at Barton Springs," he would say.

One day Johnny and Jack Kellam took the Faulk car to go courtin' the girls at Barton Springs. When Johnny backed out of his parking space, he caught the rear fender of the adjacent parked car. The son of the woman who owned the car, Robert Manlove, took down all the information from Kellam and relayed it to his mother. Johnny said he'd be there and would take care of whatever the bill would be for repairs. John Henry said, "The next afternoon, on a Sunday, Daddy came home from church to eat dinner and take a nap—he'd take one every Sunday (in fact, he had just taken one that morning in the church)—well, he was taking his nap, and everybody was gone, except me, and I was downstairs. I heard the phone ringing, and Daddy had already gotten it in his upstairs room. I heard him say 'Hello? Hello, hello?' It had interrupted his sleep. And the woman said, 'My name is Mrs. Robert Manlove, and last night your son—I'm a widow, my husband died last year, and I have to provide for myself; my son helps provide for me — well, last night, your son was out at Barton Springs, and I was out there, too, and your son backed his car out, and struck my car.'"

Johnny heard his daddy exclaim in a loud voice: "Well, you had no business out there! It ought to happen to you! I'm tellin' you, you're a grown woman, and out at Barton Springs!" Then he proceeded to deliver a lecture to the woman on the "frivolity of modern American life." He said he would, of course, cover the damages, but it broke Mrs. Manlove of ever wanting to call the Faulks again.[19]

This overwhelming Protestant work ethic and his father's constant pressure on his sons to work hard gave Johnny an extreme distaste for work that he found hard to overcome later in life.[20] Johnny would rather listen to stories than work. Constantly exposed to stories of the Texas past and the old ways of the frontier through his relatives and the Becketts, Johnny always delighted in the folk stories and yarns he heard from his elders. He enjoyed listening to stories from his Aunt Niney or Captain John Talley, who both lived at the Faulk home for a time. "Brother Talley" could resurrect events that occurred on a specific day, for example, in 1873 from part of his experiences as a traildriver and cattleman on the Texas plains.

Aunt Niney, one of his mother's kin who lived in the Faulk home for a few years, was in her nineties when she moved to Austin. She had grown up in Louisiana and lived near Lampasas, Texas, in the 1850s. A woman with sparkling, gray eyes and hair parted down the middle, she described great adventures of Comanche raids that imbued in Johnny a love for Texas folklore and frontier life.

She told him of the time she was airing out two large feather beds on a banister outside the log cabin in which she lived alone. Suddenly, she looked out her window to see a couple dozen Comanches on horseback, whooping and yelling. She bolted herself inside the cabin that was built to withstand an attack. Instead of attacking the cabin, the Indians roped the feather beds and started riding off with them to the hills.

After hours and hours of her storytelling, Johnny would often fall asleep with her in bed. He would implore her to tell him stories about "Old Three Toes," the bear that stole bacon from her smokehouse, or about the great flocks of passenger pigeons that blotted out the entire sky, or about the herd of buffalo that trampled clouds of dust on the prairies.[21]

Aunt Niney, the Talleys, and the Becketts provided much entertainment for young Faulk. He enjoyed elderly people, because they gave him attention and exposed him to the warmth and simplicity of frontier life.

4.

Professor Pancho
and the
Folklore Renaissance

N ineteen thirty-two was a taxing year for the nation. The Depression was in full force, with 13 million Americans out of work and industries down by half the production volume of 1929. Yet many Americans were optimistic, as the promise of a "New Deal" rose with the landslide victory of Franklin D. Roosevelt in November.

It was also a year of hope for young college freshman John Henry Faulk.[1] Eager to attend the University of Texas, John Henry had visions of becoming a lawyer, like his father. Living at home, he walked the four-mile trek to the university every day on gravel roads. But he was disappointed with those first two years of law classes; the subject was much too rigorous and dull for a young man eager to express himself and be creative.

John Brodie, who continued to take Johnny in his wagon during trips to his cattle farm in Oak Hill after school, disdained college, and was very disappointed that John Henry chose to go to the university. He said, "A man's got to think for himself, boy. A man that lets somebody else do his thinkin' for him is like a man who lets somebody else do his work for him."[2] On one of those trips to Oak Hill one hot summer day, both John Henry and Brodie saddled up the horses to round up a steer. After running a steer all morning, the two finally got him penned. Since the steer, which was fed a steady diet of grass, had been in the pasture all day, his bowels had become loose after all this exercise.

John Henry described what happened: ". . . Mr. Brodie was up in the front of the truck – he had run the rope around the steer's head and up through a slat in the front of the truck – and he was pulling on him and I was whipping the steer to make him walk into the truck. Brodie said 'Johnny, get him by the tail and twist it. That's the only way you're going to make the son of a bitch go forward. He's a stalling there. He's a sulling on you.' So I started to grab the tail, but it had just become a mess – almost like a garden hose – of green shit. And I made several passes at it and as he'd swing it, it would kind of throw shit like a garden hose. And Brodie was straining and said, 'Grab him, goddamn it. Twist that steer's tail.' And I said, 'Mr. Brodie, I'm not going to grab hold of that old shitty tail and get that stuff all over me.'

"Brodie turned loose the rope, looked at me in utter and total disgust for a long minute and said, 'By God, you just explained the University of Texas to me. Highly educated, that's what they teach you to be out there – to be scared of a little green cow shit, huh! By God, you know what that is? Scientific, what that is – water and grass – that's just what it is. All that steer eats is water and grass, and that's all that it is, water and grass, and you're scared of a little cow shit . . . of course, I'm not a college man like you are.' "[3]

Because John Henry delighted in that attitude of defiance, independence, and unpretentiousness, it was natural for him to gravitate toward a university teacher by the name of J. Frank Dobie. He fell under J. Frank Dobie's spell very quickly. Known as the "cowboy professor," or "Professor Pancho," Dobie was at the height of his popularity in the early 1930s. He was more than a teacher or author; he was a symbol of the state, like cattle, oil rigs, and the Alamo.

Dobie, who grew up in the South Texas brush country, came from a similar family background as Johnny. His parents were staunch Methodists; his father a county commissioner and pillar of the community in Live Oak County. He graduated from Southwestern University in Georgetown and received his master's degree in English from Columbia University in New York. He began teaching at the University of Texas in 1914, but left the university from 1923 to 1925 after incurring the wrath of some faculty members who thought his course work was too "barbaric" for the university. He was already quite well known in the Southwest by the time John Henry met him in 1934. He had worked as a journalist, served as first lieutenant in World War I, presided over the Texas Folklore Society, and written a number of books about Texas. With the publication of *A Vaquero of the Brush Country* and *Coronado's Children*, plus stories published in *The Saturday Evening Post* and *Colliers*, Dobie had gained a national recognition, both for himself and for the literature of the land he loved. Unconventional in style and in substance, Dobie disdained the teaching through records and fact-finding: "If you wish human beings, whether young or old, to regard history, then touch their imaginations," he told his good friend John H. McGinnis of Southern Methodist University.[4]

Before taking Dobie's "Life and Literature of the Southwest" class in 1934, John Henry did not know the significance of the word "folklore." Despite living with people born on the Texas frontier, Johnny didn't really learn to appreciate the natural humor of folklore as an art form until Dobie showed him that Texans had produced a rich culture of stories, songs, and ballads. To Dobie, matters of folk culture having to do with the way Texans lived and saw life were incredibly important and carried universal meanings about the nature of the human condition, and he conveyed this with rich stories about the lives of Mexican vaqueros and frontier cattlemen – the true "cowboys." He loathed the way Hollywood had portrayed the West. There was nothing "romantic" about a cowboy's life to Dobie; it was a hard, grueling existence that was a struggle for survival.

John Henry was dazzled by the way this English professor taught his 100-plus students – with stories and anecdotes rather than with textbooks. Dobie's students came from all departments, with more from English, history, and journalism. In Dobie's class, little emphasis was placed on required textbooks or note-taking, because the professor believed that the authentic history of the United States lay in people's stories about it. So he approached a course the same way he approached Southwestern life, telling personal anecdotes and stories he had heard from Texas cattlemen and ranchers. Everything the students read and wrote was embellished and enriched through Dobie's stories, which recounted the feelings and motivations of the men who herded cattle and blazed trails. He required every student to read and report on a book each week, everything from Siringo's *A Texas Cowboy* to the writings of Andy Adams and Colonel Rip Ford.

One of Dobie's peers at the university was folklorist John Lomax, who had published collections of cowboy songs with the aid of fellowships from Harvard. Lomax occasionally solicited feature articles from Dobie for the *Alcalde*, the university's only literary magazine at the time. In 1933 Lomax began a long career, with help from his son Alan, collecting not only the words but the tunes of ballads sung by black prisoners in the South. He and Alan took about 10,000 of these songs, which included ballads by Leadbelly, Iron Head, and Red Dobie (no relation to J. Frank), to the folk song archives at the Library of Congress. Dobie admired these collections, and likewise set out to collect his own tales of Texas. Dobie's tales about the wild mustangs of the Southwest and Texas cattlemen and ranchers were published by the Texas Folklore Society, which he founded in 1924, and for which he served as editor and secretary until 1943.

To Dobie, John Henry's stories about black folks in South Austin and unrefined characters like John Brodie and Alvie Gartman weren't trivial or a waste of time. Dobie saw the value in the young student's characterizations, his relationships with storytellers at home, and his use of the black folk idiom.

During a break in class, John Henry launched into one of his impersonations of a black preacher in a South Austin church:

> "Go down angel, consume the flood.
> Snuff out the sun and turn de moon to blood!
> Go down angel and close the doo'
> Times have been shain't be no mo'."

Dobie's curiosity and fascination were piqued, and he asked John Henry to take him to the Baptist Church where the Reverend A. Reese delivered his sermons in rhythmic, Miltonesque tones. Although illiterate, the old man gave an eloquent sermon, serving as the poet, preacher, and singer who gave voice to his congregation's religion.[5]

This environment was novel to Dobie. Reared in the brush country in Live Oak County in South Texas, he had been exposed to minorities (usually Mexicans) being treated in a dramatically different way from whites. He took segregation as a way of life, and didn't start considering the inequities of society before seeing rural black culture through John Henry, who gave him detailed accounts of visits to black congregations. "He began seeing a whole group of people in a new light," John Henry said, "and began to realize their individual self-worth." John Henry knew that this black religious culture was special in some way, but didn't know just how unique it was.

Dobie encouraged John Henry to look beyond the camaraderie and cheerful sense of humor of blacks and into their storytelling folklore. With Dobie's support, he began collecting material on black folklore and recording his observations from church sermons. Few scholars had regarded this a worthy pursuit, so there was no catalog or collection of such material in academia. Dobie admired his work. "You're a natural-born collector, Johnny," he told him.[6]

The admiration was mutual. John Henry found originality in the professor's recounting and examination of old Texas culture. He also found Dobie's resistance and defiance to authority very appealing, as he did with John Brodie. In 1936, Dobie was thrown in jail for a brief time because he refused to pay parking tickets. He publicly said he'd rather go to jail than pay the fine for "some ridiculous law."

"I am protesting a law," he said, "that does not permit a man to park on a street where parking space is more than sufficient to handle the demand." In lieu of a jail call, the local chief of police gave Dobie some office work to perform. Despite his vast intellect and his position at the university, Dobie didn't have much use for academicians and scholars. The Ph.D., he felt, was a meaningless ritual that derived from the Teutonic and ritualistic mind.

Dobie appreciated the stories John Henry wrote, but, as he

did with his other students, he reviewed the work with a critical eye. Although he didn't mind how bawdy John Henry's stories were, he prodded the freshman to explain his themes in greater detail, never letting him get away with anything less than his best effort. With his thick, black pencil, he'd slash away at John Henry's writings, filling the margins with pithy comment, always to the point. Dobie was a hard taskmaster, and he thought John Henry was too perfunctory in his writing.

"He wanted me to be a writer," said John Henry, "but he said writing was the hardest job in the world, with which I agree. So I found it much more efficacious to simply affect these words [of people] and make them word portraits — they came much more easily and spontaneously." [7]

One of the first pieces John Henry wrote for Dobie was on frontiersman John Wesley Hardin, as told by old cattleman John D. Talley. Talley had told John Henry a tale about Hardin driving a cattle herd on the West Texas plains in the mid-1800s. John Henry related this yarn about the cattle, the buffaloes, and Indians in his short story for Dobie.

But most of John Henry's writing at this time was confined to humor and poetry. He wrote many romantic rhythmic verses for various women he was infatuated with, like a young girl he met on the road traveling with Jack Kellam's jazz band. Kellam, who made from $4 to $10 a night playing piano in "Homer Hammity's Band of Bands," brought along John Henry as a ticket-taker for many performances. At one of the gigs in Burnet, John Henry became very enamored with a girl named Nelle, and the two held hands and warmed each other next to a woodstove on a bitter winter's night.

When he returned to Austin, he wrote Nelle a poem about the mockingbirds and the pear trees in the snow — a missive he thought very romantic — and mailed it to her. Kellam, who roomed with John Henry at the Faulk house, questioned him persistently whether he had heard from Nelle yet. One day the letter finally arrived, and John Henry nervously opened it in front of Kellam. The crude handwriting, written on scrap paper, was barely legible, but the brief message read, in part: "This leaves me well, hope you the same. Did you hear about the feller who had

the hiccups and they went down on him, and he farted himself to
death? Love, Nelle."

That killed John Henry's affection for the girl, and Kellam
would use the words "Love, Nelle" many times when John Henry
would attempt poetry.[8]

As a sophomore, John Henry encountered some more interesting and different women. Periodically, when his mother would
convince Judge Faulk that he needed to collect *some* money from
his rental houses, he'd send John Henry down to collect rent in
East Austin. There, people lived in the most abject poverty in
town; the bottom planks of their small houses rotted away, and
rats and cockroaches ran in and out at night. During one of his
trips, John Henry went with Jack Kellam to a two-story house that
had one room on each story. His father had told him to ask for
Rosa Lee.

When John Henry approached the house and knocked on
the door, a large, heavy-set black woman grabbed him by the arm
and ushered him into the tiny house. "Come on in, hon," she said
to the two. "Y'all come on in heah and sit right down." Jack and
John Henry looked at each other inquisitively and nervously
when she commented that "y'alls sure a nice lookin'," but that
Jack looked a "might chunky." John Henry thought he'd clear this
up right away: "I came to see Rosa Lee."

"Oh—you want to see Rosa Lee? I thought I recognized you.
Just a minute. Rosa Lee! Rosa Lee! Come on down heah. I got two
boys wantin' to see you!" So Rosa Lee came prancing down the
stairs wearing nothing but an undergarment, and recognized
John Henry. "Oh, shit," she said. "It's Judge Faulk's boy! He jest
want the rent—he don't want to have fun!"[9]

Afterwards, John Henry delighted in his visits to these
women just to sit and engage them in conversation. Although it
was a common tradition at the university for fraternities to take
advantage of these black prostitutes during initiations, John
Henry would go with Kellam, McNeil, or Eckhardt just to talk
with the women. To him, they not only were entertaining and
friendly, but they had the most picturesque language imaginable.

"I love the Southern people," John Henry said, "but I always
wondered, 'How can they be such animals?' Like Uncle Lee—how
can he make such a sharp distinction between his wife and the

white women, and the Negro women sexually? The answer is, they regard them as animals. And this book, *Mandingo*, came near explaining it." [10]

While in school, John Henry started writing for *The Ranger*, a monthly independent humor magazine that often criticized campus academics and ran discourses on university politics. A heady group was on this staff in 1935–36: Kellam, Eckhardt, Bob Engelking, and Charlie Black, all friends of John Henry's. Black went on to a distinguished career in constitutional law, and Eckhardt in the U.S. Congress. Johnny would write light stories as the paper's "foreign correspondent" from small towns in the state, like Canebrake.

The mid to late 1930s were times of great ferment and experimentation with new ideas among the political and social spectrum. With a boom in book publishing and government-sponsored art and theater projects, more artists were exploring the culture of the common man. Photographers and film producers discovered the documentary, stressing the independence and artistry of people who survived the Depression. The federal government, through agencies like the Farm Security Administration, sent writers and photographers to the South to document the Depression. Folk music was beginning to be viewed with respect, as musicians like Aunt Molly Jackson, Huddie Ledbetter ("Leadbelly," whom Alan Lomax discovered at Angola State Prison Farm in Louisiana), and Woody Guthrie brought to the forefront basic American musical traditions and social problems.

This cultural renaissance carried over into many classes and organizations at the University of Texas. With about 10,000 students, political activism at the school was not uncommon in this "New Deal" town, and many students belonged to organizations such as the Social Problems Council and the Young Democrats League. The university brought many liberal speakers on campus during the late 1930s: Tucker B. Smith, an industrial unionist who was director of labor for the Emergency Peace Council; Robert F. La Follette, governor of Wisconsin, and one of the founders of the Progressive Party; Mariel Lester, "the Jane Adams of England," who worked for the international peace movement; and Norman Thomas, twice presidential candidate of the Socialist Party, and a friend of Henry Faulk's. John Henry attended many meetings of the League for Industrial Democracy, which followed the teachings of Thomas. In Thomas' view, the New Deal didn't solve the economic problems of the country but only continued production for profit and increased the government borrowing from banks for public expenditures. "America is not the land of freedom," Thomas told the university crowd, "so long as we have double standards, one for the poor and one for the rich, one for the black and one for the white, one for the laborer and one for the boss." [11]

John Henry and other students were stimulated by heady discussions in classes with naturalist Roy Bedichek, historian Walter Prescott Webb (who later became president of the American Historical Association), English Professor Mody Boatright (associate editor of the Texas Folklore Society from 1936 to 1943), economics professor Bob Montgomery, and others. Forums and seminars on politics and social issues were held almost weekly. These teachers stimulated their students to engage in weighty discussions, and Dobie, Webb, and Bedichek invited groups of students to their homes for fireside debates and conversation. These discussions would often take place at Webb's ranch on Friday Mountain, at Dobie's Cherry Spring Ranch, or on one of Bedichek's hikes through the Austin Hill Country. The first hour would often be devoted to folk tales and songs discovered by John Lomax; the remainder of time focused on politics, philosophy, or other issues. Dobie, Webb, and Bedichek were teachers John Henry could identify with. He saw in these three men an idealism and egalitarianism that was highly uncommon.

A self-described naturalist and director of the University Interscholastic League, Roy Bedichek was devoted to the works of Walt Whitman, Thoreau, and of the Latin and Greek classics. Dobie considered Bedichek his greatest friend. Bedichek adored Dobie's colloquialisms and natural language, while Dobie revered Bedichek's phenomenal memory and intellect. Bedichek also had strong views on politics and social issues as much as he did on nature. "He was very supportive of the New Deal; he didn't think it went far enough. He was also very contemptuous of the reactionaries and the killers of the dream," John Henry said. "Fascism was a deep concern to Bedichek. The only progress we ever made was during a war . . . the only scientific progress made was during a war, grew out of the war experience. He couldn't tolerate that." [12]

Fascism also deeply disturbed John Henry, because he saw it as a harsh and violent means of oppressing the public. Nazi Germany had emerged its ugly head; Japan had an undeclared war on China; and the Republic of Spain was in a state of civil war. Germany and Italy had sent troops and artillery to Franco, while most of the Western democracies adopted a position of neutrality that didn't help the cause of the Spanish Loyalists. John Henry, concerned about the spread of fascism in Europe, provided some information to Dobie on this war. At the same time, Hitler was being appeased with territory by France and Britain. Yet America's posture was still one of neutrality and isolationism.

Dobie, who had been an officer in World War I, despised the Germans. After Hitler and Mussolini had attacked the Republic of Spain ("using Franco as their puppet," John Henry said), John Henry began reading literature about the Spanish Civil War and the likelihood of a second world war breaking out. He funneled this material to Dobie, who, for the first time, became interested in political activism.

"Dobie hated Catholics; hated Germans. And Pope Pious XI made the regrettable mistake, from the public's point of view, as far as Dobie was concerned, of blessing Hitler's and Mussolini's attack on the Spanish Republic, and the establishment of France and Britain and America froze out Spain and would not send any aid; let Hitler and Mussolini do unto death and set Franco up as the dictator. Dobie started reading all of this and his eyes got open; began to realize what politics were all about." [13]

In December 1937, John Henry wrote a bleak account about a family celebrating Christmas with wartime gifts: toy hand grenades, a Buck Rogers disintegrator gun, and barbed wire around the Christmas tree. "No one doubted that Santa Claus would come in," John Henry wrote, but "in a tan bomber, and that his gifts would hit the chimney of everyone who had been good and patriotic during the year." [14]

Another story John Henry wrote satirized Hitler instead of American patriotism. In a mock interview, Hitler said he would appoint a commission to investigate the "Teutonic origin of

Christmas. If all is not Aryan, then Germany goes off the old Christmas standard, and we shall change the time of celebration to my birthday and call it Hitmas. But I want all the Aryan world to know that I am eagerly looking forward to the day when I get all of the Jews and Communists killed out, so we can all enjoy peace on earth, good will toward man, together." [15]

With international events changing quickly, John Henry felt an urge to travel and get out and see the world. At age twenty-one, he had never been outside Texas, and wanted to broaden his knowledge and experiences. He also knew without a doubt that law school was not for him, and he would need time to separate himself from the pressures of academics. After a long talk with Mama, John Henry temporarily dropped out of school to go to Japan. Henry Faulk, however, was against his son leaving school to go off on some fool trip with no job. Miss Mattie won out, however, and in the summer of '36, John Henry hitchhiked to California by car and freight train. Of course, he never made it to Japan, but he did meet some fascinating travelers along the way, like the illiterate black man he caught up with in a box car between Fresno and San Francisco. Although illiterate, the man had a keen interest in current events and traveled to locations where anything he considered of historical importance took place. He supported himself by getting odd jobs along his journey.

John Henry's sojourn led him to Redwood City, just south of San Francisco, where he took jobs pumping gas and busing tables. He was more interested in literature and poetry, however. "I was bitten by the literary bug, and decided then I wanted to write," John Henry said. "And the way to write was to teach school, I thought." The year away from Travis County was an eye-opening experience for him. For the first time he saw the poverty-stricken conditions of migrant workers and their families — "dust bowl refugees" who lived in homemade shacks and underneath bridges. He also witnessed strikes by union men, making him aware of labor's plight in the West. At one of these strikes, he saw a policeman club a man, and was astonished by the violence perpetrated by someone in authority.[16]

The Depression was subsiding. Although many family farms were devastated by a widespread drought, Americans had reason to be optimistic. Farm prices rose, metal prices rose, and automobile production increased by twenty percent. Education was improving with projects like the Civilian Conservation Corps, which taught thousands to read and write.

John Henry became part of the New Deal when he returned to Texas to work with the Works Progress Administration, a federal program that gave thousands of writers, artists, and researchers new jobs. He and fellow University of Texas student Brownie McNeil made $85 per month ("good money back then") for the WPA's Historical Records Survey. The two rented a garage apartment from McNeil's mother in San Antonio and traveled frequently. A 1938 trip to Boston was the first time John Henry had been east of the Mississippi River.

Both John Henry and McNeil organized historical records in Bexar County. McNeil, who spoke and wrote Spanish fluently, researched Spanish records for the county dating as far back as 1740. John Henry's work dealt mainly with the county government history and other historical data.[17]

Brownie McNeil said the two referred to the Historical Records Survey as the "Hysterical Records Survey" because of the myriad characters they worked with at the courthouse in San Antonio. Their boss was a large, red-faced, cigar-chewing buffoon who told off-color jokes to his secretary and the other editors and stenographers in the office. Some of those who were employed there were hard-luck cases, people who couldn't hold down a job or who were still suffering from the effects of the Depression. Contrasted with the college-educated employees, the place seemed like a badly disciplined Bedlam to both John Henry and Brownie. Still, both got along fairly well as long as they had beer money.

A frequent stomping ground after work was a disreputable bar in San Antonio called The Golden Horn, on the edge of the city's red-light district. The saloon-keeper there sort of adopted them as his "young college-set," and guarded them from trouble.

This part of San Antonio belonged to the Mexican-American community, and their social life fascinated John Henry. At the Queen Plaza, John Henry and Brownie would wander through the open street markets in the evening. Vendors would sell hay and vegetables by day, but by night would purvey authentic enchiladas on portable tables. Mariachi bands would play old Mexican folk songs for fifteen cents, or two songs for a quarter.[18]

San Antonio was only the first stop for John Henry as an employee with the WPA. In March of '38, he moved to Bellville in southeastern Texas to do historical research in that county. In a letter to his friend Mary Elizabeth Dove, he described his landlady as a "charming little Jewish lady, tiny and chirping, who has taken me on as her first roomer. Her fancied role as a landlady demands that she attend my every wish with flattering enthusiasm. I am not allowed to make a single move without her assistance. Bathing is about the only solitary act I perform."[19]

By this time, John Henry had decided to return to the university the following year to complete his bachelor's and master's in English. He thought of himself as a writer, and wrote several letters, poems, and scripts. His break came when the university invited him to write a script for a play.

The play, called "Heaven in the Spring," was discovered by the wife of the editor of a San Antonio newspaper, who was so impressed by the work that she sent John Henry to Austin to meet with Herbert Well, the director of the University Light Opera Company. Well immediately commissioned John Henry to direct the production to be performed on campus at Hogg Memorial Auditorium.

Touted as the "Negro idea of heaven," the one-act play dealt with a little black boy who was on his deathbed as spring arrived on earth, with his Uncle Sy sitting up with him. Obviously very sick, the boy wakes up and asks his uncle, "Uncle Sy, when it goin' to be daylight?"

Knowing that death will come any time to the child, Uncle Sy tells him, "It's goin' to be daylight before very long now."

"But when they goin' to let me up?"

"Oh, honey, one of these days — not before very long. Any time now, a whole band of real snowy angels is goin' to sweep down here and brush through the air with their wings, comin' in on their velvet slippers. And you'll hear 'em a singin' and a laughin' and a talkin', and they're comin' to fetch you, and carry you off yonder, where every day's a Sunday and every month the month of May."

Uncle Sy proceeded to describe to this dying child the glory of heaven, "where there's always plenty to eat and where you'll be able to slop the hogs with Jesus."

Over 1,000 people came to the play on April 21, 1938, with John Henry playing Uncle Sy and an Austin High School drama student playing the dying boy. In addition to the music provided by the University Light Opera Company, sixty voices of the University Methodist Church choir sang Negro spirituals during the performance.[20]

John Henry's talents were recognized by many in the university community after this play, who perceived it as a splendid statement on black folklore. Perhaps because the one-act play was so novel, much of the white community thought John Henry had captured the poetic imagery and philosophical thinking of a culture that had heretofore been ignored. And others, like Dr. Rudolph Willard of the Linguistics Department and folklore expert Alan Lomax, persuaded John Henry to explore rural black culture in greater detail. Alan became a strong inspiration and guidance in John Henry's career, helping him organize and collect material on black folklore.

In the fall of 1939, John Henry returned to Austin when he was told his father, who had been suffering from cancer of the liver, was near death. In late September, Henry Faulk died at home at age seventy-two. The obituary in the *Austin American* referred to him as a "pioneer Austin attorney and former newspaper publisher." His body was lain in a casket at Fred Allen Memorial Methodist Church for a longer-than-usual period "to allow both races to take part in the final rites because of his philanthropic work among Negroes," the obituary said. Although despondent over the death, John Henry had little time to grieve: He suddenly found himself needed to give the rest of his family emotional support when his brother Hamilton, who had experienced episodes of mental illness in the past, had to be taken to Austin State Hospital temporarily.

John Henry's sister Martha, always the money manager of the family, took over as executor of the Faulk estate, only to find that her father had not kept records of his debts, which were numerous. She managed the estate well enough to help John Henry get back into school, so that he could continue the work he had started for his M.A., collecting black folklore.

As Dobie took a more active interest in John Henry's career, the two became much closer. John Henry's favorite experiences were with Dobie, Webb, and Bedicheck at Dobie's Paisano Ranch south of Austin. About once a month, they had informal meetings devoted almost entirely to storytelling (and eating and drinking).

"Dobie and Roy Bedichek and Henry Nash Smith, a professor of English at the university, a very distinguished historian and literary man who became editor and curator of Mark Twain's estate out at California's Huntington Library, and Mody Boatright and Webb—we had a kind of little club," John Henry said. "It was held either at Webb's ranch or Dobie's ranch, and we'd drink whiskey and talk and have supper. It was the pleasantest of pleasantest experiences for me. I developed as a storyteller. They encouraged it—always took call for two or three stories by me, my latest ones.

"Nothing bored Dobie like a joke—'Pat and Mike met, Mike said so and so'—but there's nothing he loved like real humor as part of people. And I became something of a master of that, by doing these characters. That's how I evolved a lot of my characters. Dobie absolutely ate it up. He loved to show me off when he had a literary guest come to Austin, and [would] get me to perform for him, and tell him stories.

"We'd have these suppers at the ranch at least once a month. Sometimes we'd go several months and not get together, at other times we'd do it every week. It was very informal; there was no set pattern to it." [21] The youngest of the crew, John Henry found himself very fortunate to be a part of this meeting of the minds; these scholars who held such a high mutual respect for each other's rights to hold contrary opinions. "You, see, we were of the opinion that the highest form of human intercourse is conversation. And we conceived of it to be disappearing. Under the impact of radio and television, America was becoming a listening, noise-oriented society, whereas conversation was not tolerated. People were getting to where they couldn't hardly carry on a conversation." [22] Dobie, in particular, hated radio and television (he called them the "destroyers of conversation").

John Henry recalled one incident at one of the get-togethers: "I remember there was this guy when I was coming down to

Austin from New York who invited us to his place. He said, 'Listen, you don't have to go all the way to the ranch, you can come here; I've got a swimming pool, you can go swimming. You can have a picnic out here, and you'd just be welcome as the flowers of May.' Dr. John Garcia, he fixed it up just wonderful for us, and we were sittin' around the pool there. Dobie was a big swimmer and I was a big swimmer. The fire was going, and we started telling our stories, and about that time this guy's loudspeakers (he had the place hooked up with loudspeakers) started playing music. He thought Dobie would be dying to hear some cowboy music. And it sounded like some goddamn amusement park. I thought Dobie was going to become unglued: 'Shut that goddamnthing off. Who in the hell turned on that thing?' he blared. And this guy, I thought he was going to drown himself getting over there." [23]

With Dobie's encouragement, John Henry traversed East Texas to record black preachers' sermons. In trips to the Brazos River Bottom to record these sermons, he would operate a bulky recording machine in the back pews of the small, withering churches he would visit. John Henry would spend several hours listening to the recordings of these preachers, all who used rich folk imagery from their culture and heritage intermixed with gospel singing and the only literature they knew — the Bible. With his quick ear for dialect, he learned to imitate the cadence of this "sing-preaching," now a lost art.

"These sermons," he wrote, "rang with the assurance that there was no hiding place down here, but that some day [the preacher] was going to lay down his heavy load, mount the wings of morning, and sing all over God's Heaven."

5.

The Struggle

for

Equality

"I am convinced that the simple genius and the native art that characterize the American Negro's folk religion place it in a position of importance as a genuine art form."

So began John Henry Faulk's introduction to his master's thesis, submitted to the UT Department of English in the summer of 1940. Entitled "Ten Negro Sermons," the thesis literally transcribed various black preachers John Henry had heard preach over the years. (The word "Negro" was the progressive term for blacks then; if they didn't use the disparaging word "nigger," the white community referred to them as "coloreds," "darkies," or "nigras.")

John Henry collected his sermons at black churches in Travis County, and Bexar County (in San Antonio). He would take his recording machine to a church service, take extensive notes during the sermon, then go home and write out the sermon in greater detail. The sermons he heard represented the truest expressions of black folk-religion. Dobie, Alan Lomax, and Dr. Willard guided John Henry in preparing the thesis. Willard motivated John Henry into exploring and reiterating the speech patterns of the black preachers. He would go to the black churches with John Henry and give him advice on how to pick up certain nuances of speech patterns and dialect. This encouraged John Henry that he was taking the right direction in preparing his thesis.[1]

John Henry endeavored to faithfully record the sermons of these preachers who retained folk elements in their sermons because he saw that this folk element was rapidly disappearing from existence. As blacks assimilated into the white urban society and the white system of education, they moved further away from their rural, folk religion. The poetic simplicity of this folk culture was reflected in these sermons, which gave a strong voice to the congregations. "The Negro preacher," John Henry wrote, "became the poet and the singer who gave voice to his people's religion. He was often unable to read. He was often in poverty. But he was always eloquent, and he was always convincing. His sermons, whether they were rehearsed or extemporaneous, were invariably infused with his creative genius." John Henry acknowledged that recording a sermon in written form would lose key elements of the preaching: one, the background of ecstatic comments and noises from the congregation that lended rhythm and chorus to the sermon ("a sermon without such a background is comparable to an orchestra without a rhythm section," John Henry said); and two, the captivating, melodic rhythm of the sermon itself. Several of the preachers talked in a loud, berating tone, stomping and gesticulating throughout the service. John Henry could only occasionally capture the intonations and the building crescendo of the sermons in writing, and he admitted so.

Despite help from Alan Lomax and Dr. Willard, John Henry's attempt to literally transcribe these sermons often didn't work well. Some of the language, with phonetic spellings, was too stilted and difficult to read. The eighty-five-page thesis takes an inordinate amount of time to read because he tried to spell words phonetically when the proper spelling would have sufficed. For example, he would use the word "keah" for "care," "stuhrin' " for "stirring," "tahd" for "tired," or "smawt" for "smart."

This method of phonetic spelling was the only way John Henry could think of to capture the rhythm and cadence of these sermons and the rich folk imagery invoked by the preachers — those "magnificent men who used almost Miltonic splendor" in their speech. He spent a great deal of time experimenting with different spellings to capture the idiom and dialect. While he could imitate all kinds of Southern accents and mannerisms in his speech, John Henry discovered that they could not easily be recaptured on paper. It would be a recurring problem for him in his future writings.

"All of us back then struggled with trans-literating [the words], to make it almost like phonetics," said Alan Lomax. "I don't know, it was a good effort, for the people who took the trouble to read it carefully — read Johnny carefully, and me and others who were writing this stuff down." Unfortunately, Lomax said, reading English that wasn't spelled in the conventional way managed to turn most people off. Both Lomax and John Henry would eventually give up the practice, and work more on getting the idiom down correctly.[2]

In John Henry's thesis, many of the preachers' stories build into a crescendo of rhythm and emotion, like Reverend Chester Hulen's talk of Christ's second coming. Reverend Hulen tells his congregation of the day Jesus returns to Earth, looking for men and women to join him in heaven. First he walks up to a house and knocks on the door, but no one opens the door; they're inside drinking and playing cards. Then he finds a group of children playing on a Sunday morning, and he asks them why they aren't in Sunday school; they reply they don't know what a Sunday school is. Then he finally comes across some honest, hardworking people who are praying and singing, and he announces that these are "my chillun dat's goin' to live with me in glory."

One of John Henry's favorite preachers was the Reverend Tanner Franklin, pastor of a small Baptist Church in the Brazos Bottom near Bellville. A large man in his fifties, he could neither read nor write, but spoke with a force and conviction that John Henry learned to imitate. His congregation consisted entirely of blacks who worked on farms. The church was a small, unpainted building that could not be used during a rain because it leaked so badly.

In his sermon, "Los' Sheep," Reverend Franklin said that "de Lawd got tahd of having ol' Satan steal his sheeps," so he "cided he was goin' to git hisself a shephuhd man to look aftuh his sheeps." That shepherd, of course, was Jesus.

"He love de sheep in de pen," the Reverend said, "but he loves de sheeps dat had strayed too. An' dem was de ones dat he went out aftuh. Amen. Dem was de ones dat he wanted back in the fol'."

Most of the preachers John Henry wrote about shared Franklin's background: reared on a farm, in poverty, without the benefit of formal education. Many, like Reverend Sam Buford of Pear Orchard Methodist Church near Bellville, had not been to school and could not read formal writing. "He told me that he could read reading, but that he could not read writing," John Henry said.

John Henry believed that the eloquent simplicity of these sermons made them a unique art form, and he hoped another researcher would pick up his work. Today, his study is housed at the Library of Congress.

In August 1940, after completing his master's work at age twenty-seven, John Henry intended to work toward a Ph.D. in black folklore. (He never completed the doctorate, perhaps influenced by Dobie's opinion that a Ph.D. was nothing more than "taking bones out of one graveyard and putting them in another.") With the help of Dobie and Lomax, John Henry applied for a Julius Rosenwald Foundation scholarship to study the literature of Southern blacks. In May 1941 he was one of sixty-four people chosen from 500 applicants to receive the $1,800 grant. With the one-year fellowship, he continued to visit small towns in Texas, like Rosebud, Calvert and Cameron, to interview blacks in their farm houses. Lomax helped catalog these collections in the Folk Archives of the Library of Congress.

John Henry began to be less interested in the folk religion of black people and more concerned about how they dealt with oppression. In a speech to the University Press Club, he spoke about the "Negro in the News," and how newspapers invariably gave an unfavorable and prejudiced presentation of blacks in their news stories. The Texas Folklore Society invited him to speak about his findings at their meetings, where he would present lifelike renditions of black sermons. He would attend folk festivals and go square dancing, enjoy the fiddle and country guitar, sing, and play party games.

The university recognized the importance of folklore with the opening of the University Folk Festival Center in 1941, under the directorship of Dr. William A. Owens. The center served as a collection and dissemination center for Texas folk dances, black spirituals, cowboy yarns and other types of folklore. Faulk, Dobie, Bedichek, and others would trade yarns at folk festivals on campus. Lomax, who had started a weekly broadcast on the Columbia Radio Network, would often come down from New York to play his guitar and sing folk songs that he discovered.

With the new and thriving revival in folklore at the university, Dr. Willard recruited John Henry to teach a part-time English I class for the university in 1940–1942. Traveling three to four days every two weeks for field trips for his fellowship, John Henry taught the class only once a week. He combined his master's work with credits toward a doctor of philosophy degree. Part of his class time was devoted to "A Taste of Texana," where students were entertained by John Henry's skits of growing folklore characters.

A curly blonde-haired woman named Hally Wood was one of the students in his class. A brilliant and talented young lady, she was enrolled in the Fine Arts School studying voice and piano. She also excelled in English grammar, something at which John Henry was not as adept as he was at storytelling. In class, the two had an arrangement worked out where Hally would signal to him if a student gave a correct answer to a question.[3] Within six weeks, the two were married.

John Henry never felt comfortable at faculty gatherings. During one such gathering, a small group of pretentious professors and scholars did their best to make him feel inferior and rejected in this circle. His automatic response was to tell an outlandish and bawdy joke about "four old whores from Canada who got drunk on cherry wine," shocking the sensibilities of the other instructors. This was John Henry's self-defense mechanism, used whenever he felt threatened by those hiding behind a facade of propriety and respectability.

Although he didn't quite fit the mold as a scholar, John Henry did occasionally review books for folklore journals. In one review for the Texas State Historical Association, on the subject of "the Gullah Negroes of the Carolina sea islands," he was critical of the author's "superficial" conclusions of the culture. He believed most of the books and studies by scholars of rural black culture failed to capture the essential character of the black American.

On one of his trips to the Brazos River Bottom, John Henry made an unusual discovery for someone who was considered by many as an expert in black folklore: "I have discovered, to my dismay," he wrote Alan Lomax in the fall of 1941, "that my knowledge of the Negro was most superficial. The Negro who reveals himself to other Negroes is an entirely different being from the Negro whom I imagined I knew so well."

During this trip, John Henry interviewed blacks at a plantation controlled by white landowners. He heard many stories of threats, whippings, and beatings. One woman told a story about one of her cousins who got his eye knocked out by the sheriff; another told about a pregnant woman who refused to allow her seven-year-old son to go to work for some white man, and the white man killed her. John Henry also talked to elderly blacks who recalled the Civil War. One 104-year-old man named James Johnson had seen General Sam Houston while driving an ox-cart to Mexico City.

All these individuals had something in common, John Henry noted: a feeling and experience of repression, and a deep resentment for it. These blacks were not the "happy-go-lucky, laughing bunch" John Henry thought he knew as a child.

One incident stuck in John Henry's mind from the trip. Sitting on a wagon, talking with a black minister, John Henry told him proudly that "I'm not like the other white folks. I think we ought to give you people the right to vote, the right to enter the professions, and work in whatever job your talents allow."

The old minister turned to John Henry and said, "You're awfully sweet, and you mean well, but you've got the disease. We've already got those rights. All you can do is just deprive us of them."

Initially, John Henry was perturbed by the man's reaction. Here he was, trying to be nice, sympathetic and understanding, and the man came back with a curt response like that. But on the trip back to Austin, he began to think about the old man's words, and he realized he was right. The U.S. Constitution guaranteed the equal rights of *all* people, and society could only unjustly deny blacks' rights.

John Henry felt he had made an incredible discovery. For the first time, he was aware of the abuse and ugliness of the segregated society in which Americans lived. He saw the parallel between Hitler's racism and America's racism: "I realized there was a degree of hypocrisy in our own attitude – as far as blacks were concerned, we treated them the same way the Germans treated the Jews. This disturbed me very deeply, and the more I reflected on it and investigated it, I discovered it was a very grave and great problem in our society. It was as though I discovered a new continent – my God, I have been living here all my life and didn't know this!"

Galvanized into action, John Henry joined the National Association for the Advancement of Colored People; then he joined a committee in Austin to help eliminate the poll tax, which was used along with detailed "literacy tests" to intimidate blacks and prevent them from voting. He spoke out against segregating blacks from using the same streetcars and restaurants, restrooms, and other facilities that whites used. He tried to sway others at the university to his cause. English Professor Mody Boatright supported John Henry, but Dobie wasn't an easy convert.

"Dobie thought I was a little off my rocker at first," John Henry said. But, as he listened more to Faulk's and Bedichek's arguments for equal rights, he developed more of a progressive attitude. ("We reached a conclusion that Hitler's anti-Semitic laws, his racist laws, were not at all unlike those that were on the books in most Southern states," John Henry said.) By 1945, Dobie staunchly supported equal voting and educational rights for blacks, despite severe repercussions. This was one of Dobie's traits that John Henry admired – the ability to change his view after listening to cogent and valid arguments. Dobie, John Henry said, listened with his heart and his mind, but it was the mind that continued to expand and explore. This was part and parcel of what constituted an unfettered and "liberated mind."

The issue of equal rights for all races became a passion for John Henry. "Once I got off down that road," John Henry said, "before long I was runnin' like hell on it. I mean, it became very important; I was making speeches on it, and I believed I should act on it. I really felt I had discovered something very fascinating about the American society — goddamn hypocritical society." Racism was an underlying fundamental of fascism, with Hitler's race propaganda.

With the poll tax in effect throughout the South, most blacks were prevented from voting. The argument favoring the poll tax was that some were "too ignorant" to vote. "That's so much nonsense," John Henry wrote. "Never anything the matter with democracy that a little more democracy won't help." John Henry's desire to eliminate the poll tax led him to attend the third annual meeting of the Southern Conference for Human Welfare in Nashville in April of 1942. While there, he met Southern activists Virginia Foster Durr, sister-in-law of Supreme Court justice Hugo Black, and Clark Foreman, who worked for the Rosenwald Fund and for Secretary of the Interior Harold Ickes. Durr and San Antonio Mayor (and later Texas congressman) Maury Maverick presided over a subcommittee of the Southern Conference to eliminate the poll tax.

Between ten to twenty percent of the voting population of most Southern states voted in the early 1940s. Since the white primaries and the anti-poll tax of the early 1900s in the South, blacks and poor whites were disenfranchised and the number of people who voted steadily declined. In some states, you couldn't vote unless you owned a certain amount of property.

John Henry joined the poll tax (or "Civil Rights") committee, which had expanded from mostly a Roosevelt coalition to a national civil rights group. Yet the only main support the coalition received from Congress was from Senator Claude Pepper of Florida and from Representative Vito Marcantonio of New York, until the tax was eliminated by the 24th Amendment in 1964.

John Henry drove to the three-day conference in his 1937 Dodge with others from the university. The theme that year was on "The South's Part in Winning the War for Democracy," with one segment of the conference dealing with citizenship and civil liberties.

The new University of Texas president, Homer P. Rainey, who directed a group on youth and training, was elected general chairman of the conference. One thousand delegates — labor leaders, church activists, blacks, industrialists, and students – attended the event.

John Henry impressed several people with his enthusiasm and concern for the disenfranchised, not the least of whom was the conference's chief speaker, Mrs. Eleanor Roosevelt. In her speech, she told how she and the president had fought against racism for years. She described one incident where both were on a train in Georgia, and a drunk white man walked into the "Jim Crow" car and shot a black man. "The next time we were in Georgia," she said, "we asked the sheriff what happened to the man. 'There he is,' he pointed. 'You don't go to jail here for killing a nigger.' "

John Henry, who was standing against a door, asked the First Lady,"Does it look like there's any hope for us to keep on fighting for these things?"

Mrs. Roosevelt pounded her knee, looked John Henry in the eye and said, "Never give up! That's what we're fighting for – the right to ask for these things. Progress will be slow, but progress will come. There have been tremendous changes in the last ten years. Just one good sign is the fact that in the last war there were no young people thinking like you at the time – nobody noticed injustices.

"There will come times when it will be a little easier to shut our eyes to injustice," Mrs. Roosevelt said. "But if we do that, democracy in this country can't be a reality. That's what makes a democracy so hard to live in."

During this time, the U.S. was heavily involved in the war against Japan and Germany. After two key defeats in the South Pacific, U.S. forces finally won major victories against the Japanese in the Coral Sea and in Midway. Everyone seemed united in the war effort; thousands of draft-age civilians flocked to Washington, D.C. to man the offices set up to handle the war program.

Feeling a strong sense of patriotic duty to his country, John Henry tried to get admitted into the service, but was turned down because of his bad eye. A friend suggested applying for the Merchant Marines, so he did in August 1942. Later that year, he was shipped on a tanker convoy that carried high-test gasoline, bound for the British Isles. His service overseas marked the beginning of a personal fight that would last far beyond the war.

6.

FIGHTING
FASCISM

A ssigned to anti-aircraft gunning, John Henry was issued a
pair of dungarees, a shirt, and a cap for his uniform. The
wages were poor; the rocking of the ship constant; the time on
land sparse. For nine months he saw the devastation of England
first-hand, heard horror stories about the war from Europeans,
and survived a torpedo barrage by the Germans in the North
Atlantic Ocean. The trip at sea was rough, with John Henry doing
everything from standing on watch in thick fog and biting cold,
to manning the anti-aircraft guns, to making the captain's bed.

Being a "utility man" on a tanker meant seeing a lot of action. He got a glimpse of another ship breaking up; witnessed a
fellow seaman lose five tanks and deck cargo in the heavy seas;
and heard the warning when an enemy submarine was nearby.
John Henry and the other men on the ship harbored an unspo-
ken dread of that unseen submarine stalking the tanker, and that
fear only disappeared when the tanker landed.

Being part of the Merchant Marines was not all dreadful for
John Henry, however. He enjoyed associating with his well-trav-

eled crew-mates, who could spin yarns and tell tall tales in great detail.

John Henry fell in love with the British people during his tour. He admired their spirit and "wholesomeness," and their ability to laugh a little at themselves despite blocks of leveled buildings in their neighborhoods left from the German strafing.

The first night he went ashore in Southern England he had a long session with the night porter and clerk at his hotel. Both assured John Henry that Hitler's biggest mistake was not attacking England when it was unprotected, and in thinking that he could demoralize the British people by blitzing them. All that Hitler managed to do, they told the young seaman, was to strengthen the resolve of an entire people and turn them into grim and determined fighters, never willing to give up.

Once, while spending two weeks in Britain waiting for his oil tanker to be repaired, he met two women who boasted about shooting down a German airplane with anti-aircraft guns. He was surprised that English women, serving in the Auxiliary Air Force or Royal Navy, were in uniform. At a talk to the Campus War Council of the University of Texas, after returning from overseas duty, John Henry would praise the British women, who "did everything from firing guns to manning barrage balloons." These women, he said, "have learned what this war is, by dodging bombs. They learned the hard way, and I hope that all you women don't learn that way. But it looks as if that is what might have to happen."

John Henry didn't feel alone in England. One time when he entered the town of Bath, he saw a soldier jump out of the street when a car turned on the left side and say, "Stay on your side of the street, you doggone yuh." John Henry asked the soldier where he was from and he said "Lubbock." The two made off to a local pub and talked Texas politics.

In a letter to J. Frank Dobie in October 1942, John Henry said he was slowly adjusting to his new way of life in the Merchant Marines, with no leave, poor wages, and no quarters provided when ashore. He delighted in listening to the adventures and stories of his fellow crew members: "No one can spin a yarn better than one of these fellows who has sailed the seas for 25 or 30 years. They tell their tales, as all good tales should be told, in great detail, and unhurriedly." [1]

John Henry made it clear that he did not consider himself "heroic" or courageous for serving in the Merchant Marines; on the contrary, he considered it a privilege to be part of the struggle to end fascism. "Unless I, along with millions of others who feel as I do, are not willing to give all that we've got by way of life and energy, we are not going to win this war – and a chance for a democratic society," he wrote. [2]

Texas politicians were particularly uninspiring to him, especially U.S. Representative Martin Dies from Texas, U.S. Senator W. Lee ("Pappy") O'Daniel (the former Texas governor who had just won a special election in 1941 to fill a Senate vacancy over then U.S. Representative Lyndon Johnson), and Lietuenant Governor John Lee Smith. Any labor union members who participated in strikes Smith called "scoundrels," and he left the impression that organized labor was an anathema to American democracy. O'Daniel, who spewed passages from the Bible on a radio show before he was elected governor in 1938, condemned labor and Roosevelt, and opposed proposals to tax income on oil or gas.

Dies, in the forefront of a rising anti-New Deal sentiment, chaired the "Dies Committee," which investigated "un-American propaganda activities in the United States." This "un-American" activity that Dies and the conservative-dominated committee defined included all "Communists, crackpots, Socialists." Among the groups the Dies Committee investigated and branded as subversive were the Anti-Nazi League, the American League for Peace and Democracy, the American League Against War and Fascism, the National Committee for the Defense of Political Prisoners, the Washington Committee for Democratic Action, the American Youth Congress, the American Committee for Democracy and Intellectual Freedom, and the National Negro Congress. [3] The Dies Committee would later be known as the House Un-American Activities Committee, or HUAC. John Henry's friend Maury Maverick was one of the few congressmen who opposed the creation of the Dies Committee in 1937, accurately predicting that the word "un-American" would be arbitrarily defined and would be applied inquisitionally against the advocacy of freedom of speech, a wage and hour bill, a fair living wage, etc.

Dies was able to label certain organizations "communist," "communist-front," or "un-American" not only without sufficient evidence, but also without fear of legal reprisals, because of the congressional immunity his committee held. Dies accused some labor unions of being controlled and manipulated by Communists and "criminals and racketeers," and attacked members of the former Roosevelt administration as "Communist sympathizers." To John Henry, Dies was a man chasing mirages, but a man capable of causing much damage to the U.S. and the Constitution. "I hate a damn flag waver damn near as bad as I hate a nazi," he wrote to Dobie on February 7, 1943. "Patriotism is not something a man talks about – it is something he does something about. The fellows that blow the loudest about their love for their country (Dies and O'Daniel) are usually the ones whose actions show up the sorriest."

John Henry defended American labor, as he knew one of Hitler's first actions was to crush his country's labor unions before he took power. He heard that Dies was attacking Dobie, citing Hitler's labor policy to prove his point against labor. John Henry wrote: "It reminds me of the time that Uncle Dave Beckett and I were hunting for a turkey hen's nest for grandma Beckett and found two fuzzy, white baby buzzards in a nest at the foot of a hollow tree. Uncle Dave warned me not to get too close to them. 'It ain't that they'll peck you or fight you like a baby owl or hawk would, Johnie. Hit's jest that God never gave 'em any way to perteck theyselves – and that was about the low-downdest way in the world. The only defense a buzzard ever uses is jest haul off and spew his puke at you.' "[4]

Back in Austin, Dobie took John Henry's words to heart, arguing for the right of labor to strike, even in wartime, in his Sunday newspaper column on February 21, 1943. This "automatically brought the charge that he had turned 'red,' " wrote Lon Tinkle.[5]

With his stay in the Merchant Marines up, John Henry was itching to serve in the army, but knew he was limited in action because of his bad eye. His friend from the university, Dr. David Stephens, suggested that he do some real work in the army, in interracial affairs. Since his expertise was in black culture, he believed John Henry should work with black soldiers. So Stephens helped him join the American Red Cross in April 1943, during the North African and Italian campaign.

John Henry asked to be assigned with black troops, but instead the Red Cross stationed him with white troops, to teach illiterate soldiers to read and write. It was a sobering experience to meet these men who could not read their names on their tags. Once, when he was sitting with a soldier in the barracks and reading the newspaper, he said absent-mindedly, "Hey, Spragg, did you read this tale about these three soldiers from your town?" The soldier grinned sheepishly and said, "No, I didn't read that — I can't read that. I can't read. I'd sure give a purty if I could." John Henry helped the man write letters to his family back home.

The year in Cairo, Egypt, was full of some excitement: flying, riding camel-back, and seeing exotic sights of the ancient city. But after one year of seeing how the army treated blacks and working at a "useless" assignment, he resigned. The Red Cross field office in Washington, D.C. solicited John Henry to take another assignment or go on a lecture tour for them, but he had enough of what he thought was a group of hypocrites who were more interested in keeping the contributions coming in than in correcting abuses in their own organization.

Instead of keeping the reason for his resignation a secret, he spoke and wrote about his experience when he returned to Austin. Blacks working in the Red Cross, he said, "had a universal distrust" of the Red Cross, which had allowed itself to be associated with "Jim Crowism." Black soldiers were forbidden to attend dances, and, although they were allowed to go to clubs at furlough centers, they were invariably greeted with the words: "Don't come in, you're colored."

"I found, to my surprise, many of my superiors had decidedly prejudicial views toward the Negro soldier," John Henry said. One of his superiors, for instance, said to him, "You don't understand the nigger problem, although you're a Southerner. You have to make them sweat."

On his way from Cairo to Texas, John Henry told a reporter that he was constantly reminded by his commanding officers that he had been sent overseas with American money, "to maintain the status quo. This was most apparent in the instance of Negro servicemen," he said.

"No one in the country knows what American boys overseas are going through, soldiers of all ancestry—Negro, Jew, and Gentile. And it would be doubly hard for anyone to understand what Negro troops have to put up with."

John Henry had already gotten "a belly full" of the Red Cross by the fall of 1943, when he wrote to Dobie: "When I first came [here], there was a little something to do for the soldiers. For the past month and a half, there has been nothing. They have an over-abundance of Red Cross workers here, and they don't know what to do with them. It has taken on a sort of WPAish atmosphere with a pack of highly paid administrators at the top, refusing to use common sense and send two thirds of the fellows they have under them back to the States because they prefer to clutch the prestige that a great number of workers under them give them in the eyes of the National Office in Washington. I have become about as useful to the Army as tits to a boar hoag. You would never believe the ferocious amount of just plain old everday politicking that goes on with this pack of leeches." [6]

John Henry wanted to get back in the service some way, since he firmly believed Nazism was a disease that needed to be eradicated. He was discouraged that the American government was making conditions difficult for labor, but was doing little to halt Hitler. He wasn't sure how he could continue this fight. Although he had the respect of his peers for his folklore work and the admiration of friends, he wanted to win the confidence of everyone by finding something that was worthy.

"Where can I best serve the people?" he wrote in a diary when he took a sojourn at Dr. Stephens' ranch. "Any service that does not include very real participation in defeating fascism does not deserve merit, even a thought. I should think of nothing else until Hitler is wiped from the face of the earth."

This attitude was tempered somewhat when John Henry returned to the States in February 1944, hearing several reactionary voices who wanted to oust Roosevelt and run for higher office in his own home state. To be pro-Roosevelt was considered by many to be un-American, even with the war still raging overseas.

Coke Stevenson was again running for governor — an "old coon dog," John Henry called him, "baying when the other dogs bay, with a dead nose, but snuffling around like he's in the hunt as big as the next one." [7] Although a Democrat, Stevenson had approved of harsh anti-union bills drafted by Herman Brown and Alvin Wirtz, and had initiated no broad legislative programs of his own. There was no pro-New Deal candidate to challenge Stevenson. In a moment of inspiration, John Henry thought of an excellent candidate: his most respected friend, J. Frank Dobie, who had left a year before on sabbatical from the university to teach history at Cambridge University in England. John Henry and a few like-minded friends visited Mrs. Dobie to convince her that there were serious people who wanted J. Frank to become a legitimate candidate.

He appealed to Dobie: "My position is this: my deep personal attachment for you prevents me from acting any further in the matter, although I feel that Texas is in a desperate state, for I feel that you have your reasons not to run and I do not want to be the one who urges you to do something against your own wishes. On the other hand, an issue much greater than my own and your own personal desires, is at stake. I am going to throw everything I've got in me against the O'Daniels-Stevenson reactionary flood in Texas. I would love nothing more than anything to have you as the standard-bearer." [8]

Dobie fired a telegram to John Henry indicating that he was dead against running for governor: "He wrote me in no uncertain terms, 'Goddamn it, I'm not interested, I'm not going to run, and I want you to quit getting people sending those goddamn telegrams to me, because I have to pay to have them delivered!'" [9] But the issue didn't go away immediately. Although John Henry pulled out of the role of urging him to run after receiving Dobie's letter, the "Draft Dobie" campaign raged on for a few more months.

John Henry's experiences in the Merchant Marines and Red Cross gave him an interest and curiosity about the nature of the American soldier and his motivations. So once more, he tried to join the U.S. Army. Since the army had relaxed its vision standards, and he had some overseas experience, the army accepted him on a limited basis as a medic in April 1944.

After six grueling weeks at boot camp at Camp Barkley in West Texas ("the nearest thing to hell you can get without dying"), John Henry felt like an army veteran. Even though he detested the regime, the frightful bawling of the men, and the long hours, he enjoyed army life; he liked being on an equal footing with the other hundreds of privates.

"At close view," he wrote in a random diary, "the picture is an unhappy one. Uneasy, semi-dazed fellows . . . completely innocent of the circumstances — national and international — that brought them here. How can one fail to pity them? Yet, from all the marching, dirt, grime, sweat, and heart-break, there can be forged a better citizen."

After basic training, John Henry was assigned to the medical section of Camp Swift, near Austin, as a psychiatric social worker. It was limited army work, but a grade up from private (Class T-5). His job was to interview "maladjusted" soldiers who just got out of hospitals, in order to obtain clinical material that would aid psychiatrists in diagnosing illnesses and treatments. After each interview, he prepared case histories of each patient and often assisted with any therapy work. Because of his outgoing personality and notoriety in Austin, John Henry's superiors also gave him the job of liaison between the local civilian community (including the University of Texas at Austin) and the soliders at Camp Swift.

"The N.P. staff here changes weekly," John Henry wrote friend Anthony Ostroff. "They get in three or four psychiatrists, discover that they all wet the bed, have terror dreams, and are subject to spells of profound melancholy. They send them in as patients, discharge 'em, and send them in another psychiatric staff." John Henry did enjoy the dances at the camp, and brought several friends back home for parties. He also met one of his best friends at Camp Swift, Eli Friedland, a soldier from Brooklyn.

"John Henry would tell us several stories," Friedland said. "I remember one about a black teenager who was just out crawfishing one day and got picked up by a county sheriff's deputy for stealing a sack of potatoes. He didn't steal the potatoes, but he almost got hanged by a group of white men. It was a real poignant story. John Henry would do that to you — take you into the minds of others; he taught me how to relate to people on different levels."

Working at the hospital reconditioning center at the post, John Henry ran an educational program for his medical unit, setting up a "war room" filled with "News of the World" newspaper clippings, photographs, and memorabilia from overseas. Fellow officer Harry Lerner selected him as one of the instructors/ lecturers for the INE (Information and Education) center he ran at Camp Swift. Lerner ran four programs a week at the INE, bringing in lecturers from local colleges.

Lerner (who later became a delegate to the United Nations) said John Henry encouraged him to develop and complete an entire program commemorating Franklin Roosevelt, after Roosevelt died. The event was co-sponsored by the post, the University of Texas at Austin, the City of Austin, and other army units in town.

John Henry liked the INE because it was the only place in the camp where both blacks and whites could sit together, eat together, and study together. All of the troops were segregated: Each race had their own USO, their own outfits, and even their own section of the camp. But the INE was different because Lerner and John Henry insisted on that. Lerner said he, John Henry, and Eli Friedland were all part of the same "circle" of friends and co-workers who "tended to buck the local traditions and prejudices of the day." [10]

John Henry's family was actively involved in the blacks' struggle for equal rights. After her husband died, Mattie Faulk continued to attend Democratic precinct meetings at Central Feed & Seed Store in South Austin. Only a few families went to the meetings, but the Faulks always attended. The Faulk family openly advocated the right of blacks to vote, trying to push legislation to that end. All the Faulk children can remember an incident that showed how Mrs. Faulk dealt with the common bigotry of the time.

In 1944, the U.S. Supreme Court outlawed all-white primaries in the Democratic Party. At their South Austin Democratic precinct meeting, Texana offered a resolution commending the Supreme Court for its ruling. John Henry's mother spoke in favor of the resolution at one of the precinct meetings. The precinct chairman, Raymond Canion, whose wife Mattie Faulk had taught in school, was at this meeting, and when she sat down after her talk he asked her, "Why, Mrs. Faulk, would you lie down with a nigger?" And she responded coolly and deliberately, "Raymond, I don't vote lying down."

That was the characteristic way in which Mattie Faulk dealt with prejudice of the time—not by quarreling with someone over the issue, but by rising above it. Once, when she had visitors at her home, she pointed out the rooms where the houseworkers lived. The visitors were incredulous, saying, "Oh, my goodness, aren't you afraid of having them this close? They'll steal from you!" She quickly said, "No, they don't steal from us, and we don't steal from them." [11]

Being in the army didn't mean John Henry wasn't active in Austin politics and UT affairs. In 1944 the Dies Committee, the forerunner of the House Un-American Activities Committee, blasted the university for being overrun with suspected communists. University President Homer Rainey demanded proof from the committee, or else wanted an apology. John Henry wrote letters to Rainey supporting his stance. Eventually, the Dies Committee did issue such an apology.

Also in 1944, a battle reached its pinnacle between the governor-appointed University of Texas Board of Regents and University President Rainey. Governors Pappy O'Daniel and Coke Stevenson had appointed conservative, wealthy oil men to the board, and they strongly opposed Rainey's reform proposals, which included instituting a program for black students' education and consolidating the Galveston medical school into UT. The battle was joined when the Regents fired a group of economics professors for straying from the traditional teachings of economics and for allegedly being "unpatriotic" by speaking out in support of organized labor and the Fair Labor Standards Act. One of the Regents insisted on subjecting all faculty and university employees to a "patriotism test" in the form of a questionnaire. Another charged Rainey with bringing "a nest of homosexuals" onto campus.

The Regents became a reactionary board that resisted change and vehemently opposed new ideas and new thought. Lon Tinkle wrote that these men "were (with a few exceptions) conservative men of wealth and power, haters of Roosevelt and the New Deal, fearful and resentful of intellectuals." [12] All six of the Regents opposed to Rainey were members of the Texas Regulars, conservatives opposed to FDR. Trying to explain the concept of academic freedom to these men, Roy Bedichek wrote, was "like talking to a group of East Texas hog-raisers about Hindu philosophy." The Regents engaged in several obstructive tactics against Rainey and the university as an institution of learning, including:

· firing his appointment to the director of public information office without any charge lodged against him;

· rejecting the formation of a School of Social Work, thinking it might be used to "train bureaucrats and socialists";

· proposing a resolution abolishing all faculty tenure;

· rejecting several social science research requests on arbitrary grounds;

· calling the American Association of University Professors, a group that opposed the firing of the economics instructors, "the professors' CIO Labor Union";

· and banning the book *U.S.A.*, by John Dos Passos, from university classrooms, libraries, and bookstores because the Regents called it "obscene" and part of the communist conspiracy. (The book won the Pulitzer Prize for American literature.)

In 1943, sociologist Anthony M. Orum wrote that "the Regents embarked on what can only be described as an inquisition. They undertook a long questioning of each member of the English department who used that book. The questions dealt with such unrelated matters as where the person was born and whether he was married." [13]

Rainey fought the Regents on all these measures, and triumphed on the issue of faculty tenure, influencing the state's Attorney General Department to establish the principle firmly in Texas law. Rainey gave a plea to the faculty on October 12, 1944, to halt the Regents' conduct in curtailing academic freedom: "For centuries, universities worthy of the name have been the meeting place for conflicting ideas. It is well that this is true, for conflicts in ideas, when resolved through the orderly process of society, lead to human progress. An idea, if contrary to prevailing opinion, usually gains more momentum when forced into subterranean channels through repression. I believe that history proves that the strength of democracy lies in tolerance, whether in the marketplace, or in public officials, or in institutions of higher learning."

Two weeks after his address, when Rainey refused to recant his comments to the Board, they fired him. Both Dobie and John Henry defended Rainey in letters and telegrams, with Dobie, in one of his newspaper columns, blasting the "ignoramuses" on the Board for their limited thinking. From Camp Swift, John Henry wrote a letter to Rainey right before the firing to show his support. "I read in last Sunday's paper with shame and anger that certain members of the Board of Regents have attempted to curb the freedom of speech of the President of the University," he wrote. The arbitrary, "undemocratic" action by the regents, he said, "seems particularly incongruous at this time when we should all be united in fighting this war against those who would legally abolish intellectual freedom."

The Rainey controversy embroiled Austin and eventually the state. Immediately after the firing, the entire student body went on strike. More than 5,000 students marched on the State Capitol, some carrying a black coffin with the words "academic freedom" draped over it. Henry Nash Smith, a colleague of Dobie's, followed the dismissal with his resignation.

The Texas Senate Committee on Education held hearings on the affair, and the public became aware of the connections the Regents had with large corporations. The American Association of University Professors censured the university for its actions, and the Southern Association of Colleges and Secondary Schools, which accredited the university's programs, put the school on probation.

Dobie accused the Regents of building a "Maginot Line" around the university in an attempt to keep out new ideas. Dobie thought that the Regents' attitudes threatened all people who believed differently from the millionaires and corporate lawyers of Texas. Both Dobie and John Henry felt the issue was one of freedom of expression versus fascism; of individual liberties versus forced conformity of thought. Though this might have been an oversimplification, the event did foreshadow what was to become the Red Scare of the McCarthy days in the state of Texas and the nation.

"It is curious," Dobie wrote in one of his newspaper columns, "how in this country calling a man a 'controversial figure' is tantamount to calling him 'subversive.' Without controversial figures, society would have remained unilluminated by thought.

"Forced orthodoxy through death, suppression, exile, derision, banning of books, starvation and all the other methods of self-righteous and conforming respectability has never been the answer."

7.

Johnny's Front Porch

J ohn Henry kept polishing his storytelling craft while awaiting his discharge at Camp Swift, writing a short script for a proposed radio series on Austin's KTBC Radio and speaking to various groups on campus about his experience in the war and his views on Texas politics. In an interview with the university's newspaper, *The Daily Texan,* John Henry said his humor was not to be construed as "exploiting or laughing at anyone," but as a means "to get people to laugh with, not at, themselves, and enjoy the humor and fun in everyday life." To John Henry Faulk, the most exciting literature in the world could be gleaned from plain, everyday folks talking about themselves.

Alan Lomax knew John Henry had the kind of talent that radio executives would love. While on furlough from the army in Christmas of 1945, John Henry visited Lomax, who was working at CBS Radio in New York. Lomax arranged a series of evening parties with many people he knew in the radio business. "We had about ten parties for him over a period of two to three weeks, and he performed at all of them," Lomax said. John Henry would launch into his favorite impersonations of his Aunt Edith, the

Reverend A.A. Reese and Tanner Franklin, among others, interspersing the imitations with salty commentary. The executives loved it so much, Lomax said, that "they decided they just couldn't let him go back (to Austin); so he had a contract by the time he went home. It was just like that; they found him completely irresistible, except they didn't know quite what to do with him at first, and they didn't, in a way, ever find out."

Although Dobie wanted his prize student to become a writer, being on the radio came effortlessly to John Henry. Telling stories came much more naturally to him than writing. "I like to talk," he wrote Dobie. "I reckon I was cut out to talk. But I do like to do a little acting with my talk." Dobie understood John Henry's need to grab this opportunity, but Bedichek was concerned that moving to New York would dull his sensibilities. ("I hope you keep your head above the big city's fetid atmosphere; I hope you never accept its values; I hope you stay true to your hillbillies, and continue to interpret and idealize the virtues of your raisin', and, dying, 'still babble o' green fields,' " he wrote.[1])

John Henry was excited about moving to Manhattan, a place that Dobie once described as "pregnant with humanity." What would a Southern country boy raised in the cedar-filled woods of South Austin find appealing about New York, and what did New York sophisticates find appealing about John Henry? Jaston Williams, an actor in both Texas and New York in the hit play "Greater Tuna," summed it up best: "New York is the only place majestic enough or big enough to impress Texans. There's something about the New York Texan. There is a kind of grudging respect New Yorkers have for Texans; we're brave and robust enough to walk into that crowd and hold our own."[2]

"When I met John Henry in Texas," said Lomax, "he had these long, wonderful long narratives like 'The Notorious Jumping Frog of Calaveras County' [by Mark Twain], or like one of a piece of Chekov — in *perfect* dialect — more perfect than any recording machine could ever do. And when he came to New York, they were liked by the CBS people, but they couldn't figure out how to handle these stories that lasted fifteen minutes — how the hell could they put that on the air?"

That was the problem CBS executives like Davidson Taylor had with Faulk. After the army discharged John Henry in April

'46, Taylor immediately placed him in his own weekly radio program, "Johnny's Front Porch," where he told stories each Sunday afternoon. CBS promoted Faulk as kind of a clever, corny, rural-folksy type who fit the mold of the "professional Texan" — polite and entertaining, but limited in breadth of experiences outside Texas. "Every time he told stories in a New York party," Lomax said, "he would have to come, do them quicker, and get-to-the-punch line. Finally he was looking for gag lines, just like a comic." Lomax felt that Johnny's final version of his stories, as massaged by radio executives and later book editors, were just "pieces of this great literature that he used to talk."

Short quips and comments were called for by CBS executives on John Henry's show. Stay clear of politics and controversy, they insisted. Talk to your audience about the flavor of life in rural Travis County and compare that to life in the Big Apple.

But "Johnny's Front Porch" wasn't a smash hit, although Henry Ford, who heard Faulk on the air one day, wanted to hire him to sell cars. Shortly after that announcement, Ford died.

John Henry was pleased to get the recognition, because the audience for the show didn't materialize. "They didn't get any audience back until Wednesday or Thursday," John Henry joked.

At the end of the first radio stint, John Henry expressed to Dobie that he was displeased with his first venture into radio. "They [CBS] have several schemes a-foot for me. I was not at all pleased with the sort of performances that I turned in this summer. I've got a long, grassy row ahead of me before I am going to really be chopping in the tall cotton. They are planning to continue to build me as a CBS feature, so I ain't got no complaints." [3]

Through Lomax, John Henry met folk singers Pete Seeger, Burl Ives, Woody Guthrie, and others. John Henry and Hally would go with Alan and Elizabeth Lomax to "hootenannies," which were large, unplanned parties where members of the audience would join in group singing, eat some, maybe watch a film, and perhaps dance afterwards. Seeger and Guthrie started having these hootenannies in 1943 about once a month, for different groups like the Newspaper Guild or Spanish Relief Fund (for Spanish refugees). One held in a school in Greenwich Village brought 1,000 people. Seeger asked John Henry to act as master of ceremonies for a couple of these hootenannies, and recalled that he regaled the audiences with his wonderful stories about poor sharecropper families or other rural Texans, rich with folk imagery and "all different sorts of accents." [4]

These folk singers sang mostly union and peace songs, and peace, in those days, was "a dirty word." A peace organization was suspicious even if it was on record as being anti-communist. "One of the main purposes of these organizations was to see that World War III did not break out," Seeger said. Some military hard-liners were advocating attacking Russia before that country got too strong, and that view was reflected in the media. "It's hard to believe now how scared a lot of people were," Seeger said, "but many in the Left believed they were going to be put behind barbed wire if America went to war with Russia." [5]

Seeger and Guthrie formed the People's Songs in 1946, to sing protest songs for unions and rallies. The People's Artists agency handled the bookings for many of these folk singers. Hally, a talented singer, got bookings at several People's Artists showings with other female folk singers like Jolly Smolens and Jackie Gibson. During this time, John Henry and Woody Guthrie became close drinking buddies, going together to various folk music recitals and fundraising parties. The Texan and the Okie were both children of the Depression and both spoke the same folksy, gritty language of the common man; however, unlike Guthrie, John Henry exuded charm and gentile politeness.

"Woody could be one cantankerous sonofabitch," John Henry told one interviewer. "He'd carry around this guitar with the words 'THIS MACHINE KILLS FASCISTS' on the back, and twice a week, like clockwork, he'd get into the same argument with these little old Jewish waiters at this restaurant in the Village. He'd refuse to tip 'em—said it was decadent capitalism—and told 'em to go out and form themselves a union!" [6]

Millard Lampell, one of the original members of the folk-singing group called the Almanacs with Guthrie, Seeger, and Lee Hays, described the band of folk singers and blue-collar workers: "We were all children of the Depression, who had seen bone-aching poverty, bummed freights across the country, shared gunny-sack blankets with the dispossessed and the disinherited. We had learned our songs from gaunt, unemployed Carolina cotton weavers and evicted Dust Bowl drifters. Such as they were, our politics were a crude, hand-me down cross between Eugene Debs and the old Wobblies. A primitive, folk version of what Franklin D. Roosevelt was saying in his fireside chats. We were against hunger, war and silicosis, against bankers, landlords and politicians and Dixie deputy sheriffs. We were for the working stiff, the underdog, the outcast, and those were the passions we poured into our songs. We were all raw off the road, and to New York's left-wing intellectuals we must have seemed the authentic voice of the working class. Singing at their benefits kept us in soup and guitar-string money." [7]

John Henry, however, didn't share the same friends as Guthrie's or Hally's. John Henry never really knew Hally that well during his marriage; indeed, most of his married years were spent in the Red Cross and in the army. The move to New York with Hally and his infant daughter, Cynthia Tannehill (born in November 1943), proved to be an unsettling, unstable transition. That, coupled with finding letters to Hally from a female lover, ended the marriage. [8] They divorced in 1947.

When CBS dropped "Johnny's Front Porch" after an unproductive year in 1947, John Henry decided to start near the bottom of the entertainment ladder by becoming a disc jockey for WOV Radio, a local station where he played cowboy music every morning from 5:00 to 6:00 A.M. The show could be heard by people in Connecticut and Pennsylvania as well as New York and New Jersey.

John Henry's interest in Texas politics never waned while in New York. Through letters and Texas newspapers, he closely followed the major races. When Homer Rainey announced his candidacy for governor in 1946 (after Dobie urged him to run), John Henry threw his support behind him. The other candidates in the race included corporate lawyer Beauford Jester, former railroad commissioner J.L. Smith, and State Attorney General Grover Sellers.

As this marked the first Democratic primary in which blacks could vote, Rainey courted the black vote during his campaign. This evoked a strong white backlash in the state, and all of Rainey's primary opponents accused him of being "pro-Negro" and a threat to the establishment. Regent D. F. Strickland said if

Rainey were elected, the Capitol would be taken over by "communists and Negroes." Smith, Sellers, and Jester linked Rainey to the communist conspiracy, and former governor Coke Stevenson joined in the barrage. "It's one thing to have full freedom to teach the truth, as each of us understands the truth to be," he wrote a minister in Mart, Texas, "and another thing to take advantage of one's position in a public school to teach atheism, communism, and other isms that tear down and destroy all that you and I have been taught to believe in." Anonymous circulars and flyers accused Rainey, a staunch Baptist, of atheism, degeneracy, and being a "nigger lover." [9] In the face of this onslaught, Rainey's managers began soft-pedaling his civil rights stance, and sought a safe distance away from Dobie, a noted supporter of blacks' rights.

John Henry warned Dobie that Rainey's pursuit of the "middle-of-the-road" position would have dire consequences: "Sure we are pro-Negro, I'm pro-human being in general. It is high time that some native born Texans stood up and declared that decent humane people exist in Texas as well as the better known scoundrels like Smith, Jester, and company. I lump the latter brethren together, because I think they all go to roost in the same tree—and feed off the same carcasses, the damn buzzards. I was shocked here the other day when I was discussing Rainey and his chances in the run-off with some Negro and labor people. They are mighty strong behind him, but they say that he did not even receive all of the Negro vote, because of his fear and trembling (or that of his advisers) when the Negro question was mentioned." [10] Jester won the governor's race, and Rainey came in a distant second, solidifying the conservatives' control of state government for thirty years. [11]

While visiting his alma mater in the spring of 1946, John Henry blasted the politics of senators and congressmen who represented Texas. Texas veterans who returned to the States after the war found their state overrun with "demagogues" in the capital who tried "to spread their policies of reaction." John Henry told a group of students: "The deal is, kids, we've been sold up the river. And the results are going to come out of the hides of lots of children who don't have the right places to live, or won't be able to afford the right kind of food.

"The people must seize their obligations to society," he said, "and see that their governments realize the narrowing boundaries of the world, and act so we can live as neighbors, both with ourselves and with other nations."

He didn't feel the blame should be laid on politicians alone. He recognized that every citizen has a duty to ensure that his or her government is doing its job. The complacent, apathetic U.T. student "who ignores responsibility to his society and government while day-dreaming on the banks of the Barton" doesn't aid our democracy, he said.[12]

At a 1948 benefit for Progressive presidential candidate Henry Wallace (who served as Franklin Roosevelt's vice-president from 1941 to 1945), John Henry met a slim, dark-haired New Yorker named Lynne Smith. They dated seriously for about six weeks before they decided to marry. The two were wed on June 28, 1948, and took a summer place on the Hudson River near Nyack, New York, complete with a swimming pool, tennis court, and a few acres of lawns and trees. John Henry spent his free time playing chess ("my greatest and most serious weakness," he said), reading social newsletters and bulletins (such as "The Social Questions Bulletin," published by the Methodist Federation for Social Action), and writing proposed skits and stories.

Nineteen forty-eight was an election year, and Harry S. Truman was reelected president in a major upset. The new president faced a critical housing shortage, rising food prices, and a perceived infiltration of communists into all levels of government. The year before, Truman had signed an executive order banning all members or "sympathizers" of the Communist Party from holding any office in the executive branch.

Actually, the political usage of communist subversion in the U.S. government began two years earlier. In 1946 a Republican candidate for Congress named Richard Nixon called his congressional opponent a "pinko" and a "red," marking the first time a major U.S. congressmen introduced the charge of treason in a U.S. political campaign. The charge hit political pay-dirt, and Nixon won. Other politicians began to follow the example. In 1947 the House Un-American Activities Committee (HUAC) jailed the "Hollywood Ten" screenwriters, wrote a number of defaming reports, and investigated federal employees. As a result, 526 resigned and 98 were fired. Later in December, Alger Hiss, a former State Department official, was indicted by a federal grand jury on two counts of perjury for his alleged espionage activities. The Hiss case confirmed the idea held by many Americans that to be a communist was to be a spy for a foreign government, and to be an informer on one's colleagues was an honorable calling.

Not surprisingly, the government severely restricted the rights of organized labor. The Taft-Hartley Act, passed over Truman's veto in 1947, prevented union members from striking, gave unions less rights to sue employers over breaches in contracts, and required unions to publish new financial statements. Also, the act required an affidavit of all union leaders attesting to nonmembership in the Communist Party.

From the government, the witch-hunt commenced, seeping into all other facets of American life. Communism had become the anti-Christ, the path to hell; and its servants and zealots could be found anywhere – in your government, in your schools, in the church, or in your bedroom. Mississippi Congressman John Rankin, chairman of the House Un-American Activities Committee, warned Americans that "communism is older than Christianity ... it hounded and persecuted its savior during his earthly ministry, inspired his crucifixation, derided him in his dying agony, and then gambled for his garments at the foot of the cross." [13] FBI Director J. Edgar Hoover said that communism's doctrines "threaten the happiness of the community, the safety of every individual, and the continuance of every home and fireside. They would destroy the peace of the country and thrust it into a condition of anarchy and lawlessness and immorality that passes imagination. The Party's influence," he claimed, "is exerted through the communist device of thought control." [14]

The Executive Branch began instituting new "loyalty tests" for federal workers. This gave rise to the document that would later be used to launch blacklisting – *The Attorney General's List*. This checklist screened federal workers to see if they had ties to organizations that might be linked to communist, fascist, or other totalitarian groups. Originally intended for legitimizing the investigations of federal employees, *The Attorney General's List* became an ominous and illegal tool that private groups used to deny people employment outside the government. Any citizen, "armed with the List, could impugn another citizen's loyalty with what looked like the authorization of the United States Government," wrote Lillian Hellman in her book *Scoundrel Time.* This single act, the creation of *The Attorney General's List,* fomented the whole blacklisting campaign.

In 1950, over the veto of President Truman, Congress passed the McCarran Internal Security Act, which required all members of the Communist Party to register with the attorney general, prohibited aliens who had ever been Communist Party members to enter the country, banned them from getting passports or government jobs, and authorized the president to hold them in detention camps if war broke out. Membership in any of the 78 classified "Communist front" groups constituted grounds for arrest and deportation (the number of "Communist front" groups would rise to over 600). The Internal Security Act also created the office of the Subversion Activities Control Board, which operated as an arm of the federal government until 1973.

The year 1950 also witnessed a shakeup in the movie and television industry. *The New York Times* reported that "many sponsors and advertising agencies reexamined the records of their broadcasting personnel," instituting a "virtual purge" of radio and television actors, writers, producers and directors whose names were listed in the bulletin *Red Channels.*[15] The purge began when General Foods dropped the popular television actress, Jean Muir from its cast in the *Aldrich Family,* due to charges of communist sympathies. General Foods was worried that Muir's "presence might antagonize prospective customers" of their products. After Muir's dismissal, *Red Channels* became a virtual bible for screening actors and actresses along Madison Avenue. Also in 1950, an ambitious Senator Joe McCarthy from Wisconsin delivered a speech to the Women's Republican Club in Wheeling, West Virginia, saying he had 205 (later he claimed the number was 57) names of people in the U.S. State Department with "known communist affiliations." In reality, McCarthy had no list at all; he was simply seeking publicity, which the press dutifully gave him.[16]

Also in Wheeling, it was discovered that certain bubblegum cards were corrupting our youth, informing unwitting children that the Soviet Union was the world's largest country, and its capital was Moscow. The corrupting cards were swiftly removed from circulation. The spark may have started in Wheeling, but the fire was soon to spread across the country. Several federal, state, and local committees were established that year whose sole purpose was to expiate all "communist propaganda" from libraries and bookstores. *The Grapes of Wrath* was one of the first books to be burned. The age of fear and suspicion had taken hold of the country. [17]

Both John Henry's network and his trade union (American Federation of Radio Artists) looked into ways to probe the "loyalty" of its members. CBS required all its employees to take a loyalty oath stating non-communist sympathies in 1950; AFRA proposed setting up an industrywide loyalty board. The following year, when AFRA merged with the television actors' union and became AFTRA (to which all performers belonged), a resolution was passed to expel any member who did not answer questions from a congressional committee.[18]

John Henry would commiserate about this state of affairs with friends like Edward R. Murrow, then a director of CBS and star of "See It Now." When John Henry first came to CBS, Dobie told him to look up Murrow (the two had met in England). At first, John Henry thought Murrow was too stodgy, too much the executive type. By 1951, however, the two had developed a friendship based on mutual respect and mutual interest. Over drinks they discussed the state of the country—McCarthy's popularity, the decline of the enforcement of the Bill of Rights, and the raging media hype that increased the level of fear and suspicion. Murrow agreed with John Henry on these issues, but didn't agree on what could be done. John Henry wanted to take the issues and the personalities head-on through the media; Murrow preferred a more low-key, general way that would bring people around eventually.

Years later, John Henry saw his point. "When you're dealing with hysteria, you have to get hold of it. When you're dealing with a madman, you can't tell him he's mad; you have to deal with his fears." [19] McCarthy attacked both Presidents Truman and Eisenhower, saying they were doing nothing about the communist conspiracy in government. He accused the entire Democratic Party of "20 years of treason." He wrecked the careers of many in the State Department with his unsubstantiated incriminations. No level of government was immune from his scrutiny. In 1953 he accused the U.S. International Information Agency of retaining material that was anti-American. His staffers, Roy Cohn and G. David Shein, inspected libraries in Europe to search for offending books. The State Department issued a directive vetoing the use of "material by any controversial persons, Communists, fellow travelers, etc." [20] Many books were banned and even burned.

John Henry compared McCarthy to a dog that started to kill chickens, destroying the farmer's business. The farmer was then faced with the prospect of going out of business or killing the dog: "Since the current thinking in the land seems to be that in spite of his destructive habits he is a fairly good watch dog and ought to be let run loose, I would think that there is a very real chance right now that some folks are going to have to go out of business. Just one further observation on the matter – You can waste a lot of energy and cussing on an egg sucking dog, when the real villain is the gent who owns him and turns him loose in the neighborhood, then beams piously at you in church every Sunday." [21]

At the height of this "McCarthy era," J. Frank Dobie came to visit John Henry in New York, discussing issues like "the supine way the colleges were firing the professors and librarians, the way the country was going at the time, how people were remaining silent." The two saw a theatre production of George Bernard Shaw's "The Lark," about Joan of Arc. The play dealt with how Joan of Arc stood by her principles in the midst of the Inquisition, even at the moment she was sentenced to death. At the end of the performance, John Henry and Dobie walked down Broadway Avenue, and Dobie's blood started to boil; he started to drive his right fist into his left palm and began cussing and yelling at the top of his lungs. "Damn it, Johnny," he said, "that's what's wrong with America today. Injustice has become acceptable. We've lost our capacity for indignation at injustice. We're not outraged by the abuses of our fellow citizens the way the 19th century Americans were, the way Mr. Dooley and Josh Billings and Mark Twain were. Injustice outraged them. We cower before it." [22]

John Henry, too, was concerned with the injustice in the American government's foreign policies, as he watched the seeds of the Cold War grow and the Truman administration deliver a glut of military aid to Greece, Turkey, and China. "I believe that Truman has about the same chance of affecting any real peace in the world," John Henry wrote Roy Bedichek, "or any of the domestic reforms he talks about, as a sick whore has of graduating from Harvard Law School."

In 1948 John Henry backed Henry Wallace for president, the former vice-president under Franklin Roosevelt, and he urged Dobie to get involved in the campaign too. ("Your name would do much to make the New Party a success," he wrote.) Wallace, who urged U.S. cooperation with the Soviets, believed the Truman Doctrine had polarized the world into two ideological camps, and that Truman was swiftly taking the country into an escalating nuclear arms race. Wallace was not a communist or socialist, but an American progressive who believed strongly in the fair ideal of justice. John Henry believed in the same goals of peace and prosperity that Wallace did.

Through his former wife Hally, John Henry had met some members of the Communist Party in Texas and New York and received no inspiration from their ideas. They were too "doctrinaire" for John Henry's blood; many of them seemed to harbor as much ingrained prejudices as conservatives. "Communists have about the same degree of tolerance and humanity as the Hardshelled Baptists," he told Dobie. Yet he did discover intellectual sustenance in Henry Wallace's progressive campaign. He also saw in Wallace the same traits he admired and respected in Dobie: "honesty, a respect for people, and unaffected humanitarianism — and a head full of common sense." Unlike the mainstream Democrats and the unvisionary communists, Wallace's new Progressive Party brought hope for peace in the world and an end to poverty, John Henry felt. Clark Foreman and others in the Wallace campaign tried to entice John Henry to run a campaign for U.S. senator on the third-party ticket. Foreman thought John Henry would give the average folk in Texas a clear choice in the race, and John Henry nearly took him up on it, when a Houston millionaire and another rich Texan offered to finance part of the campaign. Although he didn't give himself much chance of winning, he felt a duty and responsibility to give it a shot.

Bedichek talked him out of the idea. In a March 20 letter, Bedichek told John Henry that he had no business jumping into the race. "You lack political experience, and perhaps the necessary information. You are an artist, not a politician. Your field of service to mankind lies in another direction. We don't make overalls out of fine fabrics and we certainly shouldn't waste genuine artistic talent on a political campaign. It has never worked and it never will work. The opposition could tag you with communism, or with 'fellow-traveler' and that in itself would be sufficient to destroy your influence in Texas. Your personal affairs, your recent divorce, would all be exploited by the opposition, if you began showing any strength." [23]

Although John Henry heeded Bedichek's advice and stayed out of the race, he continued to support Wallace's campaign, attending a meeting of some Southern liberals in Washington and helping host the first statewide Wallace for President meeting at Green Pastures, the Faulks' former home that Mary Koock would turn into a fashionable restaurant in 1946, and one of the few places in Texas that would allow a racially integrated meeting. In April, John Henry performed a satirical imitation of a Southern politician begging for "Poor Old Truman" at the Wallace for President convention at Houston's Music Hall. Among the "liberal" issues endorsed by the party's platform: a $1 minimum wage, the abolition of the state poll tax, the lowering of the voting age to eighteen, racial desegregation and civil rights, day-care centers for working mothers, support for the United Nations, and a mutual end to the construction and stockpiling of nuclear weapons. As American intransigence solidified against the Soviet Union, the perception that Wallace was a "dupe" of the Communist Party took hold. The press often insinuated that Wallace was the captive of a leftist "palace guard" that controlled his actions. By June, "the pro-Communist, pro-Soviet image of the new party greatly increased." [24] Dobie got involved with the Wallace campaign, too, but as election day came closer, John Henry said, "We realized that Wallace wasn't going to win, and we were so damn afraid of the Republicans winning, that we voted for Harry Truman." Wallace, who had expected a minimum of four million votes, got only 1.15 million—less than the number received by Southern candidate Strom Thurmond.

Perhaps John Henry was thinking of politics as a career since his radio show was not very enjoyable for him at WOV. While at the station, a management group out of Paterson, New Jersey, approached him to join their network. He took the offer and moved, with his wife and their first child, Johanna, to a two-bedroom duplex apartment in the fall of '49. Although hired as a DJ by WPAT-Radio, the station made John Henry into a character he wasn't at all comfortable with: "Pat the Rancher," complete with cowboy hat, boots, and Western shirt. Prior to this, John Henry never owned a pair of cowboy boots or tight dark pants "like the movie cowboys wore." Yet this was the image of the Texas cowboy that he was hired to portray to his audience, both on the radio show and in the rodeos he was telecasting from Madison Square Garden every Sunday night, though he knew little about the particulars of rodeo. "I get some good publicity," John Henry wrote his good friend Anthony Ostroff, "albeit the cow manure is fairly oozing out my ears from an overdose of rodeo."

As he never got the opportunity to inject some of his own social and humorous commentary on the show, John Henry's radio show topics were mainly confined to raising chickens and church-going. He moonlighted by delivering talks to women's groups, civic clubs, and colleges about Texas folklore and the American heritage in the "Speaking of the People" lecture series sponsored by the Columbia Lecture Bureau. The Bureau flew him to cities all over the country, including Washington, D.C., Cincinnati, Chicago, Detroit, and Pittsburgh. "I aim to acquaint them with the cedar brakes and the piney woods of Texas," he told Dobie. John Henry relished the trips with the Lecture Bureau, because it would give him a chance to meet and talk with people. "The more I travel amongst the American people, the more respect I get for their decent instincts. I figure if a man talks to them straight, that sooner or later they will hearken to him." [25]

At these lectures, John Henry was billed as an "impersonator," "satirist," "philosopher," and "wit," among other descriptions. John Henry's own business card said: "I caint do nuthin'

but . . . authentic southern western and old timey dialects."
Speaking of the People was seen as a novel way for John Henry to
portray his rural folk characters—from the puffy, vain Congressman Guffaw, to Jim Clark, a wise, sentimental eighty-six-year-old
prone to spinning tall yarns, to Aunt Effie McDoo, the frustrated
spinster. One Buffalo advertising club newspaper proclaimed
John Henry's characters as "uproariously funny, but underneath
the wit and humor lie shrewd social comment, razor-keen report-
ing, skillful satire, and a deep appreciation of the poetic imagery
of plain folks' faith."

It was during these travels that John Henry refined his characters based on real-life Texans. Some, like Ed Snodgrass, were
used to satirize the "redneck ignoramuses" who always seemed to
be itching to beat somebody up; while others seemed to represent the honest, decent "hard-workin' " sorts who gave you a pas-
sel of homespun tales. One of John Henry's famed characters
included an illiterate farmer who spoke Shakespeare in a twangy
West Texas dialect: "Speak the speech, ah pray ya, as ah pro-
nounced it to ya, trippin'ly on the tongue."

Just before Christmas, 1949, WPAT officials finally realized
they weren't getting the full benefit of John Henry's storytelling
ability through "Pat the Rancher," so they turned him loose as
John Henry Faulk to talk and visit with his audience from 6:00
A.M. until 8:45 A.M., six days a week. John Henry was elated with
the move, because he no longer had to pretend to be something
he was not (a cowboy). As he wrote Dobie: "Now I can talk about
Barton Creek, the Brodies, Buck Simpson and the like as much as
I please. And I can also come clean and confess that I've had a
pretty wide acquaintance amongst cows, but not on the romantic
ranges of the Old West. Rather, on the hoarground and Johnson
grass flats of South Austin. Thank Heavens that happy day seems
to be arriving when I can tell my employers what I can and will
do, instead of having them tell me to take on any synthetic prose
they decree." [26]

John Henry appealed to many newly planted city dwellers
who missed their old lives on the farm, and to those who wanted
to live a slower, simpler life. His warm, homespun manner found
an audience in the fast-paced life of New York and New Jersey, an
audience that was older, rustic, and unpretentious—like John

Henry. Rarely did he use a set script each day; rather, he scrawled notes about things that came to mind from his past farm life or ideas that arose from listening to the news of the day.

After a two-week tour through the Midwest in May 1950, John Henry expressed dismay at some of the attitudes he found toward Senator Joe McCarthy. "You would shudder," he wrote to Bedichek, "if you could have heard the pink, plump, pleasant brethren of the Cincinnati Club where I spoke, with their toothy, bosomy wives, glibly chatting of the need to atomize the Russians and snarling about Roosevelt and his den of communists. McCarthy was their knight in shining armour. I am, frankly, damn glum over the immediate future—but almighty optimistic over the shape of things to come in the long run. This part of the country is cackling over the fact that a Republican got elected to Congress from Texas. Hell, I can no more tell a Democrat from a Republican in Texas than I can tell a male cat fish from a female cat fish in ten foot of water." [27]

In the fall of 1950, John Henry took his first callow steps in the booming medium of television, where he was getting some excellent reviews. He liked the adventure and thrill of television: "The public seems to enjoy just having me be myself and talk about whatever comes to mind. And of course, that makes it nice, for I have never enjoyed having to play a role. You would be astonished at how many people roar and applaud when I tell a story about daddy and a Jersey bull, or about Buck Simpson courting one of the Mostellar girls out in South Austin." [28] Bedichek was enthusiastic about seeing John Henry on television, because he believed that medium was more suited to his personality: "I wish I might hear you on the radio, but I'd much rather see and hear you give one of those numbers the circular is so enthusiastic about. I can't believe that a personality such as yours can be 'projected,' as the radio jargon says. When television really arrives, you will be sitting high on the front seat. As Emerson said to Whitman, 'I salute you at the beginning of a great career.' " [29]

Prospering with the new show and the lecture series, John Henry and Lynne found a larger, executive-style mansion for rent in North Haledon, New Jersey. Pregnant with a second child (Evelyn, born in the fall of 1951), Lynne obtained the services of a full-time housekeeper. The house, set in a heavily wooded hill, overlooked a deep green valley that was populated with an abundance of birds and deer. The country-setting pleased John Henry, who often went hiking, berry-pickin' and barbecuin' outdoors with Lynne and daughter Johanna. A typical weekday would consist of spending a couple of hours in the yard, eating breakfast inside, reading the morning paper, working in the study for a couple more hours, having lunch, working on his radio show material, tending the garden, listening to the world news, and driving down to the radio station at 10:30 P.M. for his new nightly two-hour show on KNOW Radio.

In this environment, John Henry could ripen his bird-watching abilities. He began to talk a lot on his show about various birds. One show in which he talked about how he made friends with a jenny wren out in the harness house when he was eight years old provoked fifty letters.[30] He often discussed the subject of blue jays — "those rowdy, bully-boys of the bird world." In a letter to Bedichek, he described watching the invasion of a band of blue jays in the field: "Try as I might, I can't actually loathe the bungling, awkward devils. But for all I can tell the rest of the bird world hates them to the point of trembling fury. This morning I watched one bobbing his head and calling for the near-melodic note they have, from a limb near the corner of my house. The way he peered around the limb, he looked for all the world like the devilish leering smart-alecks who used to come out to South Austin from Tenth Ward to play ball at Fulmore against us. I half-way expected him to break wind and belch. A sparrow (song) and his wife set up housekeeping in a shrub at the corner of our sunparlor and the other afternoon I heard a racket out there. I looked out the window and the sparrows and a catbird were furiously belaboring a jay in the shrub. I do not know whether he actually perpetrated the crime or not, but the eggs were out of the nest, on the ground, broken. I blamed the jay, as apparently did the birds." [31]

WPAT-Radio kept John Henry on for two years with his "Hi-Neighbor" (and later "Keep 'Em Smiling" and "New North Jersey Datebook") shows. The station advertised having "the music America loves best," which meant a staple of country music. John Henry's fast-talking Southern accent and earthy witticisms had many fans awake before the sun rose, but he carried over some of the same audience he had at CBS – the farmers and dairymen. They kept a sharp ear out for John Henry's daily farm news segment.

Lynne joined him on the show twice a week, discussing fashion, household hints, and other topics. John Henry's listeners would challenge him to milking contests and chicken frying competitions, both of which he usually won.

More listeners wrote in to say how they enjoyed hearing John Henry's unique Texas accent and ability to "reduce life in general to its simplest form." One listener said John Henry's voice was "fascinating, and I felt sure that if I listened long enough, you would sing. I associated your voice with Gene Autry [the singing cowboy]. My patience was rewarded when you sang a few little snatches from Mexican songs."

Yet talking was what John Henry did best. Much of his humor did not translate to paper, but was instead dependent on his timing, inflection, and accent. His listeners got to know him personally through his reminiscing about his family and exploits in South Austin. The characters he created were right out of his recent past: Fanny Rollins, an elderly, capricious and obese woman who sold rocking chairs at her farm house near Buda; Eloise Magness, whose daddy ran a cotton gin close to Lockhart; Grandpa Bible, Aunt Niney, or even his animal friends like dog LeRoy, the dog born without a left hind leg ("it was somethin' to see him take a pee on the run"). One story he told of a cotton gin worker who one day just "got up and fell in the machinery. He went in 6 foot-3, and came out 8 inches long. They held a vote in the town, and voted him more of a stain than a corpse." The town held a cotton bail funeral, but "held it up four days. And on the fourth day, cotton tripled in price." Other stories from his broadcasts:

· "Got a letter from Aunt Edith the other day. Her letters are always filled up with what she said to the doctor ... always threatening to carry some doctor to court if he don't operate." Aunt Edith boasts of having "at least four operations ahead of Winnie Waterson. Uncle Lee says she has been unhappy lately because she read about a lady in Kansas who had eighteen operations."

· "Daddy used to make this distinction between a politician

and a cowboy—a cowboy gets up early, decides what he wants to do, then straddles his pony and gets to work. He does the best he can and spends as little money as possible. The politician gets up late in the morning, straddles the fence, spends all the money he can get, gets all the votes lined up, and then decides what to do." (March 1950)

• "Grandpa Bible had qualities I loved: good-natured like a friendly old red rooster is friendly—liable to peck you. He used to say: 'I don't like to have folks around me that agrees with me. First place, I love to talk and argue; can't do either with somebody that thinks the same as me. Second place, I love to learn something *new,* and you can't never learn nothin' from somebody that's always agreeing with you.' " (September 1952)

John Henry used J. Frank Dobie, Roy Bedichek, Walter P. Webb, and Mody Boatright as the basis for many of his stories and his characters on his show. When he got a chance to return to Austin on breaks from work, he would naturally have a reunion with these friends. Often, the gathering would include Frank Wardlaw, Wilson Hudson, and Glen Evans. The group would go out into the country at Webb's Friday Mountain Ranch or Dobie's Cherry Springs Ranch some afternoon, drink beer, and eat steak over a campfire. Said Dobie: "I don't know who did the most talking; if John Henry Faulk were around then he liked to do more than anybody else. He would get to acting or taking off on somebody," said Dobie. Webb, who died in March 1963, rarely put stories or humor in his books, Dobie said, but "in conversation with congenial people he was full of anecdotes and sometimes rather sardonic observations, as when he said he wished birth control had been in operation before such and such a man was born." Bedichek, who became a vegetarian in his later years, "was also his own favorite cook, and he insisted on boiling his coffee and cooking the steaks at these parties, over an open fire. I've never seen him not refuse his own cooked steak." [32]

Geologist Glen Evans described these gatherings in the *Texas Observer:* "The peaceful, open-air setting had an enlivening effect on every member of the supper party. The talk was brisk and witty, and it seemed to improve steadily as the evening wore on. Certainly the three exceptional men who formed the nucleus of the group and their frinds who were present on these outings produced the most delightful and enlightening conversation that I have heard in my life." [33]

These junkets to the Hill Country would replenish John Henry and relieve the pressures he felt to perform in New York. Why was he energized by these men? Even he thought it worth analysis: "I have been trying to figure out why I sort of tingle all over when I am with you all. Of course, it is a rather silly analysis to carry on, but it does interest me. As close as I can come to it is the fact that your talk flows not only from healthy, creative minds, but from minds un-fenced by bigotry and prejudice. Minds enriched by life-longing probing and beauty and [being] unafraid of change. You are all living testimony to the truth that the biological changes that overtake the body cannot take like toll from the thinking processes of a man. I know a hell of a lot of young bucks who could outrun any one of you, but I do not know a single youngster who can out-think you ... My devoutest ambition is to retain a youthful, inquiring mind, as you gentlemen have, until I shuffle off this mortal coil. Then, regardless of what has befallen me in the material world, I shall have lived well." [34]

Dobie, Bedichek, Webb, and Boatright all reveled in good conversation, "not mere gabbing which many people mistake for conversation," Bedichek once explained, "but the entertaining and sincere interchange of thoughts, opinions, experiences" between individuals who desire to obtain the truth.[35]

One of Bedichek's favorite topics, of course, was nature. He always thought John Henry had a flair for describing and drawing nature scenes. The two often compared bird-watching stories together in their letters. Once, after reading an editorial in *The New York Times* in 1953 praising the mockingbird, John Henry wrote a letter that the paper published: "The mockingbird, as far as I am concerned, has no peer as a singer, and for that I love him dearly. However, he also sets a record of a very different sort — namely, he is one of the most independent and cantankerous fellows in the feathered world ... As a songster he is seemingly from heavenly climes — as an ill-tempered neighbor, he is surely from the opposite regions."

8.

CBS
Personality

A bout the time daughter Evelyn was born, WCBS Radio offered John Henry his own morning show again in September 1951, a program where he could play music and talk about whatever he wanted for four hours. He began his debut on December 17 at 7:15 A.M. Although pleased with the move, both he and Lynne had their eyes on the booming medium of television as a probable career.

Liking his home on the outskirts of New York but unable to meet the growing demands of his career from there, John Henry decided to move once again in the fall of 1951. With the help of friends Clark and Mairi Foreman, the Faulks moved into a three-bedroom apartment off 97th Street near Riverside Park. The spacious home, with high ceilings and long halls, overlooked a sweeping portion of the Hudson River and the Jersey shoreline. It was an ideal place to raise two children, who were often looked after by the Foremans' two older children.

"The John Henry Faulk Show," which ran for six years, combined music, time signals, and weather with John Henry's down-to-earth humor. He added a slightly political flair to the show by asking listeners to call in their opinions on current issues.

With those issues becoming dominated by the communist witch-hunt and the war in Korea, John Henry grew despondent about the country's "ever-accelerating descent into a Hell of complete militarization, [and its] subversion of free thought and expression," he wrote Bedichek. "The voices of the press, pulpit and political platform that help shape the public's thinking, are all raised, not against our part in rendering Korea a stinking desert, but in whorish unison for greater and more ghastly weapons and plans for destruction. The subtle and villainous way that 'peace' has been made to become synonymous with treason has been so thorough that even the gentle Quakers and their 'Plan for Peace,' is savagely attacked as Moscow-inspired." [1]

The war in Korea disturbed John Henry, because he discovered "ample evidence on hand that the entire Korean affair was deliberately planned by Dulles, MacArthur, and Chiang, aided and abetted by the pro-Chiang lobby of Knowlands and McCarthys here, who had to resort to something desperate last year after Truman and the State Dept. both announced that the U.S. was writing Chiang's Nationalists off the books. Certainly our arbitrary and arrogant refusal to consider Red China as anything but a target for our bombs would confirm our sinister intentions toward her. If we ain't headed for hell in a hack, we'll never be. They say that Wall Street stays in a constant state of jitters for fear that Russia will come up with a peace proposal that we can't afford to turn down and leave our flourishing War Business dangling. The only bright aspect of the whole sorry mess is that at least since Mc A's dismissal, there is some debate and the Republicans have managed to flounder themselves into the position of being the War Party. Perhaps some of the vestiges of the Roosevelt school will seize on this to set back on the reins a little. But the great and obvious picture today is that the land that I love is deliberately and systematically preparing to launch a bloody aggressive war that will leave the good earth mangled for generations. They are not even bothering to point out where Russia is threatening anymore — but simply roar 'We've got to stop her' and wave their guns." [2]

Because he felt somewhat guilty that he was sitting in a studio making money "while the jackals run loose in this land," John Henry often quoted observations from philosophers such as Thoreau, Whitman, and Twain to sneak in comments about man's quest for truth and his need to question authority. "My listeners," he wrote, "cheer on my quotations of thinkers on the subject of democracy and I have to get a negative reaction on the fun I poke at the windy politicians and possum-grin brethren who so smugly go their twilight days in Washington." [3]

The writer of a February 9, 1952, review in *Billboard* magazine gave John Henry an auspicious critique for his program, commenting that the entertainer was "aided by a captivating Texas drawl, considerable vocal savvy and a charm all his own." Faulk is "a personality," the reviewer continued, and "can tell a story with the best of the tale-spinners and his opinions are worth hearing."

Many of John Henry's colleagues felt the pressure of anxiety and fear of the times, and hesitated to say anything political that might be considered too controversial. Although they bred him to act as the "professional Texan," CBS Radio execs also urged John Henry to "play the good-humored doubter." This encouragement was all John Henry needed to inject some political humor on the air, often with a biting edge:

· "Senator McCarthy has the Democrats between a rock and a hard place. Mr. Truman and the administration cast their loyalty probe and subversive list bread upon the waters, and it's coming back to them in Republican cornbread. Sort of hard to get at McCarthy, because he's using their own lists to prove his story." (1950)

· "I'd much rather meet a man whose opinion differed from mine, than meet a man with no opinion at all. Course, I've met politicians who didn't have an opinion on anything; took both sides." (1950)

· Congressman Guffaw has been running for office since 1910 and never was elected. He says his opponents lie on him. "Now what sort of lies could they spread about a fine gentleman like you?" John Henry asks Congressman Guffaw.

"Well, the Republicans say I've got the principles of the Democrats, and the Democrats say I've got the principles of the

Republicans. Now them's ugly rumors — everybody that knows me knows I ain't got no principles." (1951)

• "Down in Washington today the Senate met, then adjourned ten seconds later. Don't know whether it was just that the boys didn't have anything on their mind, or that they had to hurry home and help their wives with the week's wash. But it does make you sort of envy the senators' jobs. It ain't everybody that can get together with his fellow workers and vote themselves a holiday, or raise in pay, too for that matter." (1951)

• "I see where Republicans had a $100-plate dinner the other night in Atlantic City. Both parties pull off those big shindigs; folks pay $100 for $5 worth of food and $95 worth of speeches. A man [who] pays $95 to hear a politician speak, Democrat or Republican, must be powerful hard up for entertainment." (February 1951)

• "Someone once said, 'Woman is a contradiction, at best.' Don't know why they confined it to women." (September 1952)

• "The stereotyped thinkin' about the role of women in society is much broader now than it ever was . . . it took women seventy-two years of uphill struggle just to earn the right to vote . . . I want to pay tribute to those women who fought to change the prevailing outdated attitudes of the day. And the attitudes have changed, and will keep changing." (1955)

"The John Henry Faulk Show" proved its popularity when 900 supermarkets cooperated in the "John Henry Faulk Merchandising Plan." Advertisers buying participation in the show received tie-in product displays in these stores in New York. "John Henry Faulk Weeks" were featured in the stores, and sponsors got the benefit of newspaper ads and special displays.

Listeners were captivated by John Henry's stories of Aunt Edith, Grandpa Bible, and Reverend Truesdale. Few New Yorkers had heard tall tales of the Southwest from a real Texan — on the air — and the others who had, liked hearing the sound of a familiar voice on the radio.

One of those listeners was another rising star at CBS, Walter Cronkite: "When I first heard the program on the air, I was, you know, panicked . . . I mean, I thought it was gritty, but I said that New Yorkers aren't going to go for this Texas country stuff. This is too sophisticated a town. I didn't know the town as well as John

Henry Faulk knew it. He obviously was very, very popular. He was really speaking for all of us. He put a Texas accent on it. Country Texas humor, allegedly, and that's in quotes. It was Everyman, wherever he lived. Whether he was living in Harlem or the Bronx, on Park Avenue, or whether he lived out in West Texas. It's the same humor. It was so darn human, right down to the base and the core of our characters."[4]

In a *Newsweek* magazine interview (December 1952), John Henry defended his regional accent and admitted to purposely emphasizing a Texas twang in his accent: "My speech may curve and vary a little, but 90 percent of the people are interested in the same things my folks were — keepin' clothes on their backs and their kids in school." Texans aren't the type of people to "whoop around and swing around the chandeliers of the Waldorf-Astoria," John Henry said. "My type are people that got conviction and strength, the people that made dye outta urine and lye. Those are the people, and they're the same all over."

Although he'd often change their names, John Henry's folk ballads and storybook arena included characters he knew or heard stories about during his boyhood: Old Man Mostellar ("the biggest liar in the world"), Aunt Effie McDoo (a frustrated spinster full of prejudices), Grandpa Bible (who lived in Austin in the nineteenth century), Lee Miner (preacher and small-town newspaper editor), Congressman Guffaw, "Minnesota" Dairy Princess, and Old Man Snodgrass (the caustic, old-fashioned man who drove a bus from Cedar Valley to Dripping Springs). Ed Snodgrass, who believed the Lord intended Austin to be the center of the universe, was a real cousin of John Henry's who lived with the Faulks in the 1920s. In "The John Henry Faulk Show," Snodgrass and the others evolved into exaggerated caricatures John Henry used to illustrate his stories. To get a point across about poverty or racial injustice, he might put a worldly observation in the mouths of Aunt Edith or Aunt Effie, imitating their Texas drawls and high-pitched voices. He quickly discovered that "Manhattan sophisticates . . . get the biggest kick out of me mentioning folks like Aunt Ollie, Cactus Pryor, and Aunt Mary Beckett." So he used to reminisce frequently about his parents and friends, adding to the show's down-home nature:

· "Mama was trying to get some plowing done; she wants to

get potatoes in the ground by February 15. Mama feels like it's a sin to own a piece of land that can't be planted and let it lay idle. Says the Lord put the earth here for us to make a better place. Even if you can't raise a garden, you can make it beautiful with flowers." (January 1950)

• Next to the Bible, looks like the most read [book] in our house was Dickens—even more than Mark Twain. Dickens, who symbolized in his novels the triumph of virtue over sin, was Victorian, and so was Mama. Mama had been raised on him. I knew David Copperfield, Aunt Pegotty, Mr. Macawber, Sam Heller, on infinitum on closest terms. It was much later that Dickens became significant to me, not only for his humor and pathos of novels. I discovered Dickens was a penetrating commentator of the social scene; not just a syrupy sentimentalist." (February 1953)

• "Daddy had struggled for an education—he was hung on it. He loved to see folks go to school. He had a couple of pet theories: 1) the university should teach you *how* to think; not *what* to think, and 2) education makes people easy to lead, but difficult to drive; easy to govern, but impossible to enslave." (March 1953)

John Henry was already being compared to Will Rogers, Mark Twain, Ruth Draper, and Cornelia Otis Skinner for his style of dry folk humor. He seemed to perform better when it was impromptu, and he often deviated from a prepared script. Famous broadcaster Edward R. Murrow told John Henry that he didn't need any special gimmicks to sell the show: "I would make a guess, too, Johnny," he wrote, "that you haven't really got anything to sell in this business except *believability.*"

Writer Studs Terkel, who met John Henry during the Henry Wallace campaign, knew he had encountered a one-of-a-kind storyteller. "In our first meeting," Terkel said, "he gave an incredible performance, narrating a story about an attempted lynching of a black man through the viewpoint of this white man who was part of it." Through John Henry's voice, expressions, and mannerisms, Terkel said, "he got into the psyche of this guy."

Terkel was so impressed with John Henry's ability that in 1952 he invited him on his radio show, "Stud's Place." Terkel remembered John Henry telling one of the "best Christmas stories I've ever heard," about the son of a poor sharecropper,

Rufus, whose father had given him an orange for Christmas. "Why, that ain't nothing but an orange," the young Johnny told him. "That ain't no real Christmas present." Rufus, hurt and dejected, said softly: "It's the onliest orange I ever had, Johnny." [5]

John Henry "was talking to a multitude when he talked. But each time he talked, it was fresh. His humor was unique in that his characters often made you fall off your chair laughing, but you were thinking as you fell off. That was his mastery." [6]

At age thirty-nine, John Henry was discovering he still had a lot to learn about the radio business and selling himself as a personality in a competitive market. By 1952, he was spending up to fourteen hours a day at work, but felt he had "a great deal to learn before I can make any claims to turning out a satisfactory performance. I am discovering rather painfully that there is absolutely no substitute for hard, grinding work in the business of making a success of oneself. If only a genial disposition and a ready smile would suffice! But no, they are only the show window. When the public comes in to look around the shop, one had best have good, serviceable merchandise, or else give up the trade and go back to milking cows in South Austin. And the foregoing, simple though it is, represents the most important lesson that I have learned in all my life."[7]

John Henry shouldn't have worried too much about his popularity. A PULSE rating of April 1954 showed his WCBS program to be in the top ten of all New York daytime radio shows. The program could also be heard on regional hook-up in Massachusetts. And he was beginning to be a commonly seen face on television, where many entertainers were moving because of the more lucrative contracts.

Goodson-Todman Productions was the acknowledged leader among television production firms in the early 1950s, especially in game shows. Mark Goodson and Jerry Todman produced several successful half-hour game shows on CBS and NBC, and they saw that John Henry had an appealing personality for game shows – quick, clever, humorous, and congenial. On one game show called *We Take Your Word,* John Henry and fellow panelists Harriet Van Horne and Abe Burrows traced words back to their Greek, Latin, French or Danish origins, noting how the word's meaning changed over time. On NBC's Sunday night show *Leave It To the Girls*, John Henry defended the male sex against the charges made by actresses Maggie McNellis, Dorothy Kilgallen and Eloise MacElhone. In one review, *Variety* called *Leave It To the Girls* one of the best comedy shows on the air, with John Henry as one of the relaxed and natural ingredients—a person who "knew how to shade his satire, and emerged so warm a personality that he should cast his iconoscopes on wider wavelengths." Later, John Henry became moderator on this show, and invited some of his Texas friends as panelists, including conservative Governor Allan Shivers.[8]

On its sixth anniversary, *Leave It To the Girls* reversed its regular format. Instead of a panel of four females "baiting" a lone male about attitudes on love and gender, four males, including John Henry, were placed in the dominant role that Sunday evening, "baiting" the one woman, Eloise MacElhone. John Henry, Ted Malone, Bill Slater, and Joey Adams demonstrated cogent and provocative opinions – some colorful, some humorous. At one point in the show, however, the line crossed from humor to what one reviewer called "brutal bad manners," with Malone, Slater, and Adams complaining about women's "nature" in general, and John Henry had to jump in and cool things down. "Come on, fellows, let up a little," John Henry intervened, proceeding to compliment Eloise and the entertainment value of the show.

For a year and a half, John Henry appeared as a panelist on another popular TV-talk show, CBS' *It's News to Me*, which covered the daily news with Quentin Reynolds, John Daly, and Nina Foch. John Henry particularly liked appearing on this show, because it gave him the chance "to have some fun at the expense of some of the gentlemen who are making the news these days."[9]

John Henry performed in one program in the summer of 1953 with fellow CBS colleague Walter Cronkite. Called *You Are There*, the program was created by comic writer Goodman Ace. Its premise was to use famous historical events reported by "state-of-the-art broadcast techniques," with the news reporters pretending to be "on the scene" doing interviews and narrating the action. Well-known reporters like Cronkite, Douglas Edwards, and Richard Hottelet filled the reporter roles, while actors played the historical roles.

For six months in 1953, John Henry emceed the NBC radio giveaway program, "Walk a Mile" (sponsored by Camel Cigarettes, the show paid John Henry about $300 to $400 a week). He also appeared in spots on TV's *What's My Line*, the *Saturday Evening Report*, *Let's Take Sides* (ABC), and *The Name's The Same*, and radio's "The George Skinner Show," "Maggie Haye's Show," and "Wendy Barrow's Show." In 1955 he performed a five-minute weekly network radio show for NBC called "Daniel Boone and the Colonel." Also that year, Senate Majority Leader Lyndon Johnson invited him to entertain on stage before the National Press Club's Congressional Night in Washington, D.C., alongside then Vice-president Richard Nixon (who played the "Missouri Waltz" on the piano). His coup was in landing a summer host spot on CBS-TV's *The Morning Show* in 1955, replacing Jack Paar. With Charles Collingwood and others, John Henry provided a balance to the sophisticated, news-oriented performers. On one program, he showed the viewers how to milk a cow. On others, he fed his pet goat.

Evidently, most viewers did not find his brand of cornpone-style humor appealing on Sunday mornings, because the ratings never materialized. The network, having trouble with this new show, dropped the program after only four weeks. Soon thereafter, CBS resurrected it with Dick Van Dyke, whom one reviewer called "too strenuous in his humor." He, too, was dropped, and was replaced by Captain Kangaroo.

After the birth of son Frank Dobie (named after John Henry's Texan mentor) in February 1953, the Faulks moved to a larger apartment behind the Museum of Natural History on 79th Street. In the continuing tradition of his father, this huge home served as a salon for intellectuals, social activists, and civil rights supporters. The Faulks brought together many entertainers, politicians, and celebrities to talk about politics. Of the many entertainers he knew, John Henry was closest to Yip Harburg (composer of such classics as Broadway's "Finian's Rainbow" and "Brother Can You Spare a Dime?") and actor Ossie Davis.

A few months after Frank Dobie was born, John Henry returned to Austin to show his new son to the family and to visit his mother, who had been stricken with cancer. At home, he received a call from an elderly woman who had taught him in Sunday

Henry Faulk (1868–1939) was born in Clio, Alabama, and was the eldest of nine children born to Henry Lafayette Faulk and Lucy Card Faulk. His family came to Texas in 1870, when he was two, and lived in Henderson, Coleman, and Williamson counties. Henry Faulk moved to Austin in 1896 and lived above a livery stable while attending law school at the University of Texas. *(Photo from Austin History Center, Austin Public Library, Map Case C-2)*

Martha ("Mattie") Faulk (1876–1956), center, was born on a farm midway between Manor and Webberville. She was the fifth of six children born to Ashford Tannehill Miner and Medora Jones Miner. Mattie was teaching school at Hornsby Bend (c. 1897–1902) when she first met Henry Faulk. *(Photo courtesy Anne McAfee)*

Henry and Martha Faulk with their three children in 1912 — Martha, Hamilton, and Mary. John Henry was born the next year, and Texana was born in 1915. *(Photo courtesy Anne McAfee)*

In 1916 the Faulk family moved to this home in South Austin, a sparsely populated region in a city of 33,000. An ideal place to bring up five children, the small farm provided all the milk, butter, eggs, and garden vegetables for the family. Note the wooden steps in this 1933 photograph. In 1946 Martha Faulk Koock transformed the home into a fashionable Austin restaurant called Green Pastures. *(Photo courtesy Anne McAfee)*

The two youngest of the Faulk children, John Henry (on the scooter) and Texana, playing on the porch of their new home in 1916. *(Photo courtesy Anne McAfee)*

Henry Faulk as seen in his law office on Congress Avenue in the late 1920s. John Henry kept an artist's rendition of this photo above his mantlepiece. *(Photo courtesy Anne McAfee)*

Henry and Martha Faulk outside their home, 1932. *(Photo from the Center for American History, University of Texas at Austin)*

The Faulk family posed for a rare photograph outside their home (c. 1928). From left are Texana, Hamilton (in back), Miss Mattie, Henry Faulk, Mary, Martha, and John Henry (kneeling). *(Photo from Austin History Center, Austin Public Library, PICB #02654)*

Annie Mae Finnin was a close friend of the Faulk family for several years. About 1930, Johnny poses with Annie Mae, her daughter Helen, Helen's sister Estel, and brothers Monroe, Jr., and Marvin at the Finnins' South Austin home. *(Photo from the Center for American History, University of Texas at Austin)*

Johnny embraces "Mother Finnin," mother-in-law of Annie Mae Finnin (right), and Annie Mae's eldest daughter Helen, when he returned to Austin from New York in 1949. This photograph was taken at the Finnin house on West Live Oak Street. *(Photo from the Center for American History, University of Texas at Austin)*

Johnny Faulk as he appeared in his 1932 graduation photo from Austin High School's yearbook, *The Comet. (Photo from Austin History Center, Austin Public Library, PICB #10950)*

John Henry Faulk in the early 1940s. *(Photo from Austin History Center, Austin Public Library, PICB #02656)*

Besides his parents, Texas writer and teacher J. Frank Dobie had the strongest influence on John Henry's life, instilling in him a lifelong interest in folklore and an inquiring search for knowledge. *(Photo from the Austin History Center, Austin Public Library, PICB #10951)*

John Henry took leave from the university in 1942 to join the Merchant Marines. *(Photo from the Center for American History, University of Texas at Austin)*

Known as an authority on black folklore, John Henry, on leave from the Merchant Marines in 1943, teamed up with Dobie to talk about women, war, and the Marines at the University of Texas. The talk was sponsored by the Campus War Council. *(Photo from the Center for American History, University of Texas at Austin)*

J. Frank Dobie with his namesake, Frank Dobie Faulk. *(Photo from the Center for American History, University of Texas at Austin)*

Naturalist Roy Bedichek, another major influence on John Henry's life, visited John Henry and his daughter Evelyn in New York City in 1955. *(Photo from the Center for American History, University of Texas at Austin)*

John Henry with (from left) J. Frank Dobie, Roy Bedichek (standing), Mody Boatright, and Walter Prescott Webb. When John Henry returned to Austin, he would always get together with the quartet to recharge his intellectual and creative skills. *(Photo from the Center for American History, University of Texas at Austin)*

John Henry was a strong supporter of Henry Wallace for president in 1948. This photo was taken when Wallace visited Austin in the summer of 1947. From left: Clark Foreman, John Henry, Henry Wallace, and James Dombrowski. *(Photo from the Center for American History, University of Texas at Austin)*

With fellow Texan Jim Wright at a party for the Texas Democratic legislators in Austin in 1947. *(Photo from the Center for American History, University of Texas at Austin)*

John Henry as "Pat the Rancher" for WPAT-Radio in Paterson, New Jersey, 1949. *(Photo from the Center for American History, University of Texas at Austin)*

At WPAT-Radio in January 1950, John Henry participated in the federal government's "Eat Chicken Week" by asking the age-old question: "Which came first, the chicken or the egg?" He offered six frozen chickens a day for the best answers. His first day's mail brought 750 letters. John Henry's show, which aired six mornings a week, was called "Hi Neighbor" and later, "Keep 'Em Smiling." *(Photo from the Center for American History, University of Texas at Austin)*

John Henry in Washington, D.C., as emcee of the National Press Club's party in April 1955. Richard Nixon is playing a waltz on the piano. *(Photo from the Center for American History, University of Texas at Austin)*

When he worked for CBS, John Henry developed a strong friendship with broadcaster Edward R. Murrow, who helped John Henry finance his lawsuit against AWARE, Inc. *(Photo from the Center for American History, University of Texas at Austin)*

John Henry returns to CBS Radio with his own daily show. *(Photo from the Center for American History, University of Texas at Austin)*

John Henry with his wife, Lynne, and entertainer Lena Horne at a 1953 NAACP rally at Madison Square Garden. *(Photo from the Center for American History, University of Texas at Austin)*

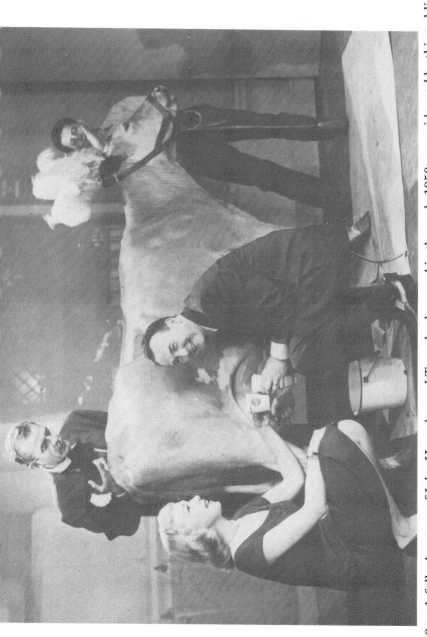

CBS took full advantage of John Henry's rural Texas background in the early 1950s, as evidenced by this publicity photo for John Henry's brief stint as host of the "CBS Morning Show" in May 1955. Here John Henry demonstrates the art of milking a cow for newscaster Charles Collingwood (holding John Henry's pet goat, Katy Gonzales) and singer/entertainer Edie Adams. (*Photo from Austin History Center, Austin Public Library, PICB #02657*)

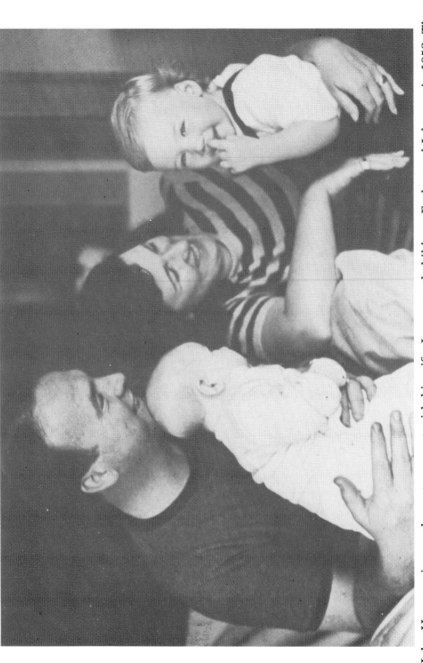

John Henry enjoys a pleasant moment with his wife, Lynne, and children, Evelyn and Johanna, in 1952. The next year, Frank Dobie Faulk was born. (*Photo from Austin History Center, Austin Public Library, PICB #02662*)

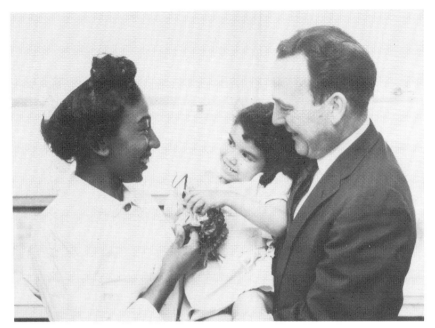

As a media personality, John Henry lent his name to several charities and non-profit groups. Here, as a member of the New York City Protestant Board, he poses with one of the children seeking foster homes. *(Photo from the Center for American History, University of Texas at Austin)*

It's News to Me was a popular panel show from 1953 to 1955. From left are: British movie acress Anna Lee, newscaster Quenten Reynolds, Broadway and Hollywood actress Nina Foch, and John Henry. *(Photo from the Center for American History, University of Texas at Austin)*

Joseph McCarthy and his assistant, Roy Cohn (left), during the Army-McCarthy hearings in 1954 that led to the senator's downfall. "McCarthyism" came to mean an anti-communist philosophy that used unproven, and usually untrue, allegations against a political adversary. *(Photo from the Center for American History, University of Texas at Austin)*

Publicity photo with attorney Louis Nizer for *Look* Magazine's article on John Henry in 1962 about his court battle against the blacklist. *(Photo from the Center for American History, University of Texas at Austin)*

John Henry with Henry Fonda in the film *The Best Man* in 1963. *(Photo from the Center for American History, University of Texas at Austin)*

George C. Scott starred as attorney Louis Nizer and William Devane as John Henry Faulk in CBS-TV's made-for-television movie in 1975, *Fear on Trial,* based on John Henry's book of the same name. *(Photo from the Center for American History, University of Texas at Austin)*

John Henry enjoys a moment with friend Ann Richards at a Watergate protest party in Austin (May 1974). *(Photo from the Center for American History, University of Texas at Austin)*

John Henry Faulk's name became well-known again when CBS-TV released its docu-drama based on his book. Here he talks to a reporter about *Fear on Trial* in 1975. *(Photo from the Center for American History, University of Texas at Austin)*

After *Fear on Trial* was dramatized and the book re-released, John Henry returned to television as a homespun philosopher on *Hee Haw* from 1975 to 1980. He posed for this photo with his good friend from Texas, Peavine Jeffries. *(Photo from the Center for American History, University of Texas at Austin)*

John Henry pauses for a moment of reflection off the set of *Hee Haw.* *(Photo from the Center for American History, University of Texas at Austin)*

John Henry with two friends, J. R. Parten (who, as a UT regent, brought Homer Rainey to the university) and Carolyn Farb, at a Houston reception in 1986, after Faulk's premiere of "Deep in the Heart" at the Chocolate Bayou Theater. *(Photo courtesy of Carolyn Farb)*

Celebrities and friends of John Henry's came to Austin in July 1989 for the John Henry Faulk Tribute. From left: writer Studs Terkel, actor Ossie Davis, actress-director Lee Grant, John Henry, and Hollywood producer Barbara Boyle. *(Photo by Michael Burton)*

John Henry Faulk in his one-man play, "Pear Orchard Texas," March 1989, as Lois Irene's kid brother who never had a pair of shoes to wear. *(Photo by Eileen Llorente)*

John Henry Faulk portrait. *(Photo by Michael Burton)*

school. Although friendly and polite about the new member of the Faulk family, she disapproved of the name he had been given.

"Honey," she said, "you jest been away from Austin too long. That ol' Frank Dobie has jest become a disgrace. When he ain't blessin' out the govmint, he's rediculin' religeon and pokin' fun at preachers. Jest disgraceful the way he goes on. I doubt if the old sinner has put foot inside a church in his life." John Henry didn't think to tell her that Dobie had been spiritually nourished in the same church she went to. When he hung up, distressed, his mother told him, "Pay her no mind, Johnny. She's a poor old simple-minded ignoramus who has little to do but sit around and stoke her prejudices with misinformation. If she knew Mr. Dobie better, she would love him as much as you do."

John Henry knew his mama was right about ignoring the remarks, but he felt she was wrong that the woman would like Dobie if she got to know him better. "She would have liked him less," he wrote. "J. Frank Dobie is an anathema to her sort. There is not a hypocrite, bigot, religious or political fraud in Texas who can stand J. Frank Dobie. The reason, I think, is easy to understand. Dobie makes them uncomfortable. Mighty uncomfortable." [10]

The city of Austin was downright proud to have one of its native sons strike it big in the entertainment world, but most Austinites couldn't hear his radio show because there was no direct hook-up with New York. Friend and local radio personality Cactus Pryor got around that by bootlegging portions of Faulk's show on Pryor's program on KTBC-Radio.

John Henry wrote Dobie in January 1954 about the difficulty in getting the show transmitted to Austin: "Yesterday, Ed Murrow called me and related to me with no little disappointment in his voice, the results of his office's investigation into line charges, etc., to Austin, Texas. It seems that the coaxial cable can carry shows into Austin (or other Texas cities) but cannot carry a show out of there. They will have to wait until dual cable to do that, which should be in use by late May, or early Fall. I thought I should tell you at once, since I made such a to-do over the show Ed wanted to do with you in late January." [11]

In April 1955, John Henry was named vice-president of the Texas Broadcasting Corporation. Senator Lyndon Johnson had worked out a deal with John Henry to be in charge of public affairs for his radio and television station at KTBC, owned by his wife, Lady Bird. Not only did Johnson want John Henry to coordinate KTBC programs in Austin and host a KTBC television show with Cactus Pryor, but he also wanted to groom him as public affairs manager for LBJ's planned campaign for the vice-presidency with Averell Harriman in 1956.[12] The Faulk family had supported Johnson and fellow Congressman Homer Thornberry in the 1940s, and Lyndon wanted to capitalize on John Henry's popularity in Texas and his connections with the New York media.

"Lyndon was courting me to come to Texas," John Henry said, and "when Lyndon courts, Lyndon courts. He was very gracious and very good. I was terribly flattered by the attention he gave me. I'd go down and spend the weekend with him and Mrs. Johnson at their home in Georgetown. We'd go to big functions: the Sam Rayburn dinner, the Harry Truman birthday party and a lot of things like this. So Johnson persuaded me to quit my job at CBS and come down to Texas as vice-president in charge of public relations for the broadcasting system."[13]

A few days after the announcement, the offer was suddenly withdrawn. John Henry canceled his plans to return to Austin. Johnson told him the Republicans were attacking him for using his senatorial influence "to promote the interests of the Texas Broadcasting Corporation." John Henry was infuriated. He got his business manager, Gerald Dickler, to contact Johnson to ask about compensating him for leaving his job. Johnson balked, and John Henry threatened a lawsuit. Soon afterwards, CBS called John Henry and offered him his old job back.

Twenty-three years later, John Henry discovered that LBJ had asked FBI director J. Edgar Hoover in 1955 for "any derogatory information the FBI might have on Faulk." The FBI had also given these files to Roy Cohn, former senior counsel to Senator Joe McCarthy (and counsel for AWARE, Inc. during part of Faulk's future lawsuit). John Henry would be able to obtain only a portion (233 pages) of the FBI documents in 1979, under the Freedom of Information Act. The rest was denied to him on the grounds of "national security."[14] When he pored through his file, John Henry noticed a notation to the "Director," meaning Hoover, from George Reedy, who was press secretary to Johnson

at the time. It said that Johnson was thinking about hiring John
Henry for his radio and television stations, and wanted to know
if the "Director" would permit him to see any FBI information on
Faulk. So Hoover prepared a summary for Johnson, listing things
like John Henry's association with J. Frank Dobie and his support
of civil rights in Texas in the 1940s.[15]

Soon after the Johnson deal fell through, John Henry discovered on a trip to the doctor that he had cancer in his lymph
glands. The malignancy was removed in time before it spread,
but he spent a great deal of time in the hospital, where he entertained the nursing staff with jokes. Being in the hospital gave
him time to work on his writing of character sketches and short
plays, and he received valuable editorial help from author Mari
Sandoz, an admirer of Dobie's who wrote *Old Jules* and *The Buffalo Hunters.*[16]

John Henry's fame in New York was growing rapidly by
1955. Even his small children knew that their daddy was a celebrity, since people would stop them in the street, and the Faulk
home would receive late-night visits from the Flamingo Dance
Troupe and other singers and entertainers. The family always had
a maid to look after the three children when the parents were
away, which was quite often, since both parents were devoted to
their careers.[17]

"He was gone a lot of the time," said son Frank Dobie, who
recalls having a lot of positive and negative feelings then. "The
way they [parents] related was so passive/aggressive. John Henry
would say, 'Tell your dear silver-haired mother to pass the salt.'
He would often make faces when Lynne would reprimand us behind her back, exactly like Chevy Chase would do." When John
Henry was upset, he would usually use humor to express his anger. "My mother was more explosive when she was angry; John
Henry would be much more subtle. It's a Faulk characteristic —
humor is used to connect us with people, but it's also used to
keep us apart. Rather than dealing with the real feelings that were
happening, let's joke about it." The intense, volatile relationship
between the two adults caused a great deal of friction in the
Faulk home.

Yet the tension was offset by the warm experiences of playing in Central Park, going to the zoo or the museums, playing

"booney-bird" on John Henry's feet, and hearing wonderful stories before bedtime. Frank recalled one in particular about "Jack Vern and the owl": "Basically, it was about a little boy who was living on the farm with his parents, and one night he was awoken by the sound of a big hoot owl, and the hoot owl knows his name, and he asks Jack Vern to get on his back and he takes him to the moon. And what I remember most was how my father would describe the little moon fairies, who had little ice cream cones, and they danced around the owl with Jack Vern and enchanted him and sang songs, and went back to the farm." [18]

After finding his niche in television, John Henry was, as he would say, "choppin' in tall cotton." In 1955 the Nielson ratings reported his program second in the ratings of seventeen radio stations — ahead of the entire NBC radio lineup. [19] During the 1956 season, John Henry's sixth year as radio talk show host, WCBS received nearly $400,000 in spot revenue from the program. His salary netted him over $35,000 a year, a handsome sum in pre-inflation days, and that didn't include the revenue from spot TV appearances and lectures. In March 1956, he flew to Washington, D.C. to serve as emcee for the opening of wealthy financier Clendenin Ryan's mansion, the Liberty House. Mingling with a throng of celebrities and politicians, including columnist Drew Pearson, former Secretary of the Senate Leslie Biffle, South Carolina Senator Strom Thurmond, and numerous other senators, John Henry enlivened the party by galvanizing the women present "to leap to their Leap Year opportunity by asking the men to dance!" One New York society columnist called John Henry "the noted CBS personality" who entertained the crowd with his energy and enthusiasm. There was one senator, however, who didn't seem to be entertained by the CBS personality from Texas, and only sat quietly at his dinner table: Senator Joseph McCarthy.

9.

BLACKLISTING:
CONFORM
OR ELSE!

J ohn Henry Faulk may have had an eerie foresight into the
future when he wrote a letter to his dear friend J. Frank
Dobie. In that letter, he noted how his career was proceeding
marvelously, but knew what might wreck it: "It looks like I'll be
sailing along up here for quite a spell, unless McCarthy decides
to crack my knuckles for un-McCarthy-like thoughts."

Ever the optimist, John Henry believed that the atmosphere
of the country was changing since Joe McCarthy was brought
down. "There is a trend toward a more enlightened attitude in
the [entertainment] industry," he told a reporter in 1955. "There
has been a very definite decline in the effectiveness of the blacklist."

Blacklisting was common in the broadcasting industry in
the late 1940s and early 1950s, a practice that sprang from the
House Un-American Activities Committee hearings into the
Hollywood Ten actors, who were jailed for contempt of Congress
after pleading the First Amendment. Before 1948, when Whittaker Chambers first accused Alger Hiss of having been a communist and then later of having spied for the Soviet Union, most

111

of HUAC's investigations were linked to "domestic concerns" and targeted the New Deal personnel and agencies under Roosevelt. After December 1948, however, HUAC "began increasingly to emphasize the internal security matters of espionage, subversion, and 'communists in government.' "[1] Ostensibly, HUAC was after the "communist conspiracy" or the "communist subversion" of the entertainment industry, a conspiracy that never existed. "Hollywood changed no person's political consciousness; at best, or worst, the movies reinforced mainstream social values. But to the right-wingers of the 1940s, even mainstream social values — if they had a liberal tinge — were anathema. 'Subversion' simply served as a pretext for silencing a cultural and humanitarian liberalism — a liberalism of the heart — which, in the eyes of the American right wing, regularly 'infected' the atmosphere in which Hollywood movies were made. To its way of thinking the movie industry had to be brought round and made to express proper American values." [2]

Like Hollywood, the networks felt more political pressures from far right groups like the American Legion, AWARE, Inc., and the Motion Picture Alliance for the Preservation of Ideals. Perhaps the most powerful — or at least the largest — of these organizations was the American Legion, with 17,000 posts and 2.8 million members in 1951. The Legion launched a virulent "public information program" in October 1951 that called for the dissemination of data of people who had "communist associations" in the entertainment industry. The organization called for its members to pressure television networks and sponsors who employed entertainers with some kind of "a record of belonging to communist fronts." A "front" group would usually comprise virtually any national organization that had anything to do with peace, disarmament, nuclear test ban, integration, civil rights, labor rights, or expanded medical care. The Legion's "Commission on Americanism" published *Firing Line*, which listed people in the entertainment world who were identified as "communist dupes" or "communist fronters."

Like the motion picture industry, where studios asked employees to write sworn testimonies that they weren't communists and did not associate with radicals, the actors' union and at least one network (CBS) required "loyalty oaths" pledging anti-communism. The blacklist also gave rise to what was known as a "whitelist" or "graylist," where casting directors were frequently asked to submit a list of names of everyone considered for hire to the production company or network for approval. Special permission was needed to hire anyone not on these laundered lists.

Author David Halberstam wrote that CBS, once considered the most liberal network, "quickly became the most sensitive to these organized pressures from the right, and acquiesced more readily than its competitors. It was a time of great cowardice, and many talented people were kept off the air." [3]

Perhaps CBS operated the most rigorous blacklist because their executives had been under criticism for shows like Fred Friendly's and Edward R. Murrow's *See It Now,* which produced a courageous television broadcast in March 1954 directly refuting Joe McCarthy's words and tactics. At the end of this broadcast, Murrow eloquently summarized with biblical allegory: "We must not confuse dissent with disloyalty. We must remember always that accusation is not proof, and that conviction depends upon evidence of due process of law. We will not walk in fear, one of another." (Eight months later McCarthy was censured from Congress, but blacklisting continued.)

Despite the independence of broadcasters like Murrow, the blacklisting system was so entrenched in the industry that people rarely challenged it. Sponsors exercised much more control over the content of shows than they do today; many, pressured from ultra-patriotic groups, hired informers to investigate entertainers. Each network had a vice-president in charge of programs who referred to little black books and responded to sponsors' concerns. Said Fred Friendly, who wrote a book about the period: "By the early 50s, the central nervous system of the vast broadcast industry was so conditioned that it responded to self-appointed policemen and blacklists as though they were part of the constitutional process." [4]

The large advertising agencies of the period also employed their own security officers and maintained their own lists. At CBS, Daniel T. O'Shea, vice-president of the network, was in charge of checking lists and issuing clearances. "There were lists on top of lists," television producer Mark Goodson said, "and networks, ad agencies and sponsors exchanged information on a regular basis. If a performer, writer, musician, producer or direc-tor was on one list, he immediately found himself on another list." [5]

Aware was one of the three major "smear and clear" orga-nizations that operated quite successfully in the 1950s. One was the Wage Earners Committee, a group that picketed selected films and published the *National Wage Earner* targeting "subver-sive" films. Another organization was American Business Con-sultants, the publisher of the "bible" of the blacklist called *Red Channels*, which listed certain entertainers who had participated in or associated with "communist-front" activities. Often, these activities could be as innocuous as belonging to a consumer's union, or being married to someone who aided the Russian War Relief. Much of the data the blacklisters used in *Red Channels* con-sisted of selected press clippings and excerpts from the House Committee; but the publishers acknowledged that they made no effort to check the accuracy of the accusations. A performer could be listed for myriad other reasons: supporting aid to Loyal-ist Spain, opposing anti-Semitism in Nazi Germany, opposing the Dies Committee, being a member of the Hollywood Anti-Nazi League, or even joining a committee to end segregation in major league baseball. Actress Madeline Lee Gilford said her listing in *Red Channels* was "by and large for supporting inter-racial employment and civil rights. Ninety percent of my listing was for my involvement in the National Negro Congress, the Arts and Sciences Committee for the Re-election of Franklin D. Roosevelt, an anti-poll tax committee, the Jackie Robinson in baseball group." [6]

Red Channels evolved into another publication called *Coun-terattack,* a newsletter devoted to the listing of actors and poli-ticians who were deemed communist sympathizers. American Business Consultants, *Counterattack*'s publisher, was heavily sub-sidized by the China Lobby and a major oil company. A yearly subscription to *Red Channels* cost $24 a year; many issues were mailed free to the press, advertising agencies, and networks. Jack Wren, former officer in Naval Intelligence, was set up in charge of "security" for the large advertising firm of Batten, Barton, Durstine and Osborn. Wren was the key liaison between *Coun-terattack* and New York's advertising agencies. Frank McNamara, who became director of anti-communist activities for the Veterans of Foreign Wars, edited *Counterattack.*[7]

A former employee of American Business Consultants, Vincent Hartnett, established AWARE, Inc., in 1953 with a group of New York actors. Its avowed mission was to "combat the communist conspiracy in the entertainment world." In the mid-1950s, its director was Godfrey P. Schmidt, a lawyer and Fordham University teacher who became one of the top men for a blacklisted person to see to get "cleared." Hartnett, Paul Milton, and Vinton Hayworth (then president of the New York local union of the American Federation of Television and Radio Artists, or AFTRA) served on Aware's board. By 1956, the organization's membership reached 600.

How did the blacklist work? For example, *Counterattack* would publish some item concerning an entertainer's "subversive" activities and/or associations. In the height of the blacklisting period, being on the list was enough to ban the entertainer from ever performing again. Often, American Business Consultants, Aware, or the American Legion members would write letters to the sponsor or network, complaining about this particular artist. Then, a representative from one of these groups might call the sponsor or his advertising agency, advising him that, in order to avoid trouble, he should hire a clearing agent to check those hired to appear on the program.

Aware even published a twelve-step, "how-to-do-it" manual called "The Road Back (to self-clearance): A Provincial Statement of View on the Problem of the Communist and the Communist Helper in Entertainment Communications Who Seeks to Clear Himself." The publication stated that anti-communism was an individual's "moral obligation," and equated hatred of communism to "the hatred of sin and error." The manual prescribed courses by which "identified suspects might achieve a change of heart or mind, perform deeds indicative of this change and thus clear themselves of suspicion and return to normal employability."

Denying one's associations or activities, even if telling the truth, was not enough to be "cleared" by the right-wing vigilantes. Before being granted complete absolution, the actor must have vigorously and formally denounced any liberal or progressive point of view, and issued a clear statement against communism to the agents set up as vindicators. Actress Kim Hunter, for example, rendered unemployable in 1953 because she used her name for a conference on world peace and attended a meeting of the Civil Rights Congress, was forced into signing a humiliating apology to Aware in 1955 "for several errors in judgment, which regrettably may have served the communist cause."

Aware, American Business Consultants, and the Wage Earners Committee called themselves "consultants," but in reality they were racketeers who charged fees ($200 per name was typical) for each clearance to the networks. Whenever a packager, or producer of television or radio shows, sent in three or four names to this consultant for a part, it would cost him about $15 to clear every name *before* hiring.

These groups essentially controlled who worked and didn't work in the motion picture/entertainment industry. With the cooperation of HUAC and the American Legion, a "clearinghouse" procedure was instituted with the networks that screened out those actors and actresses with undesirable viewpoints. From 1947 to 1955, if an actor refused to cooperate with HUAC and did not appear before that congressional committee, then he or she would officially be blacklisted by the film studios. Some 60,000 names were on this list during that period. According to writer Lillian Hellman, taking the Fifth Amendment before these committees was no defense in the public's eye. "The attempt to save jobs, or status, led men like Larry Parks and Elia Kazan and Jose Ferrer to name the guiltless in order to sweeten their own guiltlessness into what the Committee would call innocence," she wrote.[8] This "naming of names" was the subject of an investigative book by journalist Victor Navasky, who tried to psychoanalyze the motivations of the "informer."

To ferret out entertainers who had liberal political views but who were not communists, newly created blacklisting groups that profited from this racket extracted information from the performer's past speeches, meetings, and associations and linked this to completely unrelated Popular Front or Communist Party organizations. The result was a listing of what were often termed "communist front" associations—those groups that were listed in the late 1940s by the attorney general, HUAC, the

Tenney Commission in California, or some other quasi-governmental body as "subversive." Many non-communist organizations, schools, associations, and other groups were branded with the tag "communist front" during this period: the Congress of American Women, the Spanish Refugee Relief Campaign, and the Veterans of the Abraham Lincoln Brigade.

According to authors Larry Ceplair and Steven Englund, who rigorously investigated the Hollywood blacklist, "no studio was without a full set of these blacklists and graylists; no studio failed to honor these judgements from without; no studio was without its 'executive vice-president in charge of clearance.' "[9]

Hartnett was one of the major "clearing agents" that acted as judge and jury for thousands of blacklisted performers. He wrote several articles about the "infiltration" of communists into television for the *American Legion Magazine* or *The Sign*, the national Catholic magazine. "People can easily be panicked by phony 'civil liberties' bugaboos," Hartnett wrote, but the real issue, he said, was fighting communism. He believed his mission was derived from Hoover's statement in 1951 about the nature of communist terrorism: "The Communist Party has, through its increased activities, endeavored to exploit radio and television. In the communications field, they have as their primary objective the control of communications facilities in the event of an emergency."

Yet Hartnett operated solely outside the purview of the FBI or any other government agency. As early as 1954, he admitted charging individuals $5 for an initial report on alleged "communist fronters," $2 for a follow-up report, and $20 for an extensive report. He wrote several letters to major networks, studios, and sponsors offering his services as a self-appointed expert on the communist influence in radio and television. One written to the RCA Corporation in February 1951 criticized NBC for hiring "such fronters as Judy Holliday, the darling of the *Daily Worker,* Danny Kaye, and others. Obviously, for all its good intent, NBC lacks knowledge of the communist fronters.

"Some time ago, the Harly Detective Agency, on retainer to RCA, more than once solicited my information on these matters. But these roundabout ways of working are quite unsatisfactory. Would it not be better to have someone like myself, thoroughly familiar with the field, in a permanent consultative capacity?" From 1952 to 1957, Hartnett amassed $100,000 for checking, re-checking, and screening records of actors, directors, and play-wrights.

Actors who wanted to work in their profession often found themselves in the position of having to betray their beliefs and values in order to keep work; or, at the very least, privately or publicly humiliate themselves and admit their "guilt" from asso-ciating with the wrong crowd. Those who stood by their prin-ciples were forced into an alienated political exile from Holly-wood or New York, their careers, their livelihoods, and often their family life, ruined. Some were put in jail, like playwright Ring Lardner; and some, like CBS newscaster Don Hollenbeck, committed suicide.

Blacklisted screenwriters were luckier than actors and actresses, since many could submit their plays through front men, under an assumed name. Oscar-winning screenwriter Dalton Trumbo, jailed as one of the Hollywood Ten in 1950, wrote un-der thirty-five aliases while his name was on the blacklist. In a piece for *The Nation*, Trumbo assailed the blacklist as "an illegal instrument of terror which can exist only by the sufferance of and connivance with the federal government." [10]

John Howard Lawson, a 1940s screenwriter and member of the Hollywood Ten, viewed the blacklist and the "McCarthyism" movement as part of an effort to control the country's mass com-munications. For a long period, the control was effective. The national media rarely checked out the allegations made by the blacklisters, simply running unsubstantiated charges and duti-fully listing HUAC testimony. The enormous publicity McCarthy himself received also fueled the witch-hunt. The press, John Henry would later write, "behaved most slavishly in the midst of Red Scares. The media not only aided and abetted the vigilan-tism, but also instigated and orchestrated the witch-hunt, hiring 'experts' on subversion to write the inflammatory pieces on the peril threatening our community." [11] Most of the New York media denied the existence of an organized blacklist. The *New York World-Telegram & Sun*, for example, ran a four-part series by its "specialist" in communism, Frederick Woltman, in August 1955. The first article, with the headline "Networks Try to Keep 'Pink'

Files Fair," acknowledged a list of "Red-front records of prospective artists" kept by the networks.[12]

But there were a few dissenting voices in the mainstream. Jack Gould, critic for *The New York Times*, was one of the first journalists to oppose blacklisting. As early as 1951, he decried the practice. "Artists, writers, announcers and directors are being deprived of their opportunity to make a living," he wrote in 1951, and they are exiled "without hearing, publicity, or much public interest." This blacklisting underground is "the story of the futility of appeasement in the unending battle for the preservation of civil liberties. More distressingly, it is the saga of how commercial expediency, temporarily at least, has played into the hands of the foes of democracy, communists and fascists alike." [13]

A few artists did fight in court against the blacklist, but failed. In May 1950, a Hartford, Connecticut, jury was unable to reach a verdict in the libel suit of actor Paul Draper and musician Larry Adler against Hester McCullough, who called them "pro-communist." In March 1953, a group of writers, actors, and film workers (which included Gale Sondergaard, Anne Revere, and twenty-one others) filed a $51 million damage suit in Los Angeles Superior Court charging the Hollywood studios with conspiracy to blacklist. They lost on appeal to the U.S. Supreme Court in March of 1958. Other writers and artists who fought in court were also unsuccessful.

In April 1955, the New York Supreme Court dismissed a complaint by blacklisted actor Joe Julian, who had brought a libel suit against the authors of *Red Channels* for $150,000. Justice Irving Saypol's decision stated in part that the purpose of *Red Channels* was "not to accuse, but merely to list actual facts." Julian, who at that time was the only blacklisted actor who didn't drop charges and who carried his libel suit to trial, never had his case heard by a jury. The attorneys for Hartnett and American Business Consultants succeeded in disqualifying the judge for the case (Justice Abraham Geller, who later presided over the Faulk case), because he belonged to the American Civil Liberties Union, one of about 100 organizations American Business Consultants considered seditious.[14]

Part of the reason why it was so difficult to prove the exist-

ence of the blacklist was because it operated in a shadowy, un-
official capacity from a number of sources, acting both sepa-
rately and together. The parties were elusive because the basis of
the conspiracy could only thrive in a climate of fear and suspicion. It was much like Kafka's strange court in *The Trial*, where
"the nature of the offense and the charges are kept not only from
the public but from the accused as well." Garry Moore described
the process to be "like fighting with six men in a closet with the
lights out, and you can't tell who's hitting you." [15]

John Henry witnessed a number of his colleagues and
friends blacklisted and banished from their careers during the
1950s. Among them were TV writers Walter Bernstein and Yip
Harburg, and actors Ossie Davis (as well as his wife, Ruby Dee),
Madeline Lee Gilford, and Lee Grant. Another co-star with John
Henry on *It's News to Me*, Anna Lee, was targeted because a
sponsor's ad agency told the producer, Mark Goodson, that one
of their clearance forms showed she had some kind of a "record."
After talking with her, Goodson learned that she had no kind of
association that would implicate her as a communist – indeed,
she had been a Churchill Conservative in England, and her husband, a Texas Republican. He confronted the agency with this
information and discovered that another actress named Anna
Lee was the person who had been blacklisted. But the agency
representative told him, "We want you to drop her because we are
concerned about the amount of mail that may come in, about the
controversy involved, and so we would just as soon not have her
anyway." [16]

"The primary element in our national thought at that time
was fear," John Henry would later say. "The headlines were constantly full of people who had been spies ... this terrified the
American people. Consequently, by the early '50's, this fear had
more or less solidified across our country. It had enveloped it." [17]

A friend of John Henry's, investigative journalist I. F. Stone,
compared the political repression of the fifties to the witch-burn-
ing period in the 1600s. Many were hesitant to speak out because
they accepted the chief premise that there was a diabolic conspiracy against world peace and order, and the infestations should be
ferreted out. Others were simply afraid to speak out and risk
their livelihoods. It wasn't enough for an individual to be non-
communist; the individual had to be *devoutly* anti-communist.

"To doubt the power of the devil," Stone wrote in one of his columns, "to question the existence of witches, is again to read oneself out of respectable society, to brand oneself a heretic, to incur suspicion of being oneself in league with the powers of evil." [18]

Prior to the creation of the American Federation of Television and Radio Artists (AFTRA), actors and entertainers worked for very small salaries and under almost no contractual protection. Aware created both dissension and distraction in the actors' ranks, and the owners and employers in the industry, concerned over public perception, cooperated with them. By sowing fear and distrust within, Aware subverted the union's mission to serve as a collective bargaining agency. Essentially, they were union-busters. And they were very powerful in the New York chapter of AFTRA. A 1950s television reviewer, Robert Williams, noted that Aware had so controlled the local AFTRA that the "discussion on the floor was a rarity. Some members were afraid to speak or even to attend the local meetings, for fear their names would be recorded. It was understood in the industry that some persons had been blacklisted who had merely run for office against the Aware-backed administration" (at AFTRA). One actor, Philip Pine, for instance, had run for office in opposition to the established group. He soon found himself unemployable, although there was nothing in his background that could vaguely be considered pro-communist.

People within the actors' union were cooperating with the authors of *Red Channels* and *Counterattack*. Key members of Aware (vice-president, Ned Weaver, treasurer, Richard Keith, and secretary, Jean Owens Hayworth) were on the national actors' board. In 1954–55, seven of the twelve AFTRA board members also belonged to Aware, including Vinton Hayworth, first national vice-president of the union, and Godfrey Schmidt, president. These members were instrumental in drafting an AFTRA policy in 1955 that prohibited membership of a person who "knowingly promotes the special interests of, makes financial contribution to, or renders aid and assistance by lending his name and talents, to the Communist Party." (The Screen Writer's Guild had a similar amendment that it kept on the books until 1977.)

One of the informants who repudiated his past associations with such "radical" groups as the Abraham Lincoln Brigade was Leif Erickson, who publicly came out and criticized his fellow actors for being "communist dupes." He wrote a column in August 1955 for the conservative *Spotlight* publication of Syracuse: "Now that TV is dominating the entertainment scene, the actor becomes a guest in the American home, becomes almost a personal friend of the viewer. But if he gave aid and comfort to the communists at any time in his past and still refuses to fight the Reds, he has no place on the TV screen, in the movies or on the stage. Let's forget the communist-inspired squeals about 'blacklisting.' No loyal producer or director has any business hiring an actor who for ten years fronted for subversion and still refuses to tell the truth or to fight the Reds. If this type of actor doesn't know the score by now, let him starve to death and please omit the flowers." [19]

Few AFTRA members dared to speak out publicly at the union meetings. "We were all scared," said veteran actor Tony Randall, who detested Aware's methods but did not challenge them at meetings, where someone might have placed an actor on "the list." Actress Lee Grant remembered that "when anybody stood up to protest anything at a union meeting, their name was written down, and they found they didn't work the next day. It was that kind of atmosphere. Not only that, but they brought in the guy who wrote Red Channels [Hartnett] . . . to sit there at AFTRA meetings and take down names." [20]

Some actors discovered they were followed home after controversial statements at a union meeting; their trash might be ransacked, their phones tapped, and their discussions tape recorded. Actor Leslie Barrett, who spoke against Aware at a March 1955 AFTRA meeting, was followed home that night. Two days later, he received a letter from Vincent Hartnett, claiming that he had come across a photograph of someone resembling Barrett marching at the New York May Day Parade. Frantic, Barrett went to the FBI asking for a statement attesting that he did not appear at the parade. The FBI told him it didn't issue clearances. So he had his lawyer, Harvey Klein, write a letter to Hartnett assuring him that he never marched in the parade. Shortly thereafter, Barrett got a letter from Hartnett which questioned Klein's patriotism! ("Is this the same Harvey L. Klein who is listed as having signed Communist Party nominating petitions in 1939–40?" Hartnett wrote.)[21]

Barrett told the union membership at a May 1955 meeting that this letter was a flagrant and "scurrilous" attempt by Aware to subvert citizens' protections under the Bill of Rights: "They have unforgivably lumped the innocent with the guilty . . . they have ruined reputations. They have suppressed expression of views; they have killed all opposition; they have made informers; they have caused all too many of us great anxiety, great expense, and loss of self-respect. They have caused a stultifying atmosphere for years in the union of thousands; they have divided and conquered. They have made it a union of puppets and they pull the strings inside the union walls and outside the halls of employment. 'Conform or else!' is their motto, and the weapon they use is fear. Fear! Then, as they ask, are we really to thank them for this?"

After winning all thirty-five seats in the December 1954 local AFTRA election (winning for the eighteenth consecutive election), Aware officials, reckless in their confidence, published a press release (called a "bulletin") that not only bragged about the victory but asserted that AFTRA was being infiltrated with communists. The bulletin stated that "AFTRA, like most trade unions in the entertainment industry, has been subjected to leftist manipulations." It then cited twenty-six of the defeated anti-Aware candidates as either communist or pro-communist. Aware accused thirteen of the twenty-six, which included Lee Grant, Jack Gilford, Martin Balsam, John Randolph and Ruby Dee, with "significant and publicly unrepudiated records of association with the communist front apparatus." Aware called for an immediate investigation from HUAC into these actors and the "entire entertainment industry in New York." This "Bulletin No. 12" was circulated to employers, advertising agencies, sponsors, and casting directors. This type of bulletin was nothing new, but Aware officials had heedlessly typed it on AFTRA stationery and letterhead. This letter, direct evidence tying AFTRA board members to the blacklisting racket, was discovered by Madeline Lee Gilford, and circulated among Aware's opponents in the union.

With more people beginning to speak out against Aware's

influence, many New York AFTRA members launched a counteroffensive. Following the lead of the Actors Equity theatre group, some AFTRA members drafted a resolution to condemn Aware for openly interfering with union affairs and for blacklisting members. The resolution was drawn up at Madeline and Jack Gilford's house at 4:00 one morning.[22]

The resolution berated Aware for "publicly and scandalously attacking an entire slate of candidates for AFTRA, accusing said candidates of association with the 'communist front apparatus' by the now familiar smear methods of inference and innuendo from alleged 'public records.'" In addition, the resolution condemned Aware for promulgating "smear tactics or lists" and for "interfering in the internal affairs of the union."

Aware supporters and opponents argued the resolution at the monthly AFTRA meeting in May. Blacklisted actors Philip Pine and Nancy Pollack confronted Hayworth for evidence of the accusations made against them, but Hayworth said he didn't feel free to reveal information in his possession. Pollack called Aware members "liars and thieves . . . trying to steal my good name." Aware had listed her as a teacher for the Arts and Professions, although she never taught there. Actor Harold Gray told Schmidt that he was tired of anyone who opposed Aware being charged with disloyalty: "I think my fellow actors are entitled to their own ideas and opinions just so long as they don't try to use them to bludgeon, to intimidate, to blackmail, or superimpose their beliefs on me."

Aware's officials enlisted the support of many union members by coercive tactics. Hartnett contacted blacklisted actress Kim Hunter, still struggling to find work, and asked her to go to an AFTRA meeting and "speak up in support of Aware." When Hunter said she couldn't do that, Hartnett asked her to go on record in opposition to the proposed resolution. Hartnett wrote Johnson after the conversation: "If Miss Hunter comes through tomorrow night at the AFTRA meeting, as she promised me she would do, you'll hear the comrades shrieking all the way from New York to Syracuse."

Hunter did not personally attend the meeting, but she did send a telegram urging defeat of the resolution condemning Aware, which was read aloud to the AFTRA attendees. After this, she soon found work again in radio and television.

Aware bombarded the local AFTRA membership in 1955 with negative publicity about the actors on the independent platform who supported the resolution. An open but unsigned letter to the membership stated these actors had "apparently succeeded in getting some unsuspecting AFTRAns to sign that letter" condemning Aware. The letter went on to accuse these actors of having "notorious communist-front records." Without listing one name, the letter enumerated some of the "communist front activities" that these people had engaged in, such as:

· Sponsoring "the infamous Waldorf Peace Conference . . . an outspoken communist propaganda front."

· Performing at a festival sponsored by the National Council of the Arts, Sciences, and Professions – "declared subversive by the Attorney General."

· Entertaining at the Jefferson School of Social Science – "exposed by the U.S. Department of Justice as a communist training school!"

Aware's tactics didn't succeed. On May 24, 1955, 489 AFTRA members clustered into the City Theatre to vote on the controversial measure. The membership voted 197 to 149 to condemn Aware. The censure vote represented the first legitimate challenge to Aware's authority. Aware countered by attacking the vote as a communist plot. Aware lashed out like a wounded tiger; several Aware officials said some AFTRA members were "dupes" of the communists. Godfrey Schmidt said that while many AFTRA members "consider themselves anti-communist, and would not support known communists or fronters for any office, yet they shrink from public criticism of individual communists and fellow travelers." The Aware backers questioned the legality of the vote, and asked for another vote by mail referendum.

Many radio and television commentators launched into debates about the controversial vote. *The Steve Allen Show* on June 21, 1955, featured a lively war of words between Aware supporters Godfrey Schmidt and Vincent Hartnett versus actress Faye Emerson and *New York Herald-Tribune* writer John Crosby. Crosby had shown Aware to be nothing more than a racket in a scathing series in the *Herald-Tribune,* which Aware later sued. Crosby had written that one actor was dropped from a television program because he had the same name as a blacklisted actor. Hartnett, attacking Crosby's veracity, demanded a retraction. Crosby refused to name the man "because he'd be hurt."

"I say if you can't prove that statement, we want a retraction," Hartnett said.

"Take me to court," Crosby said. "I welcome a lawsuit. I welcome a lawsuit."

Again the measure passed on June 30, this time by an almost two-to-one margin, 982 to 514. Suddenly, Aware found its power undercut. Hartnett wrote a desperate letter to John Dungey, chairman of an American Legion Anti-Subversive Committee: "Those of us who are on the spot and in a position to know the facts realize that [Actors] Equity is virtually lost, and that we may well lose our solid control of AFTRA."

Suddenly, more groups felt free to openly criticize the organization. In July, the Association of Catholic Trade Unionists condemned Aware for "unjustifiable blacklisting" and for jeopardizing the "free and democratic conduct" of AFTRA. Despite the dissent, most of the New York media cast the story as one that pitted a patriotic, mainstream organization (Aware) against disruptive unionists stirring up trouble. Even the usually staid *New York Times,* in its July 22, 1955, issue, described Aware in a news story as a group that "seeks to expose the communist influence in the entertainment and communications field" and presented the conflict mostly in the view of Aware's president, Godfrey Schmidt.

It was about this time that John Henry began to take a keen interest in AFTRA's affairs. He had witnessed what had happened to Barrett and was "chilled to the bone" by it. Both Madeline Lee Gilford and Lee Grant, previous candidates defeated by the Aware-controlled opposition, urged John Henry to run for office on the local New York board. They had long talks with him about Aware's influence and the declining influence of independent actors chiefly interested in protecting other actors' livelihoods. But, since both actresses were blacklisted and discredited in the union, they had to meet John Henry late at night, secretly, to avoid suspicion. During these meetings, they'd funnel him names and information about the membership and Aware, since there was considerable spying from that group.

Gilford and Grant, as well as others of the opposition, were looking for someone with an untainted background; someone who had not been smeared by the Aware crowd; someone who might have served his country during the war; someone who hadn't been that involved in union politics, and, in Grant's words, was "squeaky clean" and one "whom they couldn't touch."

"Somebody suggested, 'You know, we ought to ask John Henry Faulk to run,' " Grant said. "So, we called him, and went over to his apartment, and laid out the situation for him . . . the only way we can beat this thing, we said, is to get rid of those people who are up there on that platform, blacklisting their fellow actors. I asked him to run for office, and that was an *enormous* step in those days, because he was setting himself up against those guys. And he said, 'I'll do it.' That was so shocking to me, that I couldn't even believe it . . . and the fact that he was so enthusiastic about it was so interesting to me. Because he knew what the situation was, but jumped in with both feet. He didn't put his toe in the water. He didn't say, 'Maybe I will, maybe I won't.' He jumped in." [23]

Just two weeks after the first vote, members of HUAC came to New York and issued subpoenas to actors in the union, apparently tipped off by Aware officials.[24] "HUAC attacked our slate, put out a letter saying reds had infiltrated the New York local of AFTRA," said John Henry. "I was outraged when I read this thing. Here was a committee of Congress, with *our* tax money, smearing us, interfering with union affairs! I wanted to write a letter. Ed [Murrow] stopped me. 'Let Charlie [Collingwood] write it.' Charlie, of course, wrote a magnificent repudiation." [25]

HUAC brought down at least three "investigators" to interview members of the union and issue subpoenas. One of those investigators interrogated John Henry. Hartnett had called HUAC investigator Donald T. Appell to check into John Henry's background and "suspicious" activities. Appell queried John Henry about his associations with Pete Seeger and the "People's Songs" folk singers, and his participation in the Progressive Citizens of America and the Southern Conference for Human Welfare. HUAC and Aware classified these organizations as communist-front groups, although they were never considered such by the FBI or Executive Branch. John Henry explained to Appell that he never heard of the People's Songs, but that he may have entertained at folk music festivals with Pete Seeger and Woody Guthrie.[26] He strongly defended his participation in the Southern Conference for Human Welfare, which he knew was not filled with communists. He also told Appell that he never was a member of the Communist Party. After the inquiry, Appell did not serve John Henry with a subpoena for the HUAC hearings in New York in August 1955.

A few days before the committee convened, these subpoenaed actors received telegrams from AFTRA's board members, which included Clayton Collyer, Rex Marshall and Conrad Nagel, forewarning them that if they exercised their constitutional right under the Fifth Amendment and declined to answer questions that might incriminate them, they would be expelled from the union. The resolution read: "If any member of AFTRA is asked by a duly constituted committee of the Senate or House of Representatives of the United States whether or not he is or ever has been a member of the Communist Party, and said member fails or refuses to answer that question, said member shall be subject to the charge that he is guilty of conduct prejudicial to the welfare of AFTRA. The accused may be investigated and charges may be heard by the board of the local of which the accused is a member. The local board may, in its discretion, fire, censure, suspend or expel the accused from membership." Aware had successfully lobbied for the national AFTRA board to pass this referendum.

Some of the witnesses placed a full-page ad in *Variety* magazine on July 27, 1955, addressed to all AFTRA members. It urged union members to vote against the referendum proposing expulsion of members who took the Fifth Amendment.

"Due process of law is something to which every union member is entitled," the ad read. "THIS REFERENDUM, if passed, would substitute a rule of AFTRA for the law of the land by possibly depriving an actor of his right to work . . . we may approve or disapprove of the manner in which any actor chooses to testify before a congressional committee, but an actor should not be compelled to testify in any particular manner and have this compulsion written into the by-laws of AFTRA."

Despite the efforts of those opposed to the referendum, the proposed rule was adopted by the national AFTRA board by a four-to-one margin.

HUAC's hearings began on August 14 and lasted four days. Twenty-seven performers were grilled before the committee about suspected communist infiltration in AFTRA, in Actor's Equity, and in the entertainment industry. Many were interrogated about past associations with such "subversive" groups as the Committee for the Negro in Arts, or the National Civil Rights Legislative Conference. The actors were allowed to bring a legal counsel with them, but this counsel was not permitted to address the committee or to argue "questions of law or of fact" with committee members. The mock trial did not protect the accused. Eighteen actors, most of them already blacklisted, took the Fifth Amendment to protect themselves from facing jail sentences; four faced contempt of Congress charges. Some of the entertainers who appeared included George Tyne, John Randolph, Stanley Prager, Martin Wolfson, Elliott Sullivan, Lee Hays, Pete Seeger, and Madeline Lee Gilford.

Those chosen to appear rehearsed extensively for the hearing. "Rehearsals were held around 11:30 at night to give Stanley Prager a chance to come from the *Pajama Game*," said Gilford. A screenwriter and director who had once been a lawyer were the head coaches in trying to prepare people to withstand the onslaught and pressure of the committee's brand of tricky questioning." [27] The group pooled its resources and its money to raise enough funds to pay a team of lawyers, which included Bella Abzug. Fundraising parties were held on Fire Island for the witnesses, and John Henry, Orson Bean, and others attended and made contributions. The group urged the acting community to turn back the tide on the inquisitors, and put an end to coercion and forced orthodoxy. [28]

Unlike most of the witnesses who refused to answer the committee's questions, Madeline Lee Gilford turned the tables on the committee and its chairman, Francis Walters. Instead of responding to the committee's questions, she asked questions of her own, charging that HUAC "coerces witnesses" and "tampers with testimony." When asked the first time by Congressman Frank Tavenner if she was a member of the Communist Party, she said: "The communist label about communist groups has been stuck on anybody and everybody who organizes against the blacklist in our industry." She was asked another time about Communist Party membership:

Miss Lee: The placing of a witness under compulsion to divulge what happens on their union floor, although it is a matter of public record, and easily accessible, is merely for the purpose of extending the blacklist and making me one of those people on the list, because I have never approved of anything this committee does.

Rep. Tavenner: Will you answer the question?

Miss Lee: And I never will. So I am trying to answer it to the best of my ability.

Rep. Scherer: I submit, Mr. Chairman, she has not answered the question, and in my opinion she is guilty of contempt. She has had an opportunity to answer it and she hasn't answered it or invoked any privilege, and I suggest we proceed to the next question.

Miss Lee: I have not stated my reasons.

Chairman Walters: Ask the next question.

Miss Lee: I object, and I decline to answer on the basis of the First Amendment.

When Rep. Tavenner repeatedly grilled her on the question, bringing out a photograph of the 1952 May Day Parade "with your likeness" in the first row, Madeline Lee invoked the First, Fourth, Fifth and Eighth amendments all in one. Exasperated, the committee dismissed her.[29]

Two of the witnesses who appeared before the committee, George Tyne and Elliott Sullivan, were cited in contempt for standing on the First Amendment. Both had to raise over $2,000 to hire a lawyer to represent them. In 1961 a district court acquitted them, because the government had not submitted the committee's resolution ordering the hearing. Pete Seeger was sentenced to a year in jail for refusing to answer questions, but his conviction was also reversed on a similar technicality.[30]

In the summers of 1954–55, the Faulks rented a summer cottage at the end of Long Island, a place called Fire Island. No automobiles were allowed on this narrow strip of land, so the only way to travel was by foot or by beach taxi. With their three children and a pet goat named Katy Gonzales, the Faulks attracted a number of actors, actresses, and writers. Mel Brooks, Carl Reiner, and Orson Bean lived on the same block and would come by frequently.

On weekend nights, various performers and broadcasters would assemble at the Faulks' house. According to Orson Bean in his 1988 autobiography, "Mrs. Faulk would serve drinks, the tanned and happy children would clamor to stay up longer, the goat would run in and out of the house, and the guests would talk politics." Bean said the goat was amazing; he would follow John Henry down the sidewalk "and do everything but carry the paper. John told wonderful stories about the poor people of Texas. He'd do them in dialect and there was one about a little girl who dreamed of some day owning a pair of shoes which always left me in tears." [31]

One night, John Henry, Bean, Charles Collingwood, Tony Randall, and a few others in AFTRA met at the Faulks' home to form the anti-blacklisting slate of officers. John Henry wanted to gather a slate of non-communists, "not left-wingers or right-wingers," he said, "but independents, who were opposed to blacklisting." The risk was great, but sitting idly by while watching friends get blacklisted by their fellow actors was not the answer. Aware's influence in the industry had to be fought, John Henry said. Some in this group feared reprisals, but John Henry reassured them. "I learned somethin' when I was a little boy diggin' for fish bait," he said, "and that's that you can't hardly get them ol' worms to crawl out from under their rocks if they think you'll dunk them in water." Run a clean slate that opposes communism, he said, and perhaps union members could then, through the democratic process, regain control of their own affairs.

John Henry's drive and determination spearheaded the "Middle-of-the-Road" slate of union officers. In the summer of 1955, the slate was set: Collingwood would run for president; Bean, first vice-president, and Faulk, second vice-president. Other candidates included Collingwood's wife, Louise Allbritton, Tony Randall, Jack Paar, Faye Emerson, and Janice Rule. The first principle of the slate was to be loyal to the entire membership; the second, to actively promote the "immediate interests of the membership's increased employment and welfare"; and the third, "to oppose denial of employment by discriminatory and intimidating practices, especially by outside organizations."

John Henry worked hard during the campaign. In one local press interview, he admitted that the Middle-of-the-Road slate was formed to replace the AFTRA members who were Aware backers. "We believed the membership [of AFTRA] was also against these men who subverted the interests of union members to a single platform of anti-communism," he said. The first and primary interest of a union member, John Henry believed, should be the employment and security of its members, "not blacklisting them."

The Middle-of-the-Road precepts included an admonition that the local board "had allowed an outside political group, Aware . . . to dominate union politics, to create a climate of fear among both employers and employees, to paralyze and emasculate the union's responsibility to its membership." Louis Van Rooten, one of the candidates, said at a Middle-of-the-Road meeting that the slate existed to demonstrate that "people can get together with different points of view and meet socially and agreeably and without fear." Garry Moore, another Middler, said the slate's members would recognize that "the greatest thing in the world is human dignity. We've all been scattered by fear." John Henry's group garnered much positive publicity for their clean and up-front campaign. A writer for *Newsday* said "the stars who have joined the fight are to be commended. At least if they can carry the ball to victory, the other players will be able to dissent at a meeting and still have a job in the morning."[32]

In December of 1955, a record number of 1,650 members turned out to cast their vote in the AFTRA elections. The "Middlers" won twenty-seven of the thirty-five seats on the board, making them in control of the local chapter. The victory, however, was short-lived.

John Henry Faulk's mentor, J. Frank Dobie, once wrote that anytime a free thinker evidences skepticism and dissent, he arouses controversy and is charged with being an "atheistic communist." The central issue is conformity, Dobie wrote, and conformity means stagnation. "The individual always has been a noncomformist, often irritating his fellows by not thinking as they think and doing as they do. Many noncomformists are put to death . . . in this country, they are put out of jobs."

If John Henry had recalled that line on February 10, 1956, the day that changed the rest of his life, then perhaps he would have been assuaged somewhat, knowing that he met Dobie's criteria for becoming a "free thinker." That was the day he received a phone call from a *New York Times* reporter asking if he'd seen the bulletin that Aware had just issued accusing him of communist activities.

10.

AWARE'S
ASSAULT

L aurence Johnson was an old war veteran who owned four large supermarkets in Syracuse, New York. His organization, the Veterans Action Committee of Syracuse Supermarkets, was composed of ex-GIs who worked in these supermarkets. The committee collaborated closely with the American Legion and the Catholic War Veterans in monitoring the activities of several entertainers. Johnson was also an influential member in the National Association of Retail Grocers, which passed a resolution at its 56th annual convention in 1955 that "called on all sponsors of radio and television programs and their agencies to exercise the constant vigilance against infiltration of their programs by communists and other subversive forces."

In his blacklisting business, Vincent Hartnett had found a powerful and rich ally in Johnson. He knew that Johnson had sent out mailings to sponsors like Kraft Foods, Swanson & Sons, and Colgate-Palmolive warning them regarding the employment of certain actors suspected of having "communist-front" records.

The two built a co-dependent relationship for their zealous activism. Johnson would often call Hartnett to check his files or to give him information about certain actors. John Henry wrote: "Sponsors who advertised in radio and television had to sell their products through Johnson's supermarkets. When Hartnett protested the appearance of an actor or an actress on a program that was sponsored by a company whose product was sold in Johnson's store, Johnson obligingly went to the sponsor himself and demanded the artist's dismissal." [1]

Johnson's letters to advertising agencies and sponsors of the offending artist all were worded much the same. Addressed to "all supermarket chain and independent operators, buyers and merchandisers" of the retail food industry, a letter would ask the distributor: "Do you realize you are helping the communists? How? By pushing the products of certain manufacturers! Yes, manufacturers who employ those people in their radio and television advertising who have contributed to communism and communist-front activities." Then the letter would insert the questionable background of the artist, and end with a plea: "Let's keep Stalin's little creatures from crawling over our merchandise." [2]

When Johnson accused the Lennen & Mitchell advertising agency of employing suspected communist-front people in the *Schlitz Playhouse of the Stars,* a number of actors never received credits for their parts in films they already completed. In 1953 he persuaded C. A. Swanson & Co., which sponsored the quiz show *The Name's The Same,* to drop Judy Holliday as a guest star. Johnson also got the president of CBS Television, J. L. Volenburg, to issue an apology to him for having hired comedian Jack Gilford on the program *Arthur Godfrey and His Friends.* [3]

Johnson was directly responsible for the blacklisting of Gilford from two CBS programs and one NBC show, according to his widow, Madeline Lee Gilford. "We got the goods on Johnson," she said, "when I faked a phone call [to Johnson] pretending to be the secretary of the president of NBC. I found out that he had gotten Jack off the Kellogg's Pet Milk Show. We then went to the union, with blacklisted actor Phil Loeb on our committee, and George Heller (AFTRA's executive secretary) kept advising Jack not to make waves, and Phil Loeb grabbed Jack by the collar and said to him: 'Don't let him do to you what he did to me.' " Eventually, Jack Gilford would settle with a compromise and take an offer to work on a local network show. [4]

Johnson and his associates from Syracuse were invited to attend Aware's membership meeting in January 1956, a meeting designed to do something about the Middle-of-the-Road slate that opposed Aware. At that meeting, "Bulletin #16," which was approved by the group's board of directors and attorneys, was introduced to the general membership. Hartnett and Paul Milton collaborated on drafting the announcement, crafted as more of a news supplement than a membership bulletin, so it could be mailed to Aware's entire mailing list of 2,285 names. Those names included representatives from the local and national news media, national advertising associations, leading ad agencies, the National Association of Retail Grocers, law enforcement agencies, and government investigating committees such as HUAC.

The five-and-one-half-page bulletin, dated February 10, 1956, prefaced with a description of Aware and the Middle-of-the-Road slate. The Middlers opposed blacklisting, the bulletin stated, but "the term 'blacklisting' is losing its plain meaning and becoming a communist jargon-term for hard opposition to the exposure of communism." (Aware consistently denied the existence of a blacklist or its involvement in it; they called themselves a "political rating service.")

The bulletin tried to portray Aware as a lone bastion in the fight against communism, and questioned whether the Middlers would have the gumption to stand up against the Communist Party "or other officially designated organizations." The bulletin then attacked Faulk: "What about his public record?"

Some of the charges included allegations that Faulk:

· appeared as "Jack Faulk" at Club 65 at 13 Astor Place, New York City, which was the meeting place of District 65 of the Distributive Workers Union (Club 65 was also known as the "Little Kremlin" and the "Proletarian Night Club");

· appeared with Will Geer (according to an article in the *Daily Worker*) at the opening of "Headline Cabaret" at Old Knick Music Hall in April 1947, sponsored by Stage for Action (another "communist front");

· contributed material to "Showtime for Wallace," a political cabaret held at the Cafe Society Downtown in New York City (according to an issue of the *Daily Worker*) and staged by the Progressive Citizens of America ("officially designated a communist front");

· entertained "with identified communist Earl Robinson and two non-communists" on April 25, 1946, "under the auspices of the Independent Citizens Committee of the Arts, Sciences and Professions (officially designated a communist front and predecessor of the Progressive Citizens of America)";

· sent "birthday greetings" to People's Songs on its second anniversary, "according to Vol. 3 Nos. 1 & 2 of the Bulletin of People's Songs (officially designated a communist front)";[5]

· spoke at a "Spotlight for Wallace" event at the Jefferson School of Social Science on February 16, 1948, an organization "found by the federal government to be what is the official training school of the communist conspiracy in New York";

· was a "sponsor of the American Continental Congress for Peace, staged in Mexico City, September 5–10, 1949," described by HUAC as "another phase in the communist world 'peace' campaign, aimed at consolidating anti-American forces throughout the Western hemisphere";

· spoke at a September 19, 1946, "street meeting" of the Southern Conference of Human Welfare (another "communist front") at 209 West 38th Street in New York City, with Dr. Clark Foreman;

· appeared at the "Gala May Day Hootenanny Cabaret" after the May Day Parade in April 1947 (also according to the *Daily Worker*). The event was sponsored by People's Songs, Inc., and Faulk entertained with Hally Wood-Faulk, Pete Seeger, Lee Hays, and Kenneth Spencer. Aware described a "hootenanny" as "a rally in which the audience, 'primed' by the entertainers, is led to group singing. Some of the songs are always of a 'topical' nature. In this instance, the House Committee on UnAmerican Activities ["witch-hunters"] was to be the butt of some of the songs."

The bulletin ended with much briefer attacks on Orson Bean and Charles Collingwood. It chastised Bean for satirizing HUAC in a summer skit in 1955 and being seen at a rally for the Emergency Civil Liberties Committee, and criticized Collingwood for responding sternly in writing to HUAC's investigation of the Middle-of-the-Road ticket.

This bulletin cleverly used innuendo, lies, deception, and guilt by association to make John Henry appear to be a disloyal, unpatriotic man. The communist newspaper, the *Daily Worker* quoted frequently in the release, neither sponsored nor sanctioned the events it publicized, but the juxtaposition of the publication's name with John Henry's activities made these events seem to be communist-sponsored. Some events were reported completely out of context, with no mention of the actual sponsors. Other events were created from conversations with later unidentified "informants." And some events were simply created when they never occurred. Most of the "officially designated communist-front" groups were never "officially designated" as such by the U.S. government;[6] many were implicated several years before by other informants who listed these "suspect" associations before HUAC. The accusers were not named, but the accused was, and the self-appointed jury in this case was a group called Aware.

John Henry's immediate reaction to the bulletin was one of indignation and anger. He had felt immune because he wasn't a communist and had signed a loyalty oath with CBS. Also, the majority of these items were total fabrications: he hadn't even heard of some of these organizations Aware said he belonged to, much less performed for some of them. But that wasn't the point; it didn't matter what organizations or associations he belonged to—he had "done the unpardonable" and opposed Aware—and this was the standard that made him a subversive.

He was reminded of Dobie's words, written in 1936: "Any strong-minded individual who does not fit the moulds determined upon for its members by a conventional society will sooner or later have his character attacked."[7] Dobie, too, was accused of being a communist, and in 1951 was listed by HUAC as being a sponsor of the Mid-Century Conference for Peace, a "communist-front" organization. During that period, a woman in an Austin crowd shouted at J. Frank Dobie: "You're nothin' but a communist!" Dobie quickly reacted: "Why, nobody but a jackass or an ignoramus would say a thing like that," and the crowd applauded him.[8]

John Henry did not sit still and take the barrage from Aware. He immediately called an emergency meeting of the

Middle-of-the-Road slate. Bean, Stan Burns, Leslie Barrett, Dennis Patrick, and fourteen others in the group assembled at John Henry's apartment at 118 West 79th Street. All of the group denounced Aware's tactics and suggested an AFTRA resolution affirming its complete and unqualified confidence in the patriotism and loyalty of each of the officers.

The Aware bulletin was designed to instill fear and intimidation in the networks and the sponsors from supporting John Henry's program. It didn't take long to take effect. Hartnett and Johnson worked hard to ensure its message had been delivered and heard. When John Henry showed the allegations to WCBS program director Sam Slate and general manager Carl Ward, both dismissed its contents as a smear tactic against the Middle-of-the-Road slate; however, a month later, when a major sponsor pulled its advertising from John Henry's show, Ward was more concerned.

On April 10, 1956, Slate asked John Henry to go into Ward's office with him. In front of Slate, Ward told John Henry: "Johnny, that groceryman from Syracuse, Larry Johnson, is in New York and he is kicking the hell out of you. He is taking that paper you showed me last month to all your sponsors and scaring them away from you. Libby's Frozen Foods canceled this afternoon, and we know others will too. [Libby's Canned Vegetables followed that week.] What do you think we can do about it?"

Ward was upset about losing more accounts. "If Johnson forces all these people off your show," he said, "you'll lose your commercial value to the station." John Henry, on the other hand, wanted to get back at Johnson some way.

"But you can't prove anything on Johnson," Ward said. "The people who told us about it made a promise that their names would not be used. They don't want to be involved."

Ward suggested that John Henry take each of the items in the bulletin, answer them point-by-point, and draw up an affidavit. John Henry balked at the idea, and reminded Ward that he already recently signed the union's anti-communist oath, as well as signed a loyalty oath at CBS.

The following morning, John Henry told Ward of his decision to go ahead with the affidavit. Ward then cautioned him not to mention a word of what he said about Johnson being in town.

Evidently, Ward slipped when he blurted that to John Henry. "Apparently," John Henry wrote later, "the legal deparment at CBS had told him that he had been a fool to tell me in the first place." That night, with help from his friends Palmer Webber and Clark Foreman, John Henry wrote the affidavit. It contained John Henry's accomplishments, membership in the Methodist Church, service in the war, and citations received from civic, business, and religious organizations. ("I have received commendations from such groups as the Daughters of the Revolution, the National Press Club in Washington, D.C., and Jewish, Catholic, and Protestant organizations," John Henry wrote.) John Henry also made sure the affidavit contained a strong statement affirming his belief in the Constitution of the United States, which included the protections of freedom of speech and of due process of law.

Then John Henry visited Slate's office. Slate said that one of the network's advertising salespeople, Howard Lally, had personal knowledge of Johnson's movements in the city.

"I then went to Howard Lally and he was very uncomfortable and evasive," John Henry said. "However, he did tell me that he knew Johnson was in town going up and down Madison Avenue smearing me with sponsors." Lally would disclose none of his sources to John Henry.

Indeed, both Johnson and Hartnett had pressured many of John Henry's sponsors. Tom Murray of Grey Advertising, which represented Hoffman Beverage Company, received a call from Johnson that March about the bulletin and Faulk. Johnson told Murray that display space in his supermarkets was "hard won space," then proceeded to describe the allegations against John Henry. "Johnson said it was a disgrace that our company was using a communist, John Henry Faulk, to advertise our product. I said I had no such knowledge. He said we'd better get in line," then intimated that if Hoffman continued to sponsor Faulk, "it might be deprived of this hard-won space." Murray continued, "I said that I had no intention of firing a man who was a first-rate salesman for our product. Johnson said, 'How would you like it if you received a letter from an American Legion post?' I said I was a veteran and I couldn't believe an American Legion post would lend itself to what was so obviously a blackmail threat." [9] A few days later, Murray got that letter from Post 41 of Syracuse. Murray was so irate about the conversation and letter that he informed Slate about Johnson's actions.

Most advertising officials were not that candid, however, and refused to go on record. Yet subsequent legal investigations did reveal the pressure some of John Henry's sponsors received. Both Johnson and Hartnett had written American Tobacco Company about their sponsorship of the radio show. Johnson also told Diamond Salt that he wanted Faulk off CBS.

A letter sent from the chairman of the Anti-Subversive Committee of the Onondaga County American Legion in Syracuse reached several sponsors of "The John Henry Faulk Show." It read:

> These are trying times not only in the field of international politics but also in the TV and Radio field.
>
> For international Communism to succeed in bringing the rest of the world under the yoke of their conspiracy, they must gain complete control of the air waves. The Communists are working around the clock to accomplish this.
>
> They must also raise money to finance their operations. As an example, four Communist fronts in the entertainment field raised over a million dollars for the Communist cause.
>
> The American Legion for years has realized the efforts that Communist(s) are exerting in the field of entertainment and has gone on record not to support programs that feature Communists or individuals who have supported the Communist cause.
>
> Therefore, we respectfully call to your attention one of your salesmen, John Henry Faulk, whose program comes through WCBS radio, New York City - 5:00 to 6:00 P.M., Monday through Friday.
>
> We are enclosing data from a publication Aware on a John Henry Faulk and would like to know if this is the same John Henry Faulk who has this WCBS program.
>
> We of the American Legion sincerely hope that you will look into this situation and we will be waiting a reply since we want our facts straight as to the person in question and his sponsors. We have previously brought to the attention of the public facts concerning Communism in the entertainment field as may be seen by copy of enclosed *Spotlight.*

Very truly yours,
John K. Dungey, Chairman
Onondaga County American Legion
1842 Bellevue Ave.
Syracuse, N.Y.

One anonymous letter, sent to Associated Food Stores, Inc., that March, assailed John Henry Faulk as a "perverted nigger lover; he should get a job on the nigger network." Cliff Poppleton, who was Associated Foods' advertising manager, sent John Henry a copy of the letter, saying that his company disagreed "with this fascist viewpoint 100 percent. We hope that you will continue to express your own point of view with your accustomed vigor."

Sponsors and ad executives weren't the only ones contacted by the blacklisters. Perhaps dissatisfied with the results of sponsor pressure, Hartnett also contacted the New York Police Department on numerous occasions about John Henry. Conversations with a Lt. Thomas Cain provided Hartnett with information about various entertainers who participated in suspicious activities or associations. In return, Hartnett let Cain review material in his private files, including stories about the Middle-of-the-Road slate and John Henry Faulk.[10]

On the advice of friends Harriet Van Horne and Ed Murrow, John Henry chose to go to Louis Nizer's law firm (Phillips, Nizer, Benjamin and Krim), which had won a famous libel suit for Quentin Reynolds in 1954 against Hearst columnist Westbrook Pegler (coincidentally, one of the many libelous statements Pegler had made included calling Reynolds a communist sympathizer). The U.S. District Court awarded Reynolds $175,000 in punitive damages—the beginning of the end of Pegler's career.

When John Henry first walked into Nizer's office, Nizer got a hint of the Texan's seemingly "dual personality," from his references to classic literature and poets, to his glib, humorous remarks filled with piquant phrases (like "the goose hangs high," or "he will lie on credit when he could have told the truth for cash"). Despite the humorous anecdotes and colorful speech, Nizer "never felt that he had a comedian's vice of sacrificing thought for satisfaction of a jest. Rather they complemented each other with such ease that one shared his concluding chuckle."[11]

After warning John Henry about the negative consequences in launching such an arduous suit, he agreed to take the case, not only because of its "high likelihood of success," but also because it "would be in aid of high principle."

John Henry's case was filed against Aware, Laurence Johnson, and Vincent Hartnett in New York Supreme Court on June 26, 1956, with a $500,000 plea for compensatory damages (which Nizer would later increase to $1 million). The legal complaint charged that Aware had entered into a conspiracy with the advertising agencies and networks to defame John Henry Faulk's reputation and professional integrity, to destroy his livelihood, to remove him from AFTRA, and to "eliminate him as a foe of the defendant's extortion of monies and use of racketeering practices to intimidate and terrorize through blacklisting."

John Henry received hundreds of letters in support of his suit; his ratings went up, and most of his sponsors returned to his program within a few months. "The men who directed the affairs of Madison Avenue, however, reacted as though I had announced I had highly contagious mumps," John Henry wrote. "It wasn't long before I realized that instead of improving my employability, the lawsuit had an adverse effect upon it; I became more controversial than ever." [12]

On August 1, 1956, John Henry went over the Aware charges with Nizer's associate, Donald Wilkes. John Henry responded to the allegations point by point. He:

· did perform at Club 65 in May of '46, but had no idea it was called "Proletarian Night Club" or "Little Kremlin" (Nizer discovered later that the event was sponsored by the Amsterdam News, a non-communist organization);

· had no knowledge of ever appearing at Headline Cabaret at Old Knick Music Hall in 1947 and actually was attending a reception for the Texas Democratic State Legislature at his sister's home in Austin on that date;

· did contribute material to "Showtime for Henry Wallace," for which he was paid $15 or $25.

· did entertain at a dinner, along with Art Carney and Eddie Mayehoff, on April 25, 1946, in San Francisco, California, but what the bulletin deliberately failed to mention was that this dinner was held to honor the first anniversary of the Security Council of the United Nations and was sponsored by the American Bar Association, YMCA, and other non-communist groups. (John Henry never saw the "identified communist" Earl Robinson at this function, but he did see a number of ambassadors and dignitaries, including Trygve Lie, the secretary general of the U.N., and Ed Stettinius, secretary of state for the U.S. The two other "known noncommunists" the bulletin referred to were likely Eleanor Roosevelt and Harold Ickes, the former secretary of the interior);

· never appeared at the May Day Parade sponsored by the People's Songs;

· was never a sponsor of American Continental Congress, and never went to Mexico City (his friend, Clark Foreman, was a sponsor);

· never heard of the Jefferson School until the year before (on the date of the "Spotlight for Wallace" event, where he was alleged to have appeared, John Henry had a speaking engagement elsewhere, but had to cancel because he had the flu);

· was an MC at a May Day hootenanny at Club 65 in May '47, but went there as a paid entertainer and was never a member of the People's Songs;

· did speak at a meeting on behalf of the Southern Conference of Human Welfare, an organization founded by Frank Graham, president of the University of North Carolina, in connection with FDR's call for national support for his program to improve the economic welfare of the South. Joe Louis and Frank Sinatra also spoke there. When Eleanor Roosevelt heard of the charge that Faulk was a member of the Southern Conference, she wrote in her column for the *New York Post*: "What of it? I have been a member of that organization myself and maybe still am. I have never heard of its trying to subvert the government."

John Henry's business manager, Gerald Dickler, advised him to contact as many of the Middlers as he could and muster support against Aware's smear campaign. Before he could take that advice, he received a call from one of the group's avid supporters, announcer Nelson Case. He urgently asked John Henry to write a letter stating that he (Case) was never a member of the Middle-of-the-Road slate. After the conversation, John Henry realized that Case had seen the Aware bulletin.[13]

Case's example was followed by announcer Dick Stark and comedian Cliff Norton, two of the original members of the Middle-of-the-Road group. At an AFTRA meeting April 11, 1956, Stark and Norton condemned the Middlers, saying they were not acting in the best interest of the union. Both said they were simply deluded into running for the group, but now knew they were wrong and misguided to get involved. The next day in his *New York Daily News* column, Ed Sullivan commended Stark for his patriotism and "courageous" stand and warned about the "sinister forces" primed to take control of the union.

The other members of the slate backed away from speaking up. Bean became apprehensive after hearing from Ed Sullivan, who saw Aware's bulletin. Sullivan queried Bean about Aware's charge that he had performed some unpatriotic satire of HUAC. "I did one of those dumb routines on your show," Bean replied. Sullivan told Bean he was sorry, but he wouldn't be able to use him on the show anymore. He explained to Bean that he was receiving pressure from his advertising agency, Kenyon and Eckhardt, not to use him. John Henry took Bean to meet his business manager/attorney, Gerald Dickler, to see if any legal action could be taken. Later next week, Sullivan denied he knew anything about the Aware bulletin. Bean soon got word from CBS that it was shelving *The Orson Bean Show* pilot scheduled for that year.

About three months later, Bean called John Henry, apologetically announcing that the pressure was too much and he had to resign from the slate to keep his career. After Bean disassociated himself from the slate, he soon reappeared on Sunday night's *Ed Sullivan Show*.

AFTRA's legal counsel, Henry Jaffe, proffered a way out for John Henry: volunteer to go to HUAC and name the names of any union members he suspected of having communist or subversive ties, and politely write to Aware recognizing and appreciating the work they had done in fighting communism. If John Henry brought charges against other members, then Aware might find some informants who could testify before HUAC, Aware's chief counsel Godfrey Schmidt said. When John Henry relayed the proposal to other members of his slate, he was astonished that many thought it was a good idea. John Henry was revolted by the thought of ruining another person's reputation in order to save his own: "I said to myself, 'I couldn't do that, that would be like wading in my own vomit! My God, I couldn't do that.' "

Independent candidates for AFTRA's national board the previous year were also not spared from Aware's vengeance. Lee Grant was targeted by Hartnett as being a communist sympathizer because she had signed a letter in support of the People's Drama group in 1949, and because she starred in *All You Need Is One Good Break* with "many communist Party members and collaborators," according to Aware. Hartnett also identified Grant's husband, Arnold Manoff, as "an identified Communist Party member."

Both Bean and Grant described the initial revelation that they were on the blacklist the same way: "I felt the blood drain from my face." They both found refuge in the theatre, which was largely immune from the blacklist, but Grant's road was much rougher because she didn't "clear" herself from her associations. Many other actors found themselves in similar situations, which left Broadway with ample talent to pick and choose from. "You had this strange phenomenon of audiences paying top price to see Zero Mostel, Jack Gilford, Phil Loeb, John Randolph, you name it, on Broadway," said Madeline Lee Gilford. ". . . You really have to picture itinerant actors living on unemployment insurance. We were not academics, nor people with income from families. We all had to go someplace to earn our living. No one gave us a penny." [14]

Aware had, in John Henry's words, "scared the hell out of the summer soldiers on our side and scattered them like a covey of quail." But John Henry refused to back down. He wrote Dobie, Webb, Bedichek, and Boatright that Aware had "grabbed the wrong sow by the ear if they think I mind becoming controversial where those heathens are concerned. And I have managed to get the biggest and best law firm in New York to take the case—Louis Nizer, who gave Pegler and the Hearst press such a thumping for Quentin Reynolds."

Just as he viewed Dies and McCarthy, John Henry saw the Aware bunch as no more than a "syndicate of blackmailers who prey on entertainers, and who use patriotism as a smokescreen for their rascality." Because they operated in the shadows for so long, with their operations remaining unexposed and unchallenged, John Henry resolved to stick with the lawsuit, although his employers and business manager urged caution. "They point out that my sponsors have come back and that if I will just forgive and forget, my hide will be safe. I point out that if AWARE, Inc. gets off this time, they will do the same thing to somebody else next month and the month after that. The reason they have flourished so long is that nobody would ever wade into them and yank them out into the bright light of day for the public to look at in all their rusty gut ugliness. So I'm going through with it." [15]

Both Dobie and Bedichek strongly supported John Henry's battle, with Dobie volunteering to go to New York to testify, even though he was ill. Bedichek thought John Henry's fight was "magnificent. It has all the essential qualities of David's walking out between the antagonistic hosts and challenging their best man. Of course, David had God on his side and didn't know it. Therefore, the greater hero, he." Still, Bedichek knew that John Henry's was "a heroic act because I feel the thrill of it." [16]

With Grant, Bean, and other Middle-of-the-Road members out of the way, Aware had effectively destroyed the backbone of the Middle-of-the-Road slate. Although CBS sent him away to be a foreign correspondent for much of this period until things cooled down, Collingwood carried on the fight that summer. In a May 1956 editorial in AFTRA's *STANDBY!* newsletter (picked up by the *New York Post* on May 25), Collingwood wrote: "I'd like to think that the character of and record of these men under assault is such that, in the end, these efforts to ruin their careers will fail. But the ugly thing is that they should be subjected to this kind of thing at all. For it seems crystal clear that the motive for this [Aware] offensive is not the purification of the union from communist influence which these people bray about so much. It's a transparent attempt to destroy opposition within the union by destroying anyone who has the temerity to run against the group which it feels it is its holy mission to direct the affairs of AFTRA."

By October, Collingwood had had enough, and decided not to run again for chapter president. While he believed in the basic principles of protection of AFTRA members from blacklisting, he wrote John Henry that he came to "increasingly feel that the

Middle of the Road group is not an effective instrument for translating these principles into Union policy." John Henry successfully spearheaded a resolution that same month that led the
AFTRA local to insert a provision in its standard contract banning blacklisting in all contracts with employers, but the provision did not pass the national board. In January 1957, the right-
wing faction took back control of AFTRA.

Even though John Henry exuded optimism about the
progress of his lawsuit to his friends back home, Vincent
Hartnett wasn't too worried about it. He and Laurence Johnson
had weathered suits before, and this one was treated as a minor
inconvenience, as evidenced in Hartnett's letter to Johnson on
June 29, 1956: "We got sued by John Henry Faulk, who wants a
million bucks. Our lawyers agreed his complaint is baseless, and
believe he does not even intend to take us to court. Still, it has to
be answered . . ." Evidently, Aware's leaders were so arrogant and
confident that they didn't take the lawsuit very seriously. They
assumed John Henry would die off the vine, like the others who
sued before him. Despite this casual disregard, Aware officials,
when learning of the lawsuit, burned the first draft of the bulletin.

John Henry, who, like his father, never had "a lick of business sense," didn't manage money well. He didn't know where to
raise the $10,000 retainer fee Nizer needed for out-of-pocket ex-
penses. He and Lynne decided to hold a fundraiser at his wealthy
friends' home, Anne and Herb Steinman, to try to come up with
the money. Famous personalities such as Myrna Loy, David and
Evelyn Susskind, Dore Schary, Max Youngstein, Matty Fox, and
Eli Landau were some of those who attended. Eleanor Roosevelt
wrote a note to the Faulks, praising John Henry for his stance,
and enclosed a check for $250. After the party, John Henry was
still $7,500 short.

One day, as he sat in his office wondering where to come up
with the rest of the money, John Henry's telephone rang. It was
Ed Murrow. He had called to ask if John Henry needed his help.
After listening to his difficulties in raising the money, Murrow
acted surprised, saying he thought CBS would take care of the
legal expenses in this matter. Just the opposite, John Henry said:
"They are putting pressure on me to drop the suit."

"Tell Louis Nizer, Johnny," he said, "that he'll have the

money tomorrow." Murrow then contacted his business manager and had him make out a check to Nizer for $7,500. When John Henry balked, telling Ed he may not be able to pay such a large sum back, Murrow replied, "Let's get this straight, Johnny. I am not making a personal loan to you of this money. I am investing this money in America." [17]

Murrow's insistence that Nizer must take the case and that John Henry must think long and hard about what he was taking on "was the closest he had come in their nine-year friendship to making a speech," according to Murrow biographer A. M. Sperber. "You're not just personally taking it on," Murrow told John Henry, "you're the catalyst here. Your union won't support you; that's why they're in the shape they're in. But remember, my office will be open to you anytime." [18]

Managing to retain most of his sponsors, John Henry may have brandished a false sense of security. And why not? He had just signed a new five-year contract with CBS at the end of 1956, and his rating and share of audience had increased since January 1956. Not until August 1957 did his PULSE rating fall below ten percent, which was still better than the overall drop for the network. His average over the year was about the same as musician Martha Wright's show. John Henry was making CBS Radio a lot of money (later figured to be a total of over a million dollars in ad revenue). Although CBS officials didn't publicly approve of John Henry's lawsuit, many told him privately that they didn't approve of Aware's tactics and hoped he would win in court. Slate also reassured him in June that he would continue to have a one-half-hour show or even a new one-hour show.

Behind the scenes, John Henry was unaware that Ed Murrow and Charles Collingwood had persuaded CBS executives to retain John Henry's radio show. Murrow used his influence as a director of CBS, while Collingwood gave notice to Hull Hays, president of CBS Radio, that AFTRA would launch an investigation of the network and the advertising agencies involved if John Henry were let go. Threatened with subpoenas, the network executives bided their time. [19]

By the end of 1957, Collingwood was no longer president of AFTRA, and Murrow had left CBS on an overseas assignment. After some time spent campaigning for Adlai Stevenson for president, John Henry left with Lynne and the children on their long-planned vacation to Jamaica. John Henry had arranged for Lanny Ross, a CBS singer, to take over his shift. In Jamaica, he spent a great deal of the vacation in the water—snorkeling, swimming, and scuba diving. The time allowed him to devote more time with his children, showing them the colorful fish encircling the coral reefs and teaching them to snorkel. "John Henry really enjoyed scuba diving," said son Frank. "I remember him taking me out in the boat and spearing these big fish and flopping them in the boat . . ." [20]

It proved to be the last time the family enjoyed a carefree moment. John Henry got a call from Dickler that August to "come to New York immediately." He had been fired.

11.

THE
PUBLIC
PARIAH

W|hen John Henry returned to New York, leaving his wife
and children to enjoy Jamaica for the remainder of the
vacation, he immediately visited Sam Slate to see what had happened. Slate explained that his ratings had slipped, and the network needed to make a programming change. His show would be
replaced with Arthur Godfrey's. He told John Henry that his
show had "gotten into a rut" and perhaps the change would do
him good. Despite John Henry's ratings adding up to be higher
than many of the artists on WCBS (including Lanny Ross, who
appeared an hour before "The John Henry Faulk Show"), CBS
always stuck by this story.

"It's what the French would call a fait accompli," John Henry
wrote Bedichek, "since it was over and done with before I ever
knew what hit me. The two gentlemen who throwed the harpoon
into my exposed rear, did such a subtle job that there is absolutely
no way to lay a hand on them. Unfortunately, they waited until a
perfect time to swing, when other circumstances (the Godfrey
show coming in) would cover up their real motives, and they
swung."[1]

Slowly but inexorably, the publicity of the blacklist and the lawsuit led to John Henry's alienation from previous friends and acquaintances. "Since I was so well known, I was an untouchable, and it was strange as hell when I got fired. It's a very strange feeling to be blacklisted. And that was unique to that period that you weren't supposed to be seen with . . . I'd go down to Colby's, which was the eating place at CBS, or any of those—Toots Shor's was kind of my headquarters over there on Fifty-First Street, you know. I knew everybody who came in. Toots had a table for me and all, and people [would] start leaving you . . . getting up and having to rush out when you come in."[2]

The alienation John Henry felt was compounded when he received news about the death of his mother, who had been fighting cancer. The yearning he felt for the closeness and camaraderie of a simpler time, when he and his family and friends capered about the live oak trees in South Austin, was reflected in an August 1 letter to Dobie:

> . . . each of us [in the family] had a sort of dependent relationship to mama, that now, that death has severed, leaves us in a state of emotional confusion. We are kind of milling around trying to get our bearings, I guess you would say. And that is the situation that I was unprepared for. It is as though a generator that sent out impulses through the family had been stilled. I noticed that the apprehension had begun to have its effect on us when I was home last. From my earliest memory, when the five of us gathered, whatever subject came up, was usually bandied about from five vociferous and different points of view. Just this side of the hair-pulling stage of such rows, mama would say "Now that will be enough of that," and invariably we shut up. This last time down in Texas, we were reluctant to launch into such a fray, sensing that mama would not be on hand to stop it. And so it is with many other aspects of our lives. I do not fully understand it even yet . . . I know now that one day I shall return to Texas to make it my home. I am at a loss, though, to explain even to myself, why. I do not believe that I will be happier there. I am happy here. And it is not because I feel that I would be in the place I love above all others on earth; I love New York, and many other places that I have been. In spite of O'Daniel's "Beautiful, Beautiful Texas," I do not think that it has any advantage beauty-wise over doz-

ens of other places that I could mention. I do not love the people of Texas more than I do New Yorkers. Indeed, there are times when I feel like an alien amongst many Texans. As near as I can come to explaining the impulse, or drive or need or whatever it is, is to say that I feel a kind of harmony with the earth there, with its rhythms and its sounds. The geographical limitations of this harmonious piece of earth are sharply defined for me. The eastern boundary runs along South Congress Ave. and on towards Llano. The sights and the sounds, a bunch of cattle standing in the shade of live oak trees near a tank or windmill in the noonday heat, a flock of bluejays announcing to the whole wide world that a chicken snake is in the limbs of the tree, these and a multitude of others have some special significance to me. I don't know the names of all the trees and plants and birds on that part of the earth, but I know the items themselves and am on a nodding acquaintance with them and feel comfortable around them. The only reason I am laboring this matter is so that I think you perhaps come as close to understanding what I mean as any other man I have ever known. And for a very real reason, your lasting influence on my thoughts and actions, I value your esteem above that of any other man's."[3]

John Henry started to have dreams harking back to his boyhood days: swimming naked in Barton Creek, listening to the sounds of the whippoorwills calling and the roosters crowing at his old Austin home. He told Bedichek about these dreams when he came to visit. Bedichek had the answer: "Why, those dreams are simple, Johnny. It is nothing more than your body and soul crying out against the unnatural environment of this terrible city. Your body is an animal's body, my boy, and your organs, every fiber in you, must have contact with nature. Your skin needs the natural heat of the summer, the natural cold of the winter; your ears need to hear the natural sounds of the earth; your eyes must behold the natural beauty of the land; your soul must have the exposure in the eternal drama of the changing seasons."[4]

Later next year, Bedichek died suddenly of a heart attack at the age of eighty. In an article honoring Bedichek in *The Texas Observer*, John Henry wrote that "Mr. Bedichek's unusual mind had as many sparkling facets as a well-cut diamond ... on matters political and social, he had firm and liberal convictions, but when friends of his, men he had known in his younger years, became opposed to him in their opinions, he maintained a warm affection for them."[5]

John Henry had had no television offers or lecture appearances since the bulletin. The year before, he had appeared on television network programs about ten times. Now television producers were telling him, "Don't call us, we'll call you." He tried every radio station in New York and found nothing available. Doggedly, he sought work outside New York state. In 1957, Minneapolis radio station WCCO paid for his trip there to cut a demo tape and interview guests in the city (including the governor). A contract was drawn up, only to be canceled without explanation. They were no longer interested in him because "some other things came up which preclude our asking you to join us." In April 1958, Wendell Campbell, an old friend, offered him a job at KFRC Radio in San Francisco. The next month, he received a letter from Campbell asking him to cut some records at New York's WOR with a Robert Leder, so that Campbell could play them for his bosses. Oddly, John Henry noticed another letter from KFRC. He opened it and saw that it was addressed to WOR's Leder. (The letter had been mailed to him by mistake.) It read: "I was concerned before going into this about Johnny's legal problems with Aware, Inc., but had been given to understand that these were all cleared up. If this is so, we will definitely be interested in him." This letter, the first concrete evidence that Aware was a factor in John Henry's employability, would later be used as evidence in the trial.

Suddenly and inexplicably, John Henry would get calls from colleagues who told him that Aware "had the goods on him." One asked him, "Have you ever been to Moscow, Johnny?" When he answered no, that the closest he had gotten was Cairo, Egypt, the man told him that Aware was spreading the rumor that he was taking his orders directly from Russia.

"It seems the defendants in this case have been carefully and persistently getting the word around that they have some devastating evidence on me and that when the trial comes off I will be unmasked for the rosy red subversive that I have always been," John Henry joked to Bedichek. "It seems that this is an old device that has been employed very effectively before to scare the hell out of any potential friends and supporters that one might have. The defendants, of course, are most anxious to keep me out of work, figuring that sooner or later I am going to go bankrupt and sit down and talk settlement. However, we have at last made them exhaust all of their legal delays and next week they are to start examinations before trial. We have first crack at them. Then they can take a flyer at me. Then a trial date is set and we have it in court. There will be no more delays, thank the Lord. We should go to trial the latter part of the Spring. As I said in my last letter, this has been a most illuminating period for me. For the first time in my life I have experienced the feeling of having erstwhile friends turn their backs, and then felt the cumulative effect of one turn down after another, week after week. It is not unlike Chinese water torture – a drop at a time on the forehead until dizziness sets in."[6]

"Nizer dug deeper and deeper into the conspiracy," John Henry wrote, relentlessly examining Hartnett's methods of investigation and clearances and the names of his associates. At one point during the pre-trial examinations, Hartnett did talk settlement. He admitted to Nizer, under persistent questioning, that he had been fed "a barrel of false information" about John Henry, and conceded that a number of items in the bulletin were in error, particularly mistaking "Jack Faulk," a black entertainer, for John Henry. Nizer said Hartnett volunteered to write a letter to a prospective employer to "clear" John Henry, then offered to issue a retraction and apology. Both Nizer and John Henry refused, because Hartnett never offered to pay a settlement fee indemnifying Faulk, and because John Henry did not want to settle out of court. "He had not begun this lawsuit for the sole purpose of restoring his career and getting some money," Nizer wrote. "He also wanted to destroy the practice of blacklisting, so that other artists would never be subjected to its fatal sting."[7]

Prevented from settling out of court, Aware hunkered down for a long, drawn-out battle, designed to whittle John Henry's will to fight on. Nizer was forced to wait two years just to get Aware's lawyers to address a series of motions to the defendants' pleadings. Aware's lawyers filed several amended answers, trying to redirect the questions to the issue of communism and the origins and nature of the Russian Revolution. [8] In 1958 Roy Cohn replaced Godfrey Schmidt as Aware's chief counsel. Cohn's first move was to announce that he was leaving for the Far East for several months, which delayed the pre-trial examinations further. Cohn also engaged in other obstructive tactics, "blustering and slicky-sliding around," said John Henry, and making several objections to Nizer's queries. At that point, John Henry had to sit it out:

> The lawsuit is in a temporary lull, on account of them not being able to get anybody but Egg Suckin Roy to represent them. However, we still have four of them to put through the wringer yet, and if the pizen keeps flowing like it has out of the first one, Hartnett, we are going to have such a case as will shake the radio-TV and movie industry from stern to stern, when it hits the papers. As I mentioned to Mr. B on the telephone, they have caved in completely and have been putting such scandalous confessions into the printed record, along with documents, letters, etc, as would set a Turkey Buzzard to puking. Nizer hits them just like Bill Modglin's cyclone hit Penn Field back in 1922, except that Nizer circles around and descends on them again and again. He ain't but 5 foot 6 inches tall, but he manages to tower up into the sky a thousand or so feet, and drop on them with such terrifying and devastating fury that it even freezes <u>my</u> blood to watch the chaos that ensues. It is difficult to believe that the cowering, whimpering wretches before us now, curled on the ground with their bellies and legs thrown up, licking out their tongues and beating the earth with their tails and whining for mercy, are the same Mighty Men who have for the past 8 years bestrode the entertainment industry, striking terror with their frowns, pronouncing sentence and executing one and all who incurred their wrath. Of course, the saddest, or rather, the shoddiest aspect of the whole mess is that our Proud and Free Citizenry, who pronounce to the world daily that they are the last defenders of True Freedom, collaborated shamefully from start to finish with the scoundrels.[9]

Aware had also been successful in getting HUAC to serve John Henry with a subpoena to appear before the committee. Nizer discovered that HUAC members were very close with the defendants. That summer, Aware held a cocktail party in honor of the committee members and their staff.

John Henry felt uneasy about testifying, because HUAC's congressional immunity permitted its interrogators to ask any question about the suspect, but didn't allow the suspect to cross-examine or question the sources of the information. John Henry wrote Dobie and Bedichek that Aware was using HUAC's subpoena as an act of blackmailing him into dropping this suit.

They figure they can smear me so completely by running roughshod with their questions, that the hideous sort of revelations we are now getting from them [Aware], will never be made public, or that they can sufficiently smear me to make me unacceptable to the newspaper folk who are rallied behind me, just waiting to start breaking the story on their conspiracy. Of course, too, they figure that the House Committee might luckily trap me into a perjury case, should I forget a date or something. The House Committee has received so much bad publicity of late that they are frantically seeking to prevent any more coming out. However, so much of our trial revolves around their cooperation with AWARE, Inc. that they are determined to whack me into silence. I got in touch with [Texas Congressman] Homer Thornberry to see about going to [House Speaker] Sam Rayburn, who happens to be a pretty good friend of mine, and who I know hates McCarthyism and the like, to get them to shut [HUAC Chairman] Walters off my trail. Walters agreed that it would be unfair to call me right in the middle of a trial in which I have put my entire career and reputation at stake, at first. But then Homer sent word to me that Walters had said that they would do it all very quietly, but that it had to be done. I have heard no further from Homer, and perhaps he is not in a fighting mood about it. But I damn sure am, and aim to move heaven and earth to butt head-in to them. I'll go to Mister Sam myself and then to my half dozen other friends down in Washington who will at least raise hell, if they insist on my observing the subpoena. It is one hell of a rough fight, but we'll win it yet.[10]

In the summer of 1958, Nizer staved off the subpoena while the litigation was active. However, the publicity of being under subpoena also prevented John Henry from obtaining work. In June, John Henry visited Homer Thornberry:

... I figured that I would go down and get Homer Thornberry to put pressure on Cong. Walters to quash the subpoena. Homer is now number one man with Sam Rayburn and Lyndon Johnson and an important figure in Congress. He spent the morning talking with me, agreed that it was a sin for the House Committee to mis-use its powers so flagrantly. But [he] became completely evasive on the matter of cracking down and knocking out the subpoena. I was embarrassed for him. Here he was, a close friend of mine and my family's since childhood, intimately acquainted with us all, fully aware that I was being victimized by a scandalous mis-use of congressional power, knowing that if he waded into the matter head-on, he could correct it quickly and easily, yet so completely cautious for fear he might compromise himself in some way that he would only make vague promises to "see what could be done." Of course, he spoke to Walters who promised to take the matter up with the chief of staff, Arens, and there the whole thing dropped. I am still under subpoena — a fact that AWARE, Inc., has made sure to publicize in every trade paper and newspaper in this part of the country. Small wonder that a big stand-up-in-the-road like old Dulles [secretary of state] can go ranging around over the globe with both feet in his mouth, spreading desolation wherever he lights, and nary a voice in Congress to say him nay.[11]

With help from his sister Texana, who prompted Texas Senator Ralph Yarborough to intercede in John Henry's behalf with Thornberry, the committee canceled its subpoena in late October.

Every avenue to land a job in his field led to a dead-end. He approached old friends like advertising executive Fred Mitchell, a former schoolmate at the University of Texas, about possible work. Mitchell checked with his talent department and told John Henry there was no prospect for him. "Johnny," he said, "you are controversial and you are dead. You won't get anything."[12] With every job in radio or television closed to him, John Henry's annual income declined to about $2,061 in 1958. Dickler told him his private savings was nearly exhausted. Desperate, he offered to work in a sit-in job putting up lights while the "stars" of the show rested, but suddenly found that job unavailable as well (John Henry had a sit-in for himself three years earlier when he was working on CBS Television, making $1,000 a week). To keep his hand in radio and to gain exposure, he started broadcasting, without pay, a one-hour midnight show on WBAI-FM in New York. These shows only lasted for three months.

The blacklisting served as a banishment from the public world, and it drained John Henry's creative talents. "The most punishing aspect of being blacklisted was not the economic hardships that it worked on its victims," John Henry said, "but the painful inability to use one's creative resources. It shuts one off from contact with the public at the most important level of existence, the creative level. I would spend frustrating and fruitless hours trying to work new material. New ideas simply would not take form. I could not create in a vacuum."[13] But this weakness was balanced by John Henry's greatest strength — his extreme desire to see the ordeal through to its final conclusion.

A trip to Austin to see Dobie and Bedichek in March 1958 had recharged his creative juices, however, and he started writing and developing character sketches with the intention of using them on a record album or in a screenplay. Writing was always one of John Henry's frustrating ambitions; for years, he harbored ideas for a novel or a long play, but he found it to be an arduous task, often because his unique colloquialisms were difficult to translate on paper. "Dobie said that writing was the hardest job in the world, which I tend to agree," John Henry said. Most of his writing came in "fits and starts," and he rarely found himself in a position to concentrate solely on the project at hand. During his broadcasting career, his radio and television work made it difficult for him to grab more than a few hours for writing every week, and, from 1956 to 1962, his mind was so preoccupied with the lawsuit and his job search that he never did develop that book of stories about his cast of Texas characters.

While in New York, the closest he came to developing a script was when Alan Lomax returned from Europe in 1958, after a seven-year stint with BBC Radio. John Henry took him in his home and the two started working on an idea for a theatrical production. Alan would work on folk songs, play his guitar for musical backgrounds and interludes, and John Henry would become the characters he wrote about from a fictional East Texas town. John Henry wanted to dramatize what could happen to an outwardly pleasant community when fear and hate-inspired violence took control. "We worked on it intensely for weeks," Lomax said, "and it had to stop in mid-career, because Lynne, basically, put her foot down and said, 'it could not happen.' " (John Henry would later re-develop this material in the mid-1980s in a play called "Pear Orchard, Texas.")[14]

After his visit to Austin, John Henry wrote to Dobie and Bedichek that events in his lawsuit had taken "a grim and mean turn. We have discovered that the Aware crowd has managed to completely shut down any chance of my getting any work whatsoever. In a way, it is a good experience for me . . . good in the sense that I would never have really been able to fully understand the violence and depravity of such people had I not been personally involved with them. You will probably remember how Mark Twain has the Conn. Yankee and King Arthur go out to travel amongst the common folk and get captured and clapped into chains and sold as slaves. And you remember how the Conn. Yankee exclaims 'Slave! The word has a new sound — and how unspeakably awful!!' That is somewhat the way I feel in this matter, everytime I am confronted with another evidence of Aware's evil dealings."[15] The blacklist also affected his wife's employability. Lynne saw her advertising job with a firm that sold gold and platinum bathroom fixtures "mysteriously stopped," and another job end with no explanation as to why she was discharged. In May, she took a job as a waitress.

By this time, John Henry realized that radio and television were off-limits to him. His daily expenses living in New York began to pile up, and he had already cut expenses to the bone. When he tried to look for work in his hometown, he discovered that even Austin was affected by the blacklist. In February 1959, a small 250-watt radio station there, KNOW Radio, committed to him a one-hour time slot each day. ("I feel sure the program will be a big success in Austin," wrote KNOW President Louis Cook to John Henry.) Walter Cronkite, John Daly, Lind Hayes, and Mary Healy all recorded promos for the station management. The next month, Cook wrote to John Henry:

"I regret to advise you that a matter, which I am not at liberty to disclose, involving some long-range program planning for our station, has unexpectedly come up and makes it necessary for us to withdraw from any further negotiation or planning in connection with the proposed John Henry Faulk Show on KNOW."

In spite of the tension and inability to find work, John Henry was glad that it was *he* the Aware bunch had gone after, "for I consider it an honor to fight the scoundrels, and my spirits are only buoyed up by their attack and the fact that I know I won't back away from them. I know that they have but one weapon — FEAR — and once they fire that at you and you don't fall over, they ain't got a thing to fight with thereafter."[16]

Unable to get work in his chosen profession, in debt up to his ears (the amount would eventually total about $60,000), and faced with an eviction notice from his landlord, John Henry finally packed his bags at the end of 1959 and took his wife and three children to his hometown, moving into a small, two-level stucco house on Airole Way.

Banned from the medium he loved, John Henry was forced into odd jobs to eke out a living. For five years, he tried operating a small public relations firm with his wife, and publishing an Austin tourist magazine called *Austin On the Go* without success. He could only muster about $4,927 as income in 1961. The family moved out of a house and into a houseboat on Lake Austin. The three children felt the increasing stress between their parents, both career-oriented persons frustrated with their inability to succeed. His sisters and other relatives supported him as best they could, but it was a trying time. "It was so hard, just watching him suffer," said sister Mary, "being cut off from what he could do, for no good reason."

Despite pressure to settle, John Henry and Nizer persisted until they faced the accusers in court. The case was finally brought to trial in New York Supreme Court in April 1962 — six years after the bulletin. *The New York Times* was one of several major daily papers that carried regular accounts of John Henry's eleven-week trial against Aware in the spring of 1962. Although blacklisting had been in existence since 1945, this was the first challenge in a state supreme court that exposed the practice. "The aim of this lawsuit," Aware attorney Thomas Bolan said during his summation, "is to eliminate private opposition to communist infiltration in the United States." Bolan tried to portray John Henry as a washed-out has-been of an actor, a "professional Texan," a "liar," a person "without talent," and a man who was fired because of low ratings.

"I felt lonely and hurt," John Henry wrote of the experience. "For the first time, I felt what a Negro or a Jew must feel when he can't strike back." But John Henry did strike back, and Nizer eloquently and convincingly, in a six-hour summation, revealed the blacklisting apparatus for the sordid money-laundering and innuendo-deploying racket it really was. "This isn't a case of mistaken fanaticism," Nizer said to the jury. "They knew John Henry wasn't a communist. They met and decided to destroy this man before he destroyed their income, their illegitimate income."

During the trial, television producer David Susskind gave crucial testimony about how he resented submitting names of actors to sponsoring advertising agencies, which in turn handed them to Aware for political "clearance." Susskind estimated that over a one-year period, he submitted about 5,000 names for one program alone. In one instance, an eight-year-old child's name came back as "unacceptable" from an agency, because her father was suspect. Susskind also testified that he believed John Henry to be "one of the very best" entertainers he had seen in 1956 and 1957. "He was warm, witty, humorous, charming, bright, articulate," he said. If it were not for the blacklisting, Susskind added, he could have reached star status in television. Garry Moore, who hosted a top-rated TV show, testified that because John Henry's "rare form of talent" was hard to duplicate, he might have earned anywhere between $200,000 to $1 million a year in network television had he not been blacklisted.

Hartnett tried to justify his work to the jury as one that served some patriotic duty, describing how he and his associates pored over old clippings from the *Daily Worker* or the *People's World* and sent in these snippets to the FBI. The FBI turned these "reports" over to HUAC, and HUAC would issue a list of the names to the press. Hartnett would, in turn, use these articles to replenish Aware's accusations. Nizer discovered that even this contorted practice didn't work in this manner all the time. Once on the stand, Hartnett admitted that he had taken a clipping commending the Middle of the Road from the *New York Herald-Tribune*, not the *Daily Worker,* as the bulletin stated. Nizer said the defense's failure to reveal the U.N. anniversary event in the bulletin was "like an accusation against a man for appearing at a function with an editor of *Pravda,* the official Communist newspaper, without revealing that the occasion was a presidential press conference."

In a key moment in the trial, Nizer smashed Hartnett's veracity. Noticing during his testimony that he had been taking notes, Nizer alertly asked him what he was writing. Hartnett replied that he was taking down the names of actors who came into the courtroom, "like Elliott Sullivan, who was sitting next to Mrs. Faulk; John Randolph; Alan Manson; Jack Gilford." Many of these performers had taken the Fifth Amendment before HUAC's questioning, he said.

Nizer, sensing an opportunity, asked Hartnett: "You have testified that Eliot Sullivan sat down next to Mrs. Faulk. Do you see Mrs. Faulk in the courtroom now?"

Hartnett gazed over the audience and pointed to a woman: "I believe she is the lady over there. I am not sure."

Nizer turned to the woman and asked, "What is your name, please?" She stood up. "My name is Helen Soffer. S-O-F-F-E-R."

The crowd let out a collective gasp, and Nizer pounced on Hartnett. "Sir, is that an example of the accuracy with which you have identified your victims over the past ten years?"

In a powerful summation, Nizer quoted Robert Frost's line, "the people I am most scared of are the people who are scared," and added, "And these people, who claim to be scared of communism, are the people most to be scared of."

When the jury returned the evening of June 27, 1962, they asked this question to the judge: "Is the jury allowed to award more than the amounts requested by the plaintiff?" The next day, the largest libel judgment in history at the time — $3.5 million — was awarded. "John Henry Faulk," Nizer said, "the lone, single man, had won the battle against blacklisting." A *New York Times* editorial on June 30, 1962, said the verdict "should have a healthy effect in curbing the excesses of super-patriots who sometimes show no more concern for the rights of individuals than the communists they denounce." The editors of *LOOK* magazine, who ran a feature story about the trial in May 1963, wrote that "no American who lived through those days has any right to feel superior to those actually involved in these cases. The guilt for John Henry Faulk's ordeal is shared by all — magazines, newspapers, radio and television, advertising agencies and just plain citizens.

He who made no protest at the time has no license for smugness now. Let us hope that we have learned our lesson well."[17] (*LOOK*'s editors did not add that they had told John Henry they would run the story four years earlier, but waited until after the trial, when it was politically safe to do so.)

The jury process vindicated John Henry and exposed the illegal and unscrupulous practices of Aware and others of their ilk. Many hailed the historic verdict as driving the nail into the coffin of the blacklist in the entertainment industry. Several blacklisted artists found work in the broadcast industry again. Writer Millard Lampell, blacklisted in 1952, did not obtain work for a major Hollywood studio again until 1962, and wasn't approached to write for a major network until 1964; Lee Grant and Madeline Lee Gilford also began working again in TV and films in 1964; Pete Seeger was hired to appear on network TV in 1967, after seventeen years away from commercial television. Nizer had skillfully revealed to the public the operation of the laundering blacklisting system, with its shadowy threads interweaving among greedy private citizens, cowardly broadcasting executives, and craven advertising agencies. Although Slate and Ward both had to deny the real causes and effects of the blacklisting operation on the witness stand, its vicious inner workings were stripped bare for everyone to see.

Despite these benefits, John Henry's case failed to confront the basic issue of the blacklist: that it is illegal and unconstitutional for quasi-official bodies to probe into the background and political beliefs of an individual. "Before my trial, they [Aware] were never obligated to prove any of their charges," John Henry said. "But what if the charges were true? My conviction is that every American citizen is entitled to his constitutional rights . . . these are guarantees. And when we start shading these because we don't like someone's opinions, it's just a matter of time till they are knocking on your door."[18]

In the late 1950s, however, the only recourse for lawyers Nizer, Martinson, and Berger was to try the case as a libel suit, and prove that John Henry was not a communist and never had been one. In doing so, the lawyers glossed over John Henry's progressive views. Rather than defending groups like the Progressive Citizens of America and the People's Songs as the legal and non-communist groups that they were, Nizer denied that his plaintiff ever was associated with them. John Henry's involvement with the Henry Wallace campaign, for example, was muffled during the trial, lest the jury suspect that he held these iconoclastic views.

"If John Henry had taken the Fifth Amendment, or had argued over the right of the government to investigate anyone's political views, we wouldn't have had a case," Paul Martinson said. "This was a libel suit, and we developed our whole suit to prove that the lies told were malicious and deliberate."[19]

Unfortunately, the court's ruling did not erase previous legal injustices against many entertainers who sought vindication from the blacklist; nor did it castigate many other clearance men ("public relations consultants") who profited from the blacklist. Had John Henry Faulk's case come to trial the year he was blacklisted, rather than in 1962, he possibly could have suffered the same fate as other blacklisted performers of the period who pursued the legal route. But the year was 1962. John F. Kennedy was president. Communism was beginning to be viewed not as an internal conspiracy in America, but as the political ideology or economic philosophy it was. Government officials began speaking of "peaceful coexistence" with the Soviet Union. Civil rights was on the U.S. domestic agenda.[20] Only in this atmosphere could the specter of blacklisting have been exposed and discredited. The suit marked the end of a terrible period, and made blacklisting a financially hazardous occupation.

Yet there was a stain on the judgment. The Appellate Division of the New York Supreme Court reduced the award to $500,000. Although the New York Court of Appeals and the United States Supreme Court affirmed the verdict, there wasn't enough money to pay the judgment. Nizer discovered that Laurence Johnson, who had died a day before the original verdict, had an estate worth less than $250,000. The administrators of Johnson's estate settled for $175,000. Of that, Nizer took $25,000 off the top to pay for filing and court fees, then equally divided the rest with John Henry — $75,000 each. John Henry used most of this money to pay off his debts accumulated in six years of virtual unemployment.

Both Nizer and Faulk expected the networks to come forth with job offers. None came.

"At first, I thought there'd be all kinds of offers," John Henry said, "but I guess I was pretty naive. Although most of the sons-of-bitches who never thought I'd get up off the floor were suddenly sweet and officious as hell, no one rushed forward with any offers. I soon discovered why — the networks were damned embarrassed by the trial's exposure of their shameful collaboration with Aware."[21]

Yet he wasn't forgotten by his friends in Austin. Dobie, still writing at age seventy-four, was pleased with the outcome. John Henry supported Dobie in his latest battle against another band of "self-appointed vigilantes" — local school groups that advocated censorship of textbooks and library books (Plato among the offending authors). Dobie set up "The Committee on Freedom to Write and Read," with Frank Wardlaw, Lon Tinkle, and Ernest Mossner. These vigilante groups, Dobie said in early 1963, believed it was their patriotic mission and moral right to protect other citizens from works that "seem to them to echo the communist line or [from] words which they believe will besmirch the innocence and undermine the morals of young people."

The following year, Dobie fell ill with a heart condition. He died peacefully at home on September 18, 1964. A funeral was held at the university's Hogg Memorial Coliseum. John Henry was one of the pall-bearers. John Henry had lost not only a friend, but a mentor. He had absorbed much of Dobie's beliefs in the freedom of every mind to explore any issue unfettered by the bonds of a government or a rigid society.

"I had great awe for him," John Henry said. "He represented something very unique to me. Our friendship emerged and developed into a very warm and ongoing affair; it was a political friendship as well as an academic one. I found it very stimulating to be around him, for he was a very unaffecting guy, very straightforward."[22] Once, in a conversation with New York publisher Angus Cameron, he analyzed that personal relationship with Dobie: "I am warmed by the knowledge that he always behaves toward me with the charity and goodness that is a part of a real friendship, rejoicing in my victories, and sorrowing in my defeats ... he was important to me on an impersonal level, too ... his way of life, his standard of values, his concern for truth and beauty, his humanity — these are all elements in the man that come closest to embodying what I believe to be the Good Life."[23]

John Henry felt the keen presence of Dobie while working on his book about his ordeal in the trial. He dedicated *Fear on Trial*, first published by Simon & Schuster in 1963, "to the three persons who influenced me the most in respecting the liberated mind and the joys and responsibilities of citizenship: my mother and father and J. Frank Dobie." The book received critical acclaim from many sources. The *Dallas Morning News* called it "a sensitive, personal, and well-told account" of the landmark trial. In the *Austin American-Statesman*, Frank Wardlaw called it "one of the most important books of our time . . . Texans who think of Johnny Faulk primarily as a comedian will be disappointed if they think they will get many laughs from his book. It starts out in low key as Faulk sketches the background of his trouble. It gradually gathers momentum and reaches its dramatic climax in the 200-odd pages which are devoted to the trial itself. Faulk handles his material effectively, with an excellent sense of proportion and timing. But, like Nizer, he never lets the reader lose sight of the main issue."[24] *New York Times* television and radio critic Jack Gould called John Henry's work "an important book because it is by far the most detailed and specific recital of how the blacklist worked, the sinister chain of events that began with undocumented political charges against an artist, extended to economic intimidation of sponsor and broadcaster – and so often ended with the exile of the individual, without hearing or compassion. All the sordid ingredients of the period – the subordination of honor to expediency, the debasement of patriotism for commercial profit and the lasting agony of the blacklist's victims – are set forth in a capsule example of McCarthyism at work."[25] John Henry culled a great deal of information for *Fear on Trial* from the transcripts of his trial before Justice Abraham Geller in New York Supreme Court. It was followed two years later by Nizer's own book, *The Jury Returns*, which dramatically recounted the trial from a lawyer's perspective.

Due to the exposure he obtained from the lawsuit, John Henry did manage to land two bit parts, in the films *All the Way Home* (co-starring Henry Fonda; directed by Alex Segall) in 1963 and *The Best Man* (directed by Franklin Shaffner and written by Gore Vidal) in 1964, but network television and radio was unattainable. His friend Norman Lear developed the idea of a network television series about the blacklisting period with Dick Van Dyke set to play John Henry, but that was scuttled when Columbia Pictures and National General backed off the funding. John Henry was tainted; damaged goods. The case brought John Henry some notoriety on the lecture circuit, but his status as a national performer and celebrity was wrecked. Like many performers who were blacklisted and later "cleared," he could not regain the momentum he lost in a highly competitive medium. Moreover, his case had embarrassed the radio and film industry to a great extent, since the networks had collaborated in the blacklist. He was sort of a forgotten man in the entertainment business. "Hell, a lot of 'em didn't even know what I did anymore," John Henry said. "I'd been out of the business for six years." Even John Henry found it difficult to recall what he did in television and radio, and began questioning his own talents. Lack of job prospects, coupled with a nasty divorce from Lynne and fight for custody of the children, left John Henry feeling isolated once again.

With his new wife, British-born Elizabeth (Liz, whom he married in 1965 and remained married to until his death in 1990), John Henry returned to Austin in 1968 to start a new life and raise a new son, Yohan.

After the marriage, Cactus Pryor said, "Johnny was a lost pup found. Liz nurtured him. She made him a home. She protected him for the rest of his life from those he chose not to suffer and smilingly indulged his childlike joy at being idolized by the masses."[26] He made a living lecturing around the country about blacklisting. "Most of them didn't know what blacklisting was," he said once to an interviewer. The only time John Henry Faulk's name appeared on CBS since the blacklist was in October 1975 when the network ran *Fear On Trial,* a docu-drama about the case that starred William Devane as John Henry and George C. Scott as Louis Nizer. Ironically, it was his old network that made money from the dramatization of John Henry's 1963 book. CBS never asked him to help publicize the TV movie, and downplayed the book and John Henry's real life experience.[27] But the movie did spark a five-year engagement as a regular homespun philosopher on *Hee Haw* (1975–1980), as well as a periodic storyteller on National Public Radio.

Notwithstanding the TV movie, John Henry rejected being portrayed as a hero. "Despising those people who were attacking the basic principles of our society, it seems to me I couldn't have taken any other action," John Henry said. "And you don't congratulate a man for doing something in his own best interest, and I regarded that as in my own best interest." And he was right. John Henry's entire makeup and background called for no other response; when asked to run for the AFTRA board, or faced with compromising his principles to work again, there was only one choice for him. His father and Dobie had instilled in him a profound sense of injustice, and a belief that "freedom; the joys of a democratic society, had to extend to all the people or it was a myth."[28] John Henry's steadfast belief in the American system of judicial justice not only led to his vindication of being called a vile Red, but it also brought an end to a vigilante system of justice that subverted that basic right of due process of law.

Touring around the country as a guest lecturer, John Henry often cited the parallel between those who blacklisted him and those who would advocate the censorship of textbooks or artwork that is not considered "morally right" to the viewer. He recognized the same anti-communist mentality of the 1950s in these attitudes — attitudes where buzz-words and labeling of people who disagreed with the norm were favored over the rational exchange of ideas. Many of his speeches were given at various colleges around the country, because John Henry wanted young people (most of whom were not even born yet when he was blacklisted) to understand what McCarthyism was all about and why it happened.

"My blacklisting wasn't about whether I was a subversive or wasn't a subversive," John Henry said. "It was about repression of our basic freedoms . . . a way of shutting off the dialogue in this country and destroying dissent." For over forty years, anti-communism was more than a philosophy or belief; it was a political tool people in power used to control the public. If one looks at the trial on a deeper, sociological level, it showed how anti-communism evolved into a societal sickness in the 1940s and 1950s; a way that one demonstrated his or her patriotism. Yet this mainstream attitude was based on fear and superstition, and the super-patriots exploited and manipulated those fears deftly. John

Henry would often give the analogy of himself and playmate Boots Cooper pretending to be a Texas Ranger and a U.S. marshal to describe the atmosphere of the period:

> We were both 12 years old and we rode the frontier between mama's back door and her hen house in the back yard, cowboying out there. We lived out in South Austin, Texas, and . . . Mama told us there was a chicken snake in one of the hen's nests out there. Would we mighty lawmen go out and execute it? We, both of us barefooted and [in] overalls, we laid aside our stick horses, got a hoe and went in. And the hens were in a state of agitation, and craning their necks. We had to stand on tiptoe to look in the top tier of nests, and in about the third top nest we looked in and a chicken snake looked out of it . . . I don't know whether you've ever viewed a chicken snake from a distance of six inches from the end of your nose, but the damn things look like a boa constrictor from that distance, although it's about the size of your finger. And Boots and I, all of our frontier courage drained out our heels. Actually, it trickled down our overall legs, and Boots and I made a new door through the hen house wall. And Mama came out and said: "Well, you've lulled me into a false sense of security. I thought I was safe from all hurt and harm and here you've let a chicken snake run you out of the hen house, and a little chicken snake at that. Don't you know chicken snakes are harmless? They can't hurt you." Boots said: "Yes, Mrs. Faulk, I know that," rubbing his forehead and behind at the same time, "but they can scare you so bad, it'll cause you to hurt yourself."[29]

That was the greatest lesson to be learned from the McCarthy period. Elmer Davis, one of John Henry's contemporaries, said that allowing the hate-mongers and fear-peddlers to scare you serves their purpose: "For the men who are trying to do that to us are scared themselves. They are afraid that what they think will not stand critical examination; they are afraid that the principles on which this Republic was founded and has been conducted are wrong. They will tell you that there is a hazard in the freedom of the mind, and of course, there is, as in any freedom. In trying to think right, you run the risk of thinking wrong. But there is no hazard at all, no uncertainty, in letting somebody else tell you what to think; that is sheer damnation."[30]

A true American patriot is not one who bends his knee to what the majority or the government tells him to believe. In a democracy, the individual's freedoms and liberties are protected from the tyranny of the majority. Unfortunately, in order to obtain those rights, someone has to actively resist when violated; someone has to be willing to be called "subversive" and "disloyal." John Henry Faulk fit the bill.

12.

JOHN
HENRY'S
LEGACY

J udge Tom Willis casually took his seat on his rocking chair and leaned forward, both hands clutching his long walking cane. His old black Texas hat cast a small, triangular shadow over his forehead. With a casual assurance that one naturally associates with crusty wisdom, he proceeds to tell his friend, Buford, about his indignation over a circulated petition.

"You're asking me to sign this petition that we padlock the ol' movie house down the street because it shows porno films and throw the owner in jail? Buford, I just can't do that. I don't advocate pornography any more than you do, but what you're doing here is wrong.

"You see, Buford, you can preach against this as much as you like, but when you start questioning people's patriotism because they don't agree with you, accusing them of being communist, that's contrary to the Constitution. The whole history of our Constitution and our First Amendment was a reaction against that sort of thinking.

"That First Amendment was worded: 'Congress shall make no law respecting an establishment of religion, or prohibiting the free exercise thereof; or abridging the freedom of speech, or of the press; or the right of the people peaceably to assemble, and to petition the Government for a redress of grievances.'

"Simple sentences—all of it. James Madison wrote that as an absolute mandate, to make us a beacon for freedom. It guarantees in perpetuity the liberties and freedoms we have. So you see, Buford, I couldn't shut you up and you couldn't shut me up. Because the people are sovereign and the government the people's servant. And that's why I can't sign your petition."

Buford's reaction to the old judge's speech was to say: "There you go with that First Amendment business again. You better watch it, or soon people will start calling you a communist."

But the gentlemanly scholar peered out into the audience and said in a wise voice: "People who founded this country knew there'd be Bufords. They realized you can't call in the government to make people believe what it wanted you to believe, so they drafted the people's Bill of Rights. We've got to protect both worlds — protect those ideas we loathe and despise as well as those we cherish and love."

The stage goes black. The audience at the small Texas theater all stand in their ovation for the last scene of a special performance by a seventy-five-year-old man. John Henry Faulk has performed his last act.

"Pear Orchard, Texas," a revised version of Faulk's "Deep in the Heart" play that premiered in Houston in 1986, consisted of much more than political messages. Although each of the ten characters John Henry created and portrayed on stage said something about the political climate of the day, they also represented the loves, hates, fears, and aspirations of all Americans. Before he was stricken with a second bout of cancer in 1989, John Henry had plans to take this show to Broadway, to be directed by Albert Marre (director of "The Man of La Mancha").

"Pear Orchard" proved endearing to Texans because the characters were people the crowds in Houston, Dallas, Austin, and San Antonio felt like they knew. John Henry would often use short, deft barbs, like when Mrs. Waters is asked whether her son had any sibling rivalry. "No," she answers, "he had measles and like that." Or he would show the false Southern pride through

Miss Effie Lou Townsin, a fixture in the local garden club for her prize sweet peas, who would express how difficult it is to get black "help" these days. Or he would show the piousness of Brother Will Boring: "Calvin Banks . . . he invented ah do-it-yourself baptismal kit. It was fer shut-ins. N'if you sent your money head-uf-time, pre-paid, Cal 'ud sent you an autographed picture of Jesus Christ that glowed in the dark. N' his eyes 'ud follow you anywhere you went in the room . . ."

Then there's Miss Fanny Rollins, who tells the story of a woman who used to be "the purtiest little thang you ever seen" at seventeen: "But one morning she was packing two buckets of milk cross the cow lot. A thunderstorm had come up a few minutes before, and lightnin' struck that chile right between the eyes. (PAUSE) Soured both buckets of that milk and gave her a severe headache! Turned out it had flattened her chest. Ironin' board flat-chested, she was. She got some foam rubber bosoms from Dallas. Nobody know'd they weren't real. Till she was sewing at the church with the quilting ladies and, absent-minded like, started using the left one as a pin cushion."

John Henry made all these characters come alive without elaborate costumes, wigs, or makeup. He only used his commanding voice, posture, and facial expressions to change from a little old Fanny Rollins rattling on about her fellow Pear Orchardians to an Aggie car dealer rejecting his son who has AIDS.

Playwright Marty Martin, author of the award-winning one-woman play "Gertrude Stein," helped John Henry organize and revise his material with a cohesive theme: "I persuaded him to get rid of his elaborate introductions for each character." John Henry skipped any explanatory narrative introducing his characters; the crowd would immediately become acquainted with them. In "Pear Orchard," Martin noted, the characters defined themselves, and when John Henry ended one character, the set would go black and he'd become a new one for the next scene. With director Mark Leonard's sensitive staging, the transitions seemed magical, for the audience saw a different person speaking to them. This allowed John Henry to adapt his storytelling style into real drama on stage.

"Pear Orchard, Texas" depicted the culmination of the folksy characters John Henry had created in the 1950s. When a reporter asked when John Henry started writing the play, he paused and answered, "I've sort of been writing it all my life. It [the show] is an accumulation of my love affair with Texans."

Many accolades were heaped upon Faulk's performance as an actor, but he was proudest of his awards and laurels in defense of the First Amendment, his real passion during the last third of his life. The list of achievements is impressive. In January 1980, he and friends Eric Sevareid and Walter Cronkite formed the "First Amendment Congress," a national forum of broadcasters and academicians organized to protect and preserve the separation of church, state, and press. His awards included the National Press Club Certificate of Appreciation (1955), the Eleanor Roosevelt Freedom of Speech Award (1976), the James Madison First Amendment Award (1980), and an award from Freedoms Foundation at Valley Forge (1985). After his death on April 9, 1990, a fund was established in his memory at the University of Texas at Austin General Libraries to support programs and activities in support of the Bill of Rights. Every two years "The John Henry Faulk Conference on the First Amendment," sponsored by the University of Texas at Austin's Center for American History, analyzes and discusses issues relating to the First Amendment.

John Henry said that the "greatest gift from the struggle I had gone through" was in discovering the history and meaning of the constitution. "I understood," he wrote, "why James Madison conceived the First Amendment as the jewel in our crown, written and nailed into the basic law of the land, the guarantee that opinions we loathe and despise would be defended and protected with the same force as those we cherish and love. No other nation had ever dreamed of this. This *is* our genius."[1]

In one of his last interviews, John Henry wanted to relate and bestow a last "will and testament" that set forth the facts reflecting the freedoms and guarantees of liberty granted by the founding fathers. He desperately wanted to communicate to the public, much of which doesn't clearly understand these tenets, "what a hell of an exciting thing it is to live in a society where these guarantees must be exercised." If you didn't understand, John Henry felt you'd do a great disservice to not only yourself but to your society as well.

John Henry Faulk was an American patriot in the true sense of the word, which made the blacklisting smear on him all the more tragic and pernicious. To John Henry, being an American was "the richest possible heritage I can have.

"Every American citizen would be as principled if they understood the Constitution and the Bill of Rights; if they know them as I do. I have particular insight into those freedoms with which it deals, because I had a unique experience that enabled me to dig into them . . . in my great lawsuit, for which I have been given a great deal of credit, none of which I deserve. The principles from that derive directly from our Constitution."

AFTERWORD

I ndividually and collectively, Americans may think we are far removed from the "McCarthy era" of the 1940s and '50s. We may think that since mainstream communism has declined, that red-baiting is a thing of the past. John Henry knew better.

He knew that the government and private vigilantes are always there lurking, waiting for the proper moment to capitalize on people's fears and paranoia. He also kept alert to government and private encroachment on individual freedoms, consistently speaking out when those freedoms were threatened or violated. John Henry was a firm believer in Thomas Jefferson's principle that held "the opinions of men are not the object of civil government, nor under its jurisdiction." He understood that if the government subjects the individual's opinion to inspection and coercion, then the self-appointed inquisitors would crop up—those people, governed by their own fears, political ambitions and private passions, who, in their effort to muzzle free thought, would destroy the reputations and careers of others.

As John Henry asserted many times, anti-communism had nothing to do with communism. Anti-communism was just a scapegoat that preyed on societal fears of conspiratorial take-over. Whether it's anti-communism or anti-Semitism, the language used is designed to incite prejudicial attitudes and inflame the mores of certain groups. The goal of these groups, John Henry said, is to stifle dissent. Today, politicians and special interest groups use hot buttons such as "the war against drugs," "family values," and "traditional values." Too often, these are only code words that legitimize bigotry and intolerance and give rise to hate crimes and gender and racial violence. Anyone who disagrees with the norm, anyone who strays from the standard mainstream, may be a target for censure or blacklisting.

The entire anti-communism crusade created by our federal government institutionalized secrecy and was used to justify illegal investigations of non-communist groups. The anti-communism psychosis was so pervasive and so effective that the government continued to exploit that red flag to go to war in Korea and Vietnam. When the Vietnam War became unpopular, anti-communism found itself replaced with "national security," and anti-war protesters were harassed. Millions of dollars of taxpayers' money have been spent to spy on artists, authors and performers, many of whom our government knew were not "enemies of the state." Despite this money, time and effort, no sufficient evidence has been found to determine that any of those suspected people served a foreign enemy.[1]

Today, the federal government, through the FBI and CIA, continues to conduct counterintelligence campaigns inside the U.S. that violate the First and Fourth Amendments. FBI Director J. Edgar Hoover's COINTELPRO secret techniques involved illegal searches and seizures, wiretapping, "dirty tricks," and other methods that lasted through 1971. Nixon continued these practices with his infamous "Plumber's" (Special Investigations) Unit.

During the 1980s, John Henry was a virulent opponent of Ronald Reagan—that "pus sac on the boil" and former president of the Screen Actors' Guild who helped participate in the Red Scare of the 1950s. Under Reagan, the FBI illegally investigated many political activists, targeting opponents of the administration's Central American policies. In 1992, the FBI, having difficulty translating new digital technology used by the phone companies, wanted Congress to pass a law requiring phone companies to reengineer their new phone networks so that the FBI could resume tapping phones.

John Henry saw the resurgence of the Red Scare during the Reagan-Bush years, when epithets and buzz-words (like the dreaded "L" word for liberal) again replaced rational political discourse in this country. In the 1988 presidential campaign, George Bush (successfully) excoriated Michael Dukakis' character, accusing him of being a "card-carrying member of the ACLU (American Civil Liberties Union). Faulk saw that as a clear "McCarthy-style" campaign tactic.

In the 1992 presidential campaign, our vice-president raised the issue of Hollywood's lack of family values when he attacked the fictional TV character Murphy Brown for having a baby out of wedlock. Bush and Dan Quayle used Bill Clinton's school trip to Moscow to raise questions about Clinton's patriotism.

As president, Bush proposed (but later dropped) a plan to use secret evidence to deport aliens suspected of terrorism, without releasing that evidence to the suspected individual or his attorney. In early 1993, both the FBI and INS (Immigration and Naturalization Service) began "monitoring" and investigating Arab-Americans for raising funds for Palestinian welfare and religious causes, and for disseminating "anti-Israel propaganda."

In the academic world, freedom of speech is often a vague concept that is strictly controlled. In the mid-1980s, Catholic University in Washington banned the Rev. Charles E. Curran from teaching theology, after he gave students information on contraception and abortion. Brigham Young University also prohibits speech that is pro-abortion, as well as any speech that "contradicts or opposes" fundamental Mormon Church doctrine. In March 1993, BYU threatened to deny tenure to an assistant professor because she spoke at an abortion rights rally. (BYU also prohibits students from drinking Classic Coke or smoking a cigarette, but requires them to salute the American flag when it is raised or lowered.) In Atlanta, a college preparatory school had a longstanding policy of requiring all its faculty members to be Christians. Even John Henry Faulk's alma mater, the University of Texas at Austin, prohibits public speech on its campus, except in a "designated free speech area."

In the entertainment industry, some television watchdog

groups want to decide what other people can watch by pressuring advertisers and networks to drop controversial shows or entertainers. Often, they go beyond attempts to influence advertisers. In April 1988, Brent Bozell's Media Research Center out of Alexandria, Virginia, launched the first issue of *TV, etc.*, which named "liberal performers." Like *Red Channels*, the newsletter listed actors and musicians who contributed time and money to purported "left-wing causes," such as Amnesty International and Greenpeace. Bozell claimed that the purpose of the newsletter was to "document the bias of the Hollywood left" and to inform the public about programs that "glorify liberal causes." The first issue of *TV, etc.*, for example, asserted that ABC's *Head of the Class* was a "study of leftist programming at its worst," and that the show "rarely fails to miss a chance to preach its leftist views to an unsuspecting audience." The same issue attacked ABC's *thirtysomething* as a show with characters who had "strident liberal political viewpoints."[2]

AFTRA passed a resolution in 1989 condemning the purpose of *TV, etc.*, and its delegates took a firm stand once again against blacklisting and political intolerance. "We only ask that if you're going to judge performers, judge them on their performance, not on what you think their beliefs are," said John Hall, national executive director of AFTRA.[3]

According to writer Michael McWilliams, a modern blacklist still exists in the television industry, based on pressure from these conservative watchdog groups. Mars, Inc., for example, has fifty shows on its list of programs it doesn't advertise, including *Golden Girls, Knots Landing,* and *Nightline.* Exxon Corporation has thirty shows on its list, but won't reveal the names.[4]

Not surprisingly, the religious right is responsible for a great many of these bullying campaigns. For example, in 1992, Representative Elizabeth Patterson from South Carolina, a conservative Democrat and a member of the National Prayer Breakfast, was ousted from office with the help of the Christian Coalition. With the exception of two small checks that had "bounced" briefly from the House bank, Patterson had a clean voting record. Yet the campaign vilifying Patterson included bumper stickers and defaced posters that read "Bounce Liz," "Lesbian Liz," and "Patterson Covers Up Cocaine Sales."[5] Referring to a proposed equal rights amendment for women in 1992, Pat Robertson was quoted as saying that it would "advance a feminist agenda . . . that encourages women to leave their husbands, kill their children, practice witchcraft, destroy capitalism, and become lesbians." In 1993, fifty years after John Henry denounced the Red Cross and the armed services for their racist, exclusionary policies toward blacks, reactionaries decried Bill Clinton's proposal to legally admit gays in the military.

The attacks are not confined to the political and entertainment worlds. School boards across the country have banned classic works by J. D. Salinger, Mark Twain, D. H. Lawrence, and others as books they deem as "morally unacceptable" to teenagers and schoolchildren. People for the American Way, an anti-censorship group, listed *Of Mice and Men, Catcher in the Rye, The Adventures of Huckleberry Finn, Slaughterhouse Five,* and *Fahrenheit 451* as on the top ten list of the most censored books. Madonna's *Sex* book, not even considered mild pornography by most critical observers, was banned from library shelves (including Austin's) because of the outcries from people who hadn't even seen the book. The censors don't confine their inspection to controversial books. In 1990 the school board of Empire, California, removed 400 copies of *Little Red Ridinghood* from classrooms because a bottle of wine was in the basket of goodies the child was taking to her sick grandmother. "It condones the use of alcohol," said one official.[6]

In the 1940s, someone might find his loyalty questioned by government investigators if he owned an album by Paul Robeson, if he read *The New Republic* or *The Nation*, if he had ever taken a class in Russian literature, or if he had been to a meeting for the "People's Songs" or the Spanish War Relief. Any progressive association, however small and unconfirmed, would be explored, investigated, and listed as "subversive."

Yet there are still groups today, like the American Family Association and others, that seek to censor materials that don't meet their own moral standards. It's not enough to simply persuade others to follow their views; they want to go one step farther, and actively compel all people to bow to their tastes by denying them a free choice in what they buy, view, or read.

Like Hartnett and Johnson, these reactionary individuals

deny any attempt to blacklist artists. Their organizations advocate censorship without admitting so, even though their goal is to control mass communications to adopt their own way of thinking (any other way is unacceptable) through a policy of intimidation, fear, and repression—just as the blacklisters did. They are easy to spot, because they use some of the same tactics. First, they appeal to people's ignorance by making exaggerated claims and half-truth charges that alarm people's values and beliefs. Second, they intimidate sponsors, networks, and producers through a sustained program of threats and innuendos. Third, they attack the credibility and character of anyone who questions their methods. And fourth, if the other three actions are successful, they might extend this questioning into a campaign of investigation and persecution.

"Wait till you hear the bleeding hearts of those who question our methods," Joe McCarthy once said, which is echoed today by radio-TV commentator Rush Limbaugh. Like McCarthy, Limbaugh uses bombastic phrases, half-truths, and self-congratulatory humor to mask his prejudices and goals. Limbaugh's attacks on Clinton, for example, strongly resemble McCarthy's impugning Adlai Stevenson ("Alger — I mean Adlai," McCarthy would quip). Also like McCarthy, Limbaugh has decried the "crackpot professors" and "communists in our schools."

Vigilante groups of the 1950s specialized in a vicious means of persecution and repression, acting outside the law. Some still carry on that tradition today, like "pro-life" organizations. John Henry satirized these anti-abortion groups through Ed Snodgrass: "Our great problem today is this business of abortion. Oh, these ol' abortion clinics is driving us mad, folks, and we've got to do something about it. If I had my way about it, I would round up every single person in any way involved in it, bring 'em down here to that University of Texas Stadium, and I'd deputize a bunch of big, husky men, give them billy clubs and sawed-off shotguns and real mean poolice dogs, and I'd go in thar and start tearin' the hide off 'em. You say, 'why?' Somebody's got to do somethin' to put down violence in this country!"[7]

Regardless of the tactics, the goal of these groups is the same: repression of opinions that are different from the mainstream. While they claim the right of "free speech" to disagree, never do these groups want to engage in a free and open dialogue on any issue—they just attack. Their purpose is not to debate or discuss, not to examine and weigh all arguments to test their own opinions, but to suppress and stifle. Their answer to speech they abhor is not to debate it, but to ban it. John Henry would point this out through the bigoted eyes of Cousin Ed:

"I'm not against free speech. I'm all for free speech. It's this damn *dissent* I'm trying to put a stop to!"

DIED APRIL 9, 1990, IN AUSTIN, TEXAS, OF CANCER.
BURIED- OAKWOOD CEMETARY AUSTIN

Appendix

Selected Letters by John Henry Faulk

May 30, 1956 / 118 West 79th St. / New York 24, NY

My Dear Brethren Dobie, Webb, Mody & Bedichek:

. . . I am involved in about the biggest fracas that I have ever managed to get into. As you know, our side won last Fall in a bitter Union fight. The defeated side, a pack of McCarthyites, took in after us with a vengeance. They scared the hell out of the summer soldiers on our side, and scattered them like a covey of quail. Then they started narrowing down their fire to the several who wouldn't back down. I think that I showed you the slander sheet they put out on Collingwood, Orson Bean and myself. After a while, Bean and Collingwood sort of started squatting behind bushes, and the next thing I knew, I was standing there on the limb all by myself, like a half-feathered jay bird, with all their ire concentrated on me. I just couldn't find it in my heart to take flight from them. Boys, I found out just how violent and merciless they could be, too. Not content to go to each of my sponsors in the dark of the night to destroy my career, they began the damndest campaign of whispered villainy in the Union and amongst the industry that you could imagine. They finally printed what is to be their own un-doing. It contained about 10 allegations, each one a clear and premeditated lie — things like my being driven out of Austin and fearing to return because of my red activities, my being fired from CBS, NBC, etc. because of my left-wing broadcasts, and that I had organized May Day celebrations in NYC in 1943 and 1944 (I was over in Egypt in the Red Cross with the Army at the time). This batch of nonsense was sent to each of my sponsors secretly, as a final volly to shake me off the limb. My sponsors turned it all over to me, thank god, with the signatures and all. Of course, the blackhearted rascals figure that they have complete immunity from a lawsuit because of two very important fac-

185

tors: 1) A public entertainer can't afford to go to court and become controversial, because he thereby loses his commercial value in radio and TV; 2) No performer can secure a first class lawyer because the cost of suit is prohibitive. They are due for a surprise on both counts. They done grabbed the wrong sow by the ear if they think I mind becoming controversial where those heathens are concerned. And I have managed to get the biggest and best law firm in New York to take the case — Louis Nizer, who gave Pegler and the Hearst press such a thumping for Quenton Reynolds. True, I have to lay down a $10,000 retainer, but that is only a fraction of the expenses of the case, and Nizer is going to bear the rest. It seems that the bunch that have been doing the dirty work are nothing more than a syndicate of blackmailers who prey on entertainers, and who use patriotism as a smokescreen for their rascality. We have about seven young lawyers from the firm digging into the past history of the evil rapscalions, and the things they have uncovered has been startling. Their reckless and heartless treatment of hundreds of entertainers in the past has gone unchallenged for so long that they have become absolutely brazen and almost open in their operations. Nizer and his firm believe that our suit will so expose them that it will never be possible for such a shameful group to operate again. CBS and my manager have gotten very frightened at my going through with the suit. They point out that my sponsors have come back and that if I will just forgive and forget, my hide will be safe. I point out that if Aware Inc. gets off this time, they will do the same thing to somebody else next month and one month after that. The reason they have flourished so long is that nobody would ever wade into them and yank them out into the bright light of day for the public to look at in all their rusty gut ugliness. So I'm going through with it. Lynne is behind me and so are all of the good souls that have a sense of responsibility for decent American life. Unfortunately, I am having to keep the whole thing quiet until Nizer hits them with the suit, and so as far as my union slate knows — and the opposition knows — I am taking it lying down. This has placed my side at a considerable disadvantage. However, the elections for Nation Board in the Union are now going on, and I have managed to get a bobtailed slate into the fray and am running myself. This in itself has astonished the opposition, for they felt that they had put me into flight along with Orson Bean, one of my lieutenants, who withdrew from the fight last week. Fear has a hideous effect on men. Bean was a decent, intelligent lad who stood right up to the rascals and, who like me, got blacklisted for doing so. They promised him if he wouldn't run with me again they would 'clear' him for more TV shows. Instead of inviting them to kiss his butt, damned if he didn't agree. I was shocked. Now he is back on the Ed Sullivan show, but he is sort of shamefaced and some of his self-respect has been destroyed. I feel sorry as hell for him and at the same time, feel even more furious than ever at the sorry scoundrels who perpetrate such things on their fellow beings, reducing them to cowards. I wrote a strong letter to the membership of the Union and got Collingwood to send it out in our union magazine under his name as president. The papers have picked it up and it is causing a lot of comment in the trade up here. I shall enclose a copy of it with this letter. I'll let you know how and when things break into the open as far as the suit is concerned.

Mama is on her last legs, and I am trying to figure out a way to slip down to see her within the next three weeks. I don't think she is going to last much longer. She told me the other night on the phone that Mayor Miller gave her a citation and it gave her such a bighead that she is thinking of running for Miss Texas in the next bathing beauty contest. I hope that all is going well with each of you kind souls and I hope that you all aren't so scattered during June that we can't have a get together if I can make it down there. Please take good care of yourselves and have a dive in Barton's for me. I sure did enjoy Stanley Walker's book. It's way out yonder the best he ever did.

Kindest regards all around,

Johnny

August 6, 1956 / 118 West 79th St. / New York 24, NY

My Dear Mr. Bedichek:

I have always been loath to pack around pictures of my children and wheel them out to show off to folks. For while this is a common practice amongst proud parents, and my children are unique and wondrous creatures to me, I have a sort of inherited sense of proportion in such matters. I realize that other's children are unique and wondrous to them. I have the same sense of reluctance when it comes [to] spraying broadcast over the country the virtues of Beautiful Texas and its inhabitants.

However, there is no denying it, that stretch of earth called Travis County and some of the folk who live there have a deep and permanent place in my heart and thoughts. Since my last visit there I have been thinking at some length on just what those elements are, which compound to make it so dear to me. I know that those elements have special meaning and significance to me, but I have been trying to assay their meaning in terms of the world. Two of them, you and Mr. Dobie, while having something very special for me, have meaning to the world in general. Society has come to recognize that you are two originals. There ain't no more Dobie and Bedichek nowhere else. However, other elements, namely mama and daddy, are not recognized generally and I have now become convinced that they, too, have a social significance that is indeed unique. What I am trying to say is, that not just in terms of my own close and devoted relationship with them are they meaningful, but in terms of society's own standards.

Now you take mama. Seemingly the very quintessence of an orthodox South Austin housewife and mother, she possessed qualities that completely removed her from the area of orthodoxy. She was a devout and dedicated Methodist, with firm and positive views about her religious beliefs. Yet, she had a daughter become a Catholic and raise a Catholic family and there was never the slightest hint of misgivings on her part, but to the contrary a complete acceptance of the fact. She had a son marry a Jew, and there was never even a slight suggestion of intolerance. Her other son became an avowed atheist, and always held the same warm and genuine place in the bosom of the family. Whether this was an inherited tolerance, I do not know. She certainly did not come from a tolerant people. But to the contrary, a bigoted and rather self-righteous pack. I think that it must have been a learned trait. After all, mama did live with a rather un-orthodox man for some forty odd years. At any rate, her tolerance for matters outside the religious world, political differences, social differences, was equally unorthodox. She could be narrow and severe in her opinions at times. Cussing and alcohol and the general area of sin were objects of considerable contempt to mama. Yet, when each of us moved into those fields at one time or another, mama never let it become a source of prolonged discomfiture in family relations. From the time women were first allowed to vote in Texas, to the absentee balloting this summer, mama never missed making her opinions known at the polls one single time. Had she been a widely travelled woman or a well-read scholar, these aspects of her personality would not have been so unique, perhaps. But she was for all practical purposes nothing more than a South Austin housewife, and never regarded herself as being anything else. But she was. She had a profound and mysterious grasp of philosophies that are fundamental to man's forward movement in this experience called life on earth. She and daddy were two of the first people I ever knew who clearly understood that the brotherhood of man is a reality, not a sought-after dream, and that the stupid walls of race and creed that divide mankind into a multitude of camps are built on ground that will give way before the march of Time . . .

Take good care of yourself and munch a fig for me.

With much affection . . .

Johnny

February 13, 1958 / 118 West 79th St. / New York 24, NY

Dear Mr. Dobie and Mr. Bedichek:

I reckon mankind is a pretty hopeless proposition. He's got a little goodness tucked away in him, maybe, but for the most part his inherent meanness is his strongest instinct. I'm talking from firsthand experience. Here I am — blacklisted, damn near broke and harried out of my business by a pack of rascals, sitting around licking my wounds and bemoaning my sad lot. And does this experience teach me charity? Does it impel compassion and sympathy for those fellow beings who have fallen on hard times? Not one whit of it. My spirits have absolutely soared for the past week, with each additional account of abuse and hardship the Jack Porters of Houston and Republikins have suffered. I have rejoiced at the squirming and sweating of the whole brotherhood of privilege-seekers in the FCC probe. I am even so callous that I am looking forward to the appearance of one Senior Senator from Texas in the lists of persons who have been exposed by the radio-TV scandal in Washington. Mark Twain was right when he said, "Man is the only animal that blushes — or needs to." The hell of it is that I don't even blush as I revel in oil and gas lobby's hard luck . . .

We have at last figured out what has happened to me as far as employment is concerned. It seems that the defendants in the case have been carefully and persistently getting the word around that they have some devastating evidence on me and that when the trial comes off I will be unmasked for the rosy red subversive that I have always been. It seems that this is an old device that has been employed very effectively before to scare the hell out of any potential friends and supporters that one might have. The defendants, of course, are most anxious to keep me out of work, figuring that sooner or later I am going to go bankrupt and sit down and talk settlement. However, we have at last made them exhaust all of their legal delays and next week they are to start examinations before trial. We have first crack at them. Then they take a flyer at me. Then a trial date is set and we have at it in court. There will be no more delays, thank the Lord. We should go to trial the latter part of the Spring. As I said in my last letter, this has been a most illuminating period for me. For the first time in my life I have experienced the feeling of having erstwhile friends turn their backs, and felt the cumulative effect of one turn down after another, week after week. It is not unlike Chinese water torture — a drop at a time on the forehead until dizziness sets in . . .

Johnny

Notes

Chapter 1: Miss Mattie and Judge Faulk

1. "Bench & Bar of Austin, Travis County, Texas," S. Solomon, Publisher, San Antonio, c. 1912.

2. Bruce Bringhurst, *The Anti-Trust and the Oil Monopoly: The Standard Oil Cases, 1890–1911* (Westport, CT: Greenwood Press, 1979).

3. Interview, Anne McAfee, July 1989.

4. Some issues of the *Austin Daily Tribune*, later called the *Daily Tribune*, are available at the Austin History Center on microfiche. The paper went out of business in 1915.

5. *State of Texas vs. Security Oil Co., et. al,* October 26, 1909, Travis County Courthouse records.

6. Audrey Bateman, "Waterloo Scrapbook," *Austin American-Statesman,* February 24, 1979.

7. Interviews, Emmett Shelton and Mary Koock (née Faulk), 1989.

8. See *The Decline of Socialism in America, 1912-1925* (New York: Monthly Review Press, 1967).

9. Interviews, Hamilton Faulk and Emmett Shelton, 1989.

10. Nick Salvatore, *Eugene V. Debs: Citizen and Socialist* (Chicago: University of Illinois Press, 1982).

11. Debs' speech on "Black Persecution," *American Appeal* magazine, February 20, 1926.

12. Interview, Mary Koock (née Faulk), May 1989.

13. *Ibid.*

14. *Texas Observer* benefit honoring John Henry Faulk and Ernie Cortes, Austin, Texas, May 1990.

15. *Travis County vs. Henry Brock,* May 1912, Travis County Courthouse records.

16. Interview, Martha Stansbury (née Faulk), June 1989.

Chapter 2: Greener Pastures

1. The Faulks would buy the car, but Henry still refused to drive. Miss Mattie would take him to work at his office on Congress and 11th Street and pick him up later in the day.

2. Interview, Texana Conn (née Faulk), June 1989.

3. Interview, Mary Koock (née Faulk), May 1989.

4. *Ibid.*

5. Interview, Jack Kellam, August 1989.

6. Interviews, Anne McAfee and Mary Koock, May and July 1989.

7. Angela Farris Fannin, *Porch Chatter* (Austin: Eakin Press, 1984); interviews with Anne McAfee and Mary Koock, 1989.

8. Interview, Lester Kitchens; interview, Anne McAfee, July-August 1989.

9. Interview, Martha Stansbury (née Faulk), June 1989.

10. *Austin Statesman,* May 24, 1956.

11. Interview, Texana Conn, July 1989.

12. *Ibid.,* June 1989.

13. Interviews with Mary Koock, May 1989, and John Henry Faulk, March 1990.

14. Interviews with John Henry Faulk, August 1989, and Mary Koock, May 1989.

15. Interview, Arleatha Williams, August 1989.

16. Greg Olds' interview with John Henry Faulk, Center for American History, University of Texas at Austin.

17. Interview, John Henry Faulk, June 1989.

18. Greg Olds' interview with John Henry Faulk, Center for American History.

19. *Ibid.*

20. Interview, John Henry Faulk, August 1989.

21. Greg Olds' interview, John Henry Faulk, Center for American History.

22. Interview, John Henry Faulk, July 1989.

23. *Ibid.,* June 1989.

24. Greg Olds' interview with John Henry Faulk, Center for American History.

25. Interview, Texana Conn (née Faulk), June 1989.

26. Greg Olds' interview with John Henry Faulk, Center for American History.

27. *Ibid.*

28. Interview, Texana Conn, June 1989.

29. Interviews, John Henry Faulk, March 1990; and Martha Stansbury (née Faulk), May 1990.

30. Interview, Martha Stansbury, June 1989.

31. Greg Olds' interview with John Henry Faulk, Center for American History.

32. John Henry Faulk "On Humor," in *The Uncensored John Henry Faulk* (Austin: Texas Monthly Press, 1985), 5; and interview, John Henry Faulk, August 1989.

33. *Austin Statesman,* November 28, 1940.

34. Interview, Mary Koock, May 1989.

35. Interview, Texana Conn, June 1989.

36. Roy Bedichek letters, April 4, 1956, Center for American History.

37. *Austin American-Statesman,* August 27, 1978.

38. Interview, Texana Conn, June 1989.

39. Interview, John Henry Faulk, August 1989.
40. Interview, Mary Koock, July 1989.
41. Interview, John Henry Faulk, May 1989.

Chapter 3: Formation of a Raconteur

1. Interview, Texana Conn (née Faulk), June 1989.
2. Interview, Texana Conn; John Henry Faulk, *The Uncensored John Henry Faulk* (Austin: Texas Monthly Press, 1985).
3. John Henry Faulk, *The Uncensored John Henry Faulk* (Austin: Texas Monthly Press, 1985).
4. Interview, Lester Kitchens, December 1989.
5. Interview, John Henry Faulk, August 1989.
6. Interview, Texana Conn, June 1989.
7. Interview, John Henry Faulk, August 1989.
8. *Ibid.*
9. Bob Eckhardt, "Remembering Johnny and Things Gone By," at the Second Annual *Texas Observer* Benefit Dinner, May 5, 1990.
10. Interview, Creekmore Fath, August 1989.
11. Interview, Mary Koock (née Faulk), July 1989.
12. Interview, Texana Conn, June 1989.
13. *Ibid.*
14. Interview, John Henry Faulk and Jack Kellam, August 1989.
15. Interview, John Henry Faulk, August 1989.
16. *Ibid.*
17. *Ibid.*
18. *Ibid.*
19. *Ibid.*
20. *Ibid.*
21. *Ibid.*, December 1989.

Chapter 4: Professor Pancho and the Folklore Renaissance

1. Although John Henry would continually be referred to as "Johnny" by his friends in school and until his career in New York, for the purposes of this book he is referred to as "John Henry" when indicating his adult life. (He was known by both names throughout his life.)
2. John Henry used this quote for his made-up character of Grandpa Bible on "The John Henry Faulk Show." Grandpa Bible was a composite of Brodie, Dobie, and Henry Faulk.
3. Greg Olds' interview, Center for American History, University of Texas at Austin.
4. Lon Tinkle, *An American Original: The Life of J. Frank Dobie* (Austin: University of Texas Press, 1978).
5. Interviews, John Henry Faulk, August 1989, and Faulk on "Alternative Views," Alternative Information Network, Austin Access Television, 1985.
6. Interview, John Henry Faulk, December 1989.
7. *Ibid.*

8. Interview, Jack Kellam, December 1989.

9. John Henry Faulk tape recording with J. Frank Dobie, Roy Bedichek, Mody Boatright and Wilson Hudson, 1958, Center for American History, University of Texas at Austin.

10. *Ibid.*; *Mandingo* by Kyle Onstott, was published in 1958 by Fawcett, Greenwich, CT.

11. *The Daily Texan,* March 11, 1936.

12. John Henry Faulk interview, December 1989.

13. Greg Olds' interview with John Henry Faulk, Center for American History.

14. *Texas Ranger* magazine, October 1937, University of Texas at Austin.

15. *Ibid.,* December 1937.

16. Interviews, John Henry Faulk, August and December, 1989.

17. Interviews, Brownie McNeil and John Henry Faulk, September and December 1989.

18. Interview, Brownie McNeil, September 1989.

19. John Henry Faulk letters, 1938, Center for American History.

20. *The Daily Texan,* April 20, 1938, and interviews with John Henry Faulk in 1989.

21. Interview, John Henry Faulk, December 1989.

22. The *Dallas Times Herald,* December 24, 1977.

23. Interview, John Henry Faulk, December 1989.

Chapter 5: The Struggle for Equality

1. Interview, John Henry Faulk, August 1990.

2. Interview, Alan Lomax, July 1990.

3. Interview, Anne McAfee, 1989.

Chapter 6: Fighting Fascism

1. J. Frank Dobie letters, October 2, 1942, Harry Ransom Humanities Research Center, The University of Texas at Austin.

2. *Ibid.,* January 19, 1943.

3. *Congressional Record,* February 1, 1943.

4. J. Frank Dobie letters, February 7, 1943, Harry Ransom Humanities Research Center.

5. Lon Tinkle, *An American Original, The Life and Times of J. Frank Dobie* (Austin: University of Texas Press, 1978).

6. J. Frank Dobie letters, October 31, 1943, Harry Ransom Humanities Research Center.

7. *Ibid.,* February 24, 1944.

8. *Ibid.,* March 27, 1944.

9. Interview, John Henry Faulk, December 1989.

10. Interview, Dr. Harry Lerner, July 11, 1990.

11. Interview, Mary Koock, May 1989.

12. Lon Tinkle, *An American Original.*

13. Anthony M. Orum, *Power, Money and the People* (Austin: Texas Monthly Press, 1987).

Chapter 7: Johnny's Front Porch

1. Roy Bedichek letters, February 13, 1948, Center for American History, University of Texas at Austin.

2. Interview, Jaston Williams, July 28, 1989.

3. J. Frank Dobie letters, August 14, 1946, Harry Ransom Humanities Research Center, University of Texas at Austin.

4. Interview, Pete Seeger, April 1993.

5. *Ibid.*

6. Harry Stein, "The Ballad of John Henry," *New Times* magazine, fall 1975.

7. Millard Lampell, "I Think I Ought to Mention I Was Blacklisted," *The New York Times*, August 21, 1966.

8. Greg Olds' interview with Faulk, Center for American History, University of Texas at Austin; interview with Anne McAfee.

9. George Norris Green, *The Establishment in Texas Politics: The Primitive Years, 1938–1957* (Westport, CT: Greenwood Press, 1979).

10. J. Frank Dobie letters, August 14, 1946, Harry Ransom Humanities Research Center.

11. Chandler Davidson, *Race and Class in Texas Politics* (Princeton, NJ: Princeton University Press, 1990).

12. The *Daily Texan*, April 4, 1946.

13. Steven Carr wrote in his 1993 doctoral thesis on "Communism and the Jewish Conspiracy, 1880–1940," presented at the University of Texas at Austin, Department of Radio-TV Film, that the political environment arising from the Smith Act "both legitimized accusations of Jewish control, and offered any overt signs of anti-Semitism through its monomaniacal anti-communism."

14. J. Edgar Hoover, *Masters of Deceit: The Story of Communism in America and How to Fight It* (New York: Henry Holt & Co., 1958).

15. *The New York Times*, August 30, 1950.

16. For a detailed look at how "McCarthy had maneuvered the media into utter concentration on him and the issues he raised," read Edwin R. Bailey's book, *Joe McCarthy and the Press* (University of Wisconsin Press, 1981).

17. *The Movie: The Illustrated History of the Cinema*, no. 38 (London: Orbis Publishing Ltd., 1980).

18. David Caute, *The Great Fear* (New York: Simon and Schuster, 1978).

19. A. M Sperber (interview), *Murrow, His Life and Times* (New York: Freundlich Books, 1986).

20. Richard M. Fried, *Nightmare in Red: The McCarthy Era in Perspective* (Oxford University Press, 1990).

21. Roy Bedichek letters, November 7, 1952, Center for American History.

22. John Williams, "J. Frank Dobie," *Lower Colorado River Review*, Third Quarter, 1979.

23. Roy Bedichek letters, March 20, 1948, Center for American History.

24. Norman D. Markowitz, *The Rise and Fall of the People's Century* (New York: The Free Press, 1973).

25. J. Frank Dobie letters, December 5, 1949, Harry Ransom Humanities Research Center.

26. *Ibid.,* January 6, 1950.
27. Roy Bedichek letters, May 15, 1950, Center for American History.
28. *Ibid.,* October 30, 1950.
29. *Ibid.,* February 13, 1948.
30. *Ibid.,* June 25, 1951.
31. *Ibid.,* May 19, 1951.
32. Interview, J. Frank Dobie, June 26–July 3, 1963, Austin History Center.
33. Glen L. Evans, "Free of Both Hate and Fear" in *Three Men in Texas,* Ronnie Dugger, ed. (Austin: University of Texas Press, 1967).
34. J. Frank Dobie letters, January 8, 1954, Harry Ransom Humanities Research Center.
35. Roy Bedichek letters, February 26, 1951, Center for American History.

Chapter 8: CBS Personality

1. Roy Bedichek letters, November 21, 1951, Center for American History, University of Texas at Austin.
2. *Ibid.,* May 19, 1951.
3. *Ibid.,* April 22, 1951.
4. *Texas Observer,* May 5, 1990.
5. Interview, Studs Terkel, March 27, 1990.
6. John Henry Faulk Tribute, Paramount Theater, July 1989.
7. J. Frank Dobie letters, January 13, 1952, Harry Ransom Humanities Research Center, University of Texas at Austin.
8. Louis Nizer, *The Jury Returns* (Garden City, NY: Doubleday & Co., 1966).
9. Roy Bedichek letters, June 25, 1951, Center for American History.
10. John Henry Faulk, "Whatever's The Matter With America, Mr. Dobie Ain't," *The Texas Observer,* July 24, 1964.
11. J. Frank Dobie letters, January 8, 1954, Harry Ransom Humanities Research Center.
12. *Ibid.,* April 30, 1955.
13. John Henry Faulk interview, *UTmost* magazine, fall 1982.
14. *The Daily Texan,* April 25, 1979.
15. John Henry Faulk interview, *UTmost* magazine, fall 1982.
16. American Cancer Society video, "John Henry on Wellness and Aging," Austin 1985; J. Frank Dobie letters, September 24, 1955, Harry Ransom Humanities Research Center.
17. Interview, Evelyn Faulk, April 4, 1990.
18. Interview, Frank Dobie Faulk, April 4, 1990.
19. Louis Nizer, *The Jury Returns* (Garden City, NY: Doubleday & Co., 1966).

Chapter 9: Blacklisting: Conform or Else!

1. Robert Griffith, *The Specter: Original Essays on the Cold War and the Origins of McCarthyism* (Franklin Watts, Inc., 1974).
2. Larry Ceplair and Steven Englund, *The Inquisition in Hollywood: Politics in the Film Community 1930–1960* (University of California Press, 1979).

3. David Halberstam, *The Powers That Be* (New York: Alfred A. Knopf, 1979).

4. Fred Friendly, *Due to Circumstances Beyond Our Control* (New York: Vintage Books [Random House], 1967.

5. Mark Goodson, "If I'd Stood Up Earlier . . . ," *New York Times Magazine,* January 13, 1991.

6. Interview, Madeline Lee Gilford, March 1993.

7. David Caute, *The Great Fear* (New York: Simon and Schuster, 1978).

8. Lillian Hellman, *Scoundrel Time* (Bantam Books, 1976).

9. Larry Ceplair and Steven Englund, *The Inquisition in Hollywood: Politics in the Film Community, 1930–1960.*

10. *The Nation,* May 1957.

11. John Henry Faulk, Foreword in *The Red Scare,* by Don Carleton (Austin: Texas Monthly Press, 1985).

12. *Variety,* August 9, 1955.

13. *The New York Times,* August 22, 1951.

14. Karen Sue Foley, *The Political Blacklist in the Broadcast Industry: The Decade of the 1950s* (New York: Arno Press, A New York Times Co., 1979).

15. *John Henry Faulk vs. Aware, Inc.,* et. al, New York Supreme Court, April 1962 trial.

16. Louis Nizer, *The Jury Returns* (Garden City, NY: Doubleday Co., 1966).

17. *The Daily Texan,* September 30, 1971.

18. I. F. Stone, *The Haunted Fifties* (Little, Brown & Co., 1963).

19. Leif Erickson, "A Time for Honesty," *Spotlight: Facts for Fighting Communism,* vol. II, no. 12, August 1955 (Syracuse, NY).

20. Interview, Lee Grant, April 1993.

21. *John Henry Faulk vs. Aware, Inc.,* New York Supreme Court, 1962.

22. Interview, Madeline Lee Gilford, March 1993.

23. Interview, Lee Grant, April 1993.

24. *The Nation,* August 20, 1955.

25. A. M. Sperber (interview), *Murrow, His Life and Times* (New York: Freundlich Books, 1986).

26. "John Henry's crime was in *knowing* communists like me and others of my ilk," said Pete Seeger, who was a brief Party member in the 1940s but rarely attended meetings. "John Henry didn't care what we belonged to, he liked our music." (Interview, Pete Seeger, 1993.)

27. Kate Mostel and Madeline Gilford with Jack Gilford and Zero Mostel, *170 Years of Show Business* (New York: Random House, 1978).

28. Interview, Madeline Lee Gilford, March 1993.

29. Hearings before the Committee on Un-American Activities, House of Representatives, 84th Congress, First Session (Washington, DC: U.S. Government Printing Office, 1955).

30. Walter Goodman, *The Committee* (New York: Farrar, Strauss and Giroux, 1968).

31. Orson Bean, *Too Much Is Not Enough* (Secaucus, NJ: Lyle Stuart, Inc., 1988).

32. *Newsday,* November 21, 1955.

Chapter 10: Aware's Assault

1. John Henry Faulk, *Fear on Trial* (Austin: University of Texas Press, 1983).

2. Letter from Veterans Action Committee of Syracuse Supermarkets to merchandisers, March 7, 1952; *John Henry Faulk vs. Aware, Inc.*, New York Supreme Court, 1962.

3. David Caute, *The Great Fear: The Anti-Communist Purge Under Truman and Eisenhower* (New York: Simon and Schuster, 1978).

4. Interview, Madeline Lee Gilford, March 1993.

5. The People's Songs was claimed to have been "filled with Communists" by some HUAC congressmen. In August 1955, Pete Seeger was questioned extensively about the political nature of the group's songs by the 84th Congress.

6. In the *Faulk vs. Aware* lawsuit, a judge dismissed the designations of "communist front" groups, ruling that the House Committee's citations were not, in a legal sense, "official designations."

7. Wilson M. Hudson, "Love of Life and Freedom," *Three Men in Texas: Bedichek/Webb/Dobie* (Austin: University of Texas Press, 1975).

8. Interview, John Henry Faulk, 1989.

9. Thomas Murray testimony, *John Henry Faulk vs. Aware*, Vincent Hartnett and Laurence Johnson, New York Supreme Court, May 1962.

10. Stefan Kanfer, *A Journal of the Plague Years* (New York: Atheneum, 1973).

11. Louis Nizer, *The Jury Returns* (Garden City, NY: Doubleday, 1966).

12. John Henry Faulk, *Fear on Trial.*

13. *Ibid.*

14. Interview, Madeline Lee Gilford, March 1993.

15. J. Frank Dobie letters, Harry Ransom Humanities Research Center, and Roy Bedichek letters, May 30, 1956, Center for American History, University of Texas at Austin.

16. Roy Bedichek letters, June 23, 1956, Center for American History.

17. John Henry Faulk, *Fear on Trial.*

18. A. M. Sperber (interview), *Murrow, His Life and Times* (New York: Freundlich Books, 1986).

19. Louis Nizer summation in *John Henry Faulk vs. Aware*, June 27, 1962, trial in New York Supreme Court.

20. Interview, Frank Dobie Faulk, April 4, 1990.

Chapter 11: The Public Pariah

1. Roy Bedichek letters, September 6, 1957, Center for American History, The University of Texas at Austin.

2. Faulk interview with Bill Moyers, Public Broadcasting System, aired on August 1, 1990.

3. J. Frank Dobie letters, August 1, 1956, Harry Ransom Humanities Research Center, The University of Texas at Austin.

4. John Henry Faulk remembering Bedichek in *The Texas Observer*, June 27, 1959.

5. *Ibid.*

6. Roy Bedichek letters, Center for American History, and J. Frank Dobie letters, February 13, 1958, Harry Ransom Humanities Research Center.

7. Louis Nizer, *The Jury Returns* (Garden City, NY: Doubleday & Co., 1966).

8. *Ibid.*

9. J. Frank Dobie and Roy Bedichek letters, July 8, 1958, Harry Ransom Humanities Research Center and Center for American History.

10. *Ibid.*, June 11, 1958.

11. *Ibid.*, August 26, 1958.

12. *LOOK* magazine, May 7, 1963.

13. John Henry Faulk, *Fear on Trial* (New York: Simon & Schuster, 1963).

14. Interview, Alan Lomax, July 1990.

15. J. Frank Dobie and Roy Bedichek letters, May 15, 1958, Harry Ransom Humanities Research Center and Center for American History.

16. Roy Bedichek letters, June 2, 1958, Center for American History.

17. *LOOK* magazine, May 7, 1963.

18. John Henry Faulk interviewed on "Alternative Views," Alternative Information Network, Austin Access Television, January 7, 1978.

19. Interview, Paul Martinson, July 1990.

20. The House Un-American Activities Committee renamed itself the Internal Securities Committee in 1967, and finally, mercifully, ceased to exist in 1970, after thirty-one years.

21. Harry Stein, "The Ballad of John Henry," *New Times* magazine, fall 1975.

22. Interview, John Henry Faulk, December 1989.

23. J. Frank Dobie letters, January 9, 1957, Harry Ransom Humanities Research Center.

24. *Austin American-Statesman*, December 13, 1964.

25. *The New York Times*, November 22, 1964.

26. Cactus Pryor, "He Called Me Puddin," *Texas Monthly*, March 1992.

27. John Henry Faulk letter to David Halberstam, September 5, 1975, Center for American History.

28. John Henry Faulk, *The Dallas Times-Herald*, February 11, 1990.

29. This particular version of the chicken snake story is taken from an interview with Bill Moyers on PBS Television August 1, 1990, entitled: "The Man Who Beat the Blacklist."

30. John Hohenberg, *Free Press, Free People, The Free Press* (New York: Collier-Macmillan Publishers, 1973).

Chapter 12: John Henry's Legacy

1. John Henry Faulk, "To Secure the Blessings of Liberty," lecture, the National Convention of Professional Journalists, 1980.

Afterword

1. For a chilling account of the FBI and CIA espionage campaign of American writers, read *Dangerous Dossiers, Exposing the Secret War Against America's Greatest Authors,* by Herbert Mitgang (Donald I. Fine, Inc., 1988).

2. *Newsday,* September 27, 1989.

3. *Ibid.*

4. Michael McWilliams, *Playboy,* December 1989.

5. The *Washington Post,* November 12, 1992.

6. The *Washington Spectator,* The Public Concern Foundation, September 1, 1990.

7. John Henry Faulk performance at Esther's Follies 12th Anniversary Show, Paramount Theatre, October 14, 1989.

Bibliography

Bibliographic Notes

The author is grateful to the Faulk family for interviews that provided the background and history of life in early twentieth-century Austin. John Henry Faulk also graciously gave much of his time during the period that he was courageously fighting cancer. His widow, Liz, also gave support during this difficult time.

Chapters 1, 2 and 3:
John Henry's niece, Anne McAfee, was particularly helpful in giving valuable information about the Faulk and Tannehill genealogy. For these three chapters, most of my research came from personal interviews with John Henry Faulk and his sisters, Martha, Mary and Texana; and John Henry's schoolmates, Jack Kellam, Bob Eckhardt, Lester Kitchens, Creekmore Fath, and others. Interviews with his brother Hamilton Faulk and attorney Emmett Shelton also aided my research into the political atmosphere of the period, particularly with the Standard Oil case and Eugene V. Debs' speeches. Travis County Attorney Ken Oden helped in researching two of Henry Faulk's law cases.

Chapters 4 and 5:
Information on J. Frank Dobie was culled from several different sources. The Austin History Center's biographical files on Faulk and Dobie proved very helpful, particularly in regards to actual interviews with Dobie. Lon Tinkle's book, *An American Original: The Life of J. Frank Dobie*, published by The University of Texas Press in 1978, was an excellent reference source. The nucleus for John Henry's relationship with Dobie, however, resides in interviews with John Henry and the letters he wrote to him. These letters are housed at the Harry Ransom Humanities Research Center at the University of Texas at Austin.

Chapters 6, 7 and 8:
The bulk of my research for this book comes from the *John Henry Faulk Papers, 1881 –, 1936–1990*, at the Center for American History

(formerly the Eugene Barker Texas History Center) at the University of Texas at Austin.

In 1982, John Henry began donating some of his papers to the Center. By the time of his death in April 1990, the center had accumulated sixty linear feet of material in the John Henry Faulk Papers. The collection includes Faulk's correspondence, literary productions, lectures, transcripts, notes, diaries, journals, news clippings, interviews, photographs, and sound recordings.

In addition to the Faulk Papers, Faulk's letters to Dobie and Bedichek were very useful. The Roy Bedichek Papers collection is housed at the Center for American History.

Chapters 9, 10 and 11:

Much of the research for these chapters is derived from the *John Henry Faulk vs. Aware Inc., Laurence A. Johnson, and Vincent Hartnett* case records, donated in 1982 to the Center for American History by the law firm of Phillips, Nizer, Benjamin, Krim and Balloon. Personal interviews with blacklisted artists Madeline Gilford, Lee Grant, and Pete Seeger were also extremely helpful for these chapters.

Books on the Blacklisting Period:

Reading material on the blacklist is scarcely found in public libraries and bookstores. Nearly all of the books adequately covering the history of the blacklist in the entertainment field are out of print, which leaves one to research material at the university libraries. The University of Texas libraries have a good selection of reading material (most of which are listed in the bibliography), particularly the Perry-Castenada Library and the Law Library.

The best published works on the period are also the hardest to find. John Cogley, together with Michael Harrington, produced an incisive, investigative *Report on Blacklisting* in 1956. The two-volume report, funded by the Ford Foundation's Fund for the Republic, led in part to the decline of the blacklister. Unfortunately, much of the information comes from anonymous sources because of the fear of reprisals the entertainers had. (Cogley was called before the House Un-American Activities Committee a few days after publication of his work in 1957 and refused to reveal his notes.)

John M. Pope, reporter for the *New Orleans Times-Picayune*, developed a fine master's thesis in 1972 for the University of Texas at Austin, "Trial Without Jury: A Study of Blacklisting," which is available at PCL Reserves. Another thesis, *The Political Blacklist in the Entertainment Industry*, by Karen Sue Foley for Ohio State University, was published by Arno Press in 1979. It contains much information about Aware and blacklisted artists.

One of the most comprehensive works on the blacklist is David Caute's *Great Fear*, which details the methods of Hartnett, Johnson, and their ilk. Also worth mentioning is Robert Vaughn's *Only Victims*, a study of the blacklist in the entertainment industry. The most comprehensive work on the House Un-American Activities Committee (and its various names) is *The Committee*, by Walter Goodman, first published in 1964. Although Goodman traps himself in labeling progressive organizations "communist fronts," and partially justifies the investigation of innocent victims, his book is a good source of the history of the committee and its investigations.

John Henry's own book, *Fear on Trial*, first published in 1963, poignantly and dramatically illustrates the atmosphere of the period and how he dealt with his blacklisting. Yet the trial itself is more thoroughly revealed in Louis Nizer's 1966 book, *The Jury Returns*.

BOOKS

Chapters 1 and 2:
Barkley, Mary Starr. *The History of Travis County and Austin, 1839–1899.* Waco: Texian Press, 1963.
Bringhurst, Bruce. *The Antitrust and The Oil Monopoly, The Standard Oil Cases, 1890–1911.* Westport, CT: Greenwood Press, 1979.
Salvatore, Nick. *Eugene V. Debs: Citizen and Socialist.* Chicago, IL: University of Illinois Press, 1982.
Weems, John Edward. "Austin: 1889–1989," *Austin American-Statesman,* April 16, 1989.
Willoughby, Larry. *Austin: A Historical Portrait.* Norfolk, VA: The Donning Company/Publishers, 1981.

Chapter 3:
Faulk, John Henry. *The Uncensored John Henry Faulk.* Austin, TX: Texas Monthly Press, 1985.
Kellam, Jack. *Johnny 'n Me.* Thumbnose Press, 1985.
Orum, Anthony M. *Power, Money and the People, The Making of Modern Austin.* Austin: Texas Monthly Press, 1987.

Chapters 4 and 5:
Dos Passos, John. *U.S.A.* New York: Modern Library, 1937.
Goodwyn, Lawrence. *The Populist Movement in America.* Oxford: Oxford University Press, 1976.
Manchester, William. *The Glory and the Dream, A Narrative History of America.* New York: Bantam Books, 1990.
Meltzer, Milton. *Brother, Can You Spare a Dime? The Great Depression.* Paddington Press, 1976.

Rodnitzky, Jerome L., Frank Ross Peterson, Kenneth R. Philp, and John A. Garraty. *Essays on Radicalism in Contemporary America.* The Walter Prescott Webb Memorial Lectures. University of Texas Press at Arlington, 1972.

Tinkle, Lon. *An American Original: The Life of J. Frank Dobie.* Austin: University of Texas Press, 1978.

Chapters 6 and 7:

Davidson, Chandler. *Race and Class in Texas Politics.* New Jersey: Princeton University Press, 1990.

Dugger, Ronnie, ed. *Three Men in Texas.* Austin: University of Texas Press, 1967.

Green, George Norris. *The Establishment in Texas Politics, The Primitive Years, 1938-1957.* Westport, CT: Greenwood Press, 1979.

Griffith, Robert. *The Specter: Original Essays on the Cold War and the Origins of McCarthyism.* New York: New Viewpoints, 1974.

Klein, Joe. *Woody Guthrie, A Life.* New York: Ballantine Books, 1980.

Owens, William A. *Three Friends: Dobie, Bedichek, Webb.* Austin: University of Texas Press, 1967.

Owens, William A., and Lyman Grant, ed. *Letters of Roy Bedichek.* Austin: University of Texas Press, 1985.

Chapter 8:

American Business Consultants. *Red Channels: The Report of Communist Influence in Radio and Television.* New York: 1950.

Carleton, Don. *Red Scare!* Austin: Texas Monthly Press, 1985.

Caute, David. *The Great Fear.* New York: Simon and Schuster, 1978.

Ceplair, Larry, and Steven England. *The Inquisition in Hollywood: Politics in the Film Community, 1930-1960.* Berkeley and Los Angeles: University of California Press, 1983.

Cogley, John. *Report on Blacklisting.* Arno Press and the New York Times, 1971. (Originally published by the Fund for the Republic, New York, 1956.)

Durr, Virginia. *Outside the Magic Circle.* University, AL: University of Alabama Press, 1985.

Hellman, Lillian. *Scoundrel Time.* Boston: Little Brown, 1976.

Hoover, J. Edgar. *Masters of Deceit: The Story of Communism in America.* New York: Henry Holt and Co., 1958.

Markowitz, Norman D. *The Rise and Fall of the People's Century, Henry A. Wallace and American Liberalism, 1941-1948.* New York: The Free Press, 1973.

O'Reilly, Kenneth. *Hoover and the Un-Americans: The FBI, HUAC, and the Red Menace.* Philadelphia: Temple University Press, 1983.

Stone, I. F. *The Haunted Fifties, 1953-1963.* Boston: Little, Brown & Co., 1989.

Persico, Joseph E. *Edward R. Murrow: An American Original.* New York: McGraw-Hill Publishing Co., 1988.

Chapter 9:
Bean, Orson. *Too Much is Not Enough.* Secaucus, NJ: Lyle Stuart, Inc., 1988.
Cook, Fred J. *The Nightmare Decade.* New York: Random House, 1971.
Foley, Karen Sue. *The Political Blacklist in the Broadcast Industry.* New York: Arno Press, 1979.
Fried, Richard M. *Nightmare Red: The McCarthy Era in Perspective.* New York/Oxford: Oxford University Press, 1990.
Griffith, Robert. *The Politics of Fear.* 2nd ed. Boston: University of Massachusetts Press, 1987.
Hentoff, Nat. *The First Freedom.* New York: Delacorte Press, 1980.
Kanfer, Stefan. *A Journal of the Plague Years.* New York: Atheneum Publishers, 1973.
Navasky, Victor. *Naming Names.* New York: Viking Press, 1980.
Vaughn, Robert. *Only Victims: The Study of Show Business Blacklisting.* New York: Putnam, 1972.

Chapter 10:
Faulk, John Henry. *Fear on Trial.* Austin: University of Texas Press, 1983.
Nizer, Louis. *The Jury Returns.* Garden City, NY: Doubleday, 1966.

Afterword:
Beck, Melvin. *Secret Contenders: The Myth of Cold War Counterintelligence.* New York: Sheriden Square Press, 1984.
Churchill, Ward, and Jim Vander Wall. *COINTELPRO Papers: Documents from the FBI's Secret Wars Against Dissent in the United States.* Boston: South End Press, 1988.
Demac, Donna A. *Liberty Denied: The Current Rise of Censorship in America.* New York: PEN American Center, 1988.
Levin, Murray B. *Political Hysteria in America – the Democratic Capacity for Repression.* New York: Basic Books, 1971.
Linfield, Michael. *Freedom Under Fire: Civil Liberties in Times of War.* Boston: South End Press, 1988.
Morgan, Richard E. *Domestic Intelligence: Monitoring Dissent in America.* Austin: University of Texas Press, 1980.
Wise, David. *The American Police State.* New York: Random House, 1976.

Index

A

ABC, 106, 180
abortion, 179, 182
Abraham Lincoln Brigade, 122
Abzug, Bella, 129
Ace, Goodman, 105
Actors Equity, 124, 126, 129
actors' union, 112, 115, 121–132 (see also AFTRA)
Adams, Andy, 43
  Joey, 105
Adler, Larry, 119
Adventures of Huckleberry Finn, The, 21, 181
AIDS, 173
Alcalde, 43
Aldrich Family, 86
Allbritton, Louise, 131
Allen, Mrs., 25
  Steve, viii
All the Way Home, 166
All You Need Is One Good Break, 145
Almanacs, 81
American Association of University Professors, 75, 76
American Bar Association, 143
American Business Consultants, 114–115, 116, 119
American Civil Liberties Union, xv–xvi, 119, 179
American Committee for Democracy and Intellectual Freedom, 67
American Continental Congress, 136, 143

American Family Association, 181
American Federation of Radio Artists (AFRA), 87
American Federation of Television and Radio Artists (AFTRA), 87, 115, 121–132, 138, 144, 145, 146–147, 148, 180
American Historical Association, 48
American League Against War and Fascism, 67
American League for Peace and Democracy, 67
American Legion, 112, 115, 116, 126, 133, 139–141
American Legion Commission on Americanism, 112
American Legion Magazine, 117
American Railway Union, 7
American Red Cross, 69–70, 71, 181
American Socialist Party, 6, 48
American Tobacco Company, 140
American Youth Congress, 67
Amnesty International, 180
Amsterdam News, 142
Angola State Prison Farm, 47
Anti-Nazi League, 67
anti-trust law, 3-4, 6
Appeal to Reason, The, 6
Appell, Donald T., 127–128
Arens, ——, 157
Arthur Godfrey and His Friends, 134
Arts and Sciences Committee for the Re-election of Franklin D. Roosevelt, 114
Associated Food Stores, Inc., 141

207

Association of Catholic Trade
Unionists, 126
Atlanta, Georgia, 179
Attorney General's List, The, 85–86
Aunt Edith, 78, 95, 101, 102
Aunt Effie McDoo, 92, 102
Aunt Niney, 38-39, 95
Austin American, 5
Austin City Council, xvii
Austin City Planning Commission,
xv–xvii
Austin Daily Statesman, 5
Austin Daily Tribune, 5
Austin On the Go, 160
Austin High, 32, 34, 36, 53
Austin Maroon, 33
Austin State Hospital, 53
Austin, Texas, 2, 15, 34, 73, 107, 159
Autry, Gene, 95
Auxiliary Air Force, 66
AWARE, Inc.: and AFTRA, 121–
132, 144-145, 146-147; and
"Bulletin #16," 135–137, 138;
defines blacklisting, 135; denies
use of blacklisting, 135; estab-
lished, 115; fees charged by,
116, 117–118; Laurence Johnson's cooperation with, 133–135,
138; manual of self-clearance,
115; media involvement with,
112, 165, 167; mission of, 115;
New York Police Department
cooperation with, 141; opposition to, 123–127, 131–132; sued
by Faulk, 141-144, 147, 154-156,
160-164

B
Bailey, Joe, 4, 5
Balsam, Martin, 123
Banks, Calvin, 173
Barrett, Leslie, 122–123, 126, 138
Barton Creek, 92, 152
Barton Springs, 34, 37–38
Bates, Snooky, 13, 17–18
Bath, England, 66
Batten, Barton, Durstine and
Osborn, 114
Batts family, 17

BBC Radio, 158
Bean, Orson, 129, 130–131, 136,
138, 144, 145, 146
Beckett, Aunt Mary, 19–20, 23, 102
Aunt Ollie, 19–20, 23, 102
Dave, 68
Grandma, 19–20, 23, 68
Beckett family, 19-20, 38, 39
Bedichek, Roy, ix, 48–49, 54, 60, 62,
75, 79, 89, 90, 93, 94, 96–97,
146, 152–153, 158
Bell, Charles, 4
Bellville, Texas, 52, 58, 59
Benford, Mary, 13
Berger, ——, 163
Bernstein, Walter, 120
Best Man, The, 166
Bexar County, Texas, 51, 56
Biffle, Leslie, 110
Biles family, 17
Billboard magazine, 100
Billings, Josh, 88
Bill of Rights, 87, 123, 172, 174, 175
Birth of a Nation, 7
Black, Charlie, 47
Hugo, 63
blacklisting: advertising agencies'
use of, 113–114, 140, 141, 144,
161, 163; artists' fight against,
119, 131–132, 135, 138;
Attorney General's List used as
tool for, 85–86; in broadcasting,
111; CBS' use of, 113; challenged in state supreme court
for first time, 160; defense
against, 115–116, 118, 131;
defined by AWARE, 135; of
entertainers, 86, 111–132, 134,
164; as exists today, 178–183;
exposed in Faulk trial, 163–164;
informants in, 116, 122, 137;
media involvement in, 118–119,
126, 165, 167; motion picture
studios' use of, 117, 119; organizations which provided, 114,
116; publications used as ve-
hicle for, 114–115, 123, 135;
sponsors' effect on, 113, 133–

134, 138, 139–141; working of, 115–116, 119–120, 166
Boatright, Mody, 48, 54, 62, 96–97
Bolan, Thomas, 160
Bolshevik Revolution, 6
books, banned, 88
Boring, Brother Will, 173
    Marvin, 31–32
Bozell, Brent, 180
Brady, John, 5
Brazos River Bottom, 55, 58, 61
Brigham Young University, 179
Brock, Henry, 8–10
Brodie, John, 20–21, 35, 40–41, 43, 44
    Marie, 21
    Mrs., 20, 25
Brodies, 92
Brooks, Mel, 130
Brown, Herman, 71
Brownwood, Texas, 1
bubblegum cards, 86–87
Buffalo Hunters, The, 109
Buford, Reverend Sam, 59
"Bulletin #12," 123
"Bulletin #16," 135–137
Burnet, Jack, 30
Burnet, Texas, 45
Burns, Stan, 138
Burrows, Abe, 104
Bush, George, 179

C
Cafe Society Downtown, 135
Cain, Lieutenant Thomas, 141
Cairo, Egypt, 69
Calhoun, George C., 3
Calhoun Debate Club, 33
Calvert, Texas, 59
Cambridge University, 71
Camel Cigarettes, 106
Cameron, Angus, 165
Cameron, Texas, 59
Camp Barkley, 72
Campbell, Wendell, 153
Camp Swift, 72, 76
Campus War Council, 66
Canebrake, Texas, 47
Canion, Raymond, 73-74

Captain Kangaroo, 106
Carney, Art, 142
Carrington, Mollie, 8-9
Case, Nelson, 143-147
Catcher in the Rye, 181
Catholic University, 179
Catholic War Veterans, 133
CBS, 113–114
CBS News, 118
CBS Radio, 78–80, 82, 87, 100, 108, 147, 148
CBS TV, 104, 105, 106, 134, 144
censorship, 165, 168, 181–182
Central Feed & Seed Store, 73
Ceplair, Larry, 117
Chambers, Whittaker, 111
Chase, Chevy, 109
Cherry Springs Ranch, 48, 96
Chiang Kai-shek, 99
China Lobby, 114
Christian Coalition, 180
Chum's Feed Store, 30
CIA, 178
Cincinnati Club, 93
Citizens Against Pornography, xv–xvi
Civilian Conservation Corps, 51
civil rights, 63, 82–83, 90, 109, 112, 114, 164
Civil Rights Congress, 116
Civil War, 61
Clark, Jim, 92
Clay-Pierce, Henry, 5
"clearing agents," 117
Clinton, Bill, 179, 181, 182
Clio, Alabama, 1
Club 65, 135, 142, 143
Cohn, Roy, 88, 108, 154-155
COINTELPRO, 178
Colby's, 151
Cold War, 89
Coleman, Texas, 1
Colgate-Palmolive, 133
Colliers, 42
Collingwood, Charles, 106, 127, 131, 136, 146–147, 148
Collyer, Clayton, 128
Colquitt, Oscar, 10

Columbia Lecture Bureau, 91
Columbia Pictures, 167
Columbia Radio Network, 60
Columbia University, 42
Comet, The, 33
Committee on Freedom to Write
    and Read, 165
Committee for the Negro in Arts,
    129
communism: changes in perspective
    about, 164; individuals allegedly
    connected with, 84–86, 88, 114,
    120, 123, 129–130, 132, 140–
    141, 144-145; organizations al-
    legedly connected with, 86, 114,
    116–117, 129, 137; "propagan-
    da" of, 87; U.S. Government
    warnings about, 84, 85, 112,
    117, 168; U.S. Government
    actions against "sympathizers"
    of, 84-86, 87 (*also see* House Un-
    American Activities Commit-
    tee)
"communist-front" associations, 86,
    112, 114, 116–117, 125, 127,
    135–136, 137
Congress of American Women, 117
Conn, Texana Faulk, 15, 22, 26, 27,
    29, 31, 73, 157 (*see also* Faulk,
    Texana)
consumer's union, 114
Cook, Louis, 159
Cooper, Boots, 13, 19, 169
Coronado's Children, 42
Counterattack, 114–115, 121
Cousin Florence, 36
Cousin Teck, 36
Cronkite, Walter, 101, 105, 159, 174
Crosby, John, 125-126
Culpepper, Reverend, xvii
Curran, Rev. Charles E., 179

D
Daily Texan, The, 78
Daily Worker, 117, 135, 136, 137, 161
Dallas family, 17
Daly, John, 105, 159
"Daniel Boone and the Colonel,"
    106

Daughters of the Revolution, 139
Davis, Elmer, 169
    Ossie, 106, 120
day-care centers, 90
Debs, Eugene, 6–7, 82
Dee, Ruby, viii, 120, 123
"Deep in the Heart," 172
Democratic Party, 87–88, 100–101
Devane, William, 167
Diamond Salt, 140
Dickens, Charles, 33, 103
Dickler, Gerald, 108, 143, 144, 149,
    157
Dies, Martin, 67–68, 145
Dies Committee, 67–68, 74, 114
Distributive Workers, 135
Dixon, Thomas, 7
Dobie, J. Frank, ix, 41–45, 48, 49,
    54–55, 56, 59, 60, 62, 66, 68,
    71, 76–77, 79, 80, 82, 83,
    88–89, 92, 96–97, 106–107,
    111, 132, 137, 146, 158, 165,
    168
    Mrs., 71
    Red, 43
Dooley, Mr., 88
Dos Passos, John, 75
Dove, Mary Elizabeth, 52
Downs, Janie Miner, 4
    Oscar, 4
Draper, Paul, 119
    Ruth, 103
Dukakis, Michael, 179
Dulles, 99, 157
Dungey, John, 126, 141
Durr, Virginia Foster, ix, 63

E
Eckhardt, Bob, 8, 32–33, 46, 47
Ed Sullivan Show, 144
Edwards, Douglas, 105
Eisenhower, Dwight D., 87
Eleanor Roosevelt Freedom of
    Speech Award, 174
Emergency Civil Liberties Commit-
    tee, 136
Emergency Peace Council, 47
Emerson, Faye, 125, 131
    Ralph Waldo, 16, 28, 93

Engelking, Bob, 47
Englund, Steven, 117
entertainers, blacklisting of *(see blacklisting)*
equal rights amendment, 181
Erickson, Leif, 122
Evans, Glen, 96–97
Exxon Corporation, 6, 180

F

Fabulous Baker Boys, 33
faculty tenure, 75
Fahrenheit 451, 181
Fairbanks, Douglas, 34
Fair Labor Standards Act, 74
family values, 179
Farm Security Administration, 47
fascism, 48–49, 63, 67, 70, 76
Fath, Creekmore, 33, 36
Faulk, Cynthia Tannehill, 82
    Elizabeth (Liz), 167
    Evelyn, 98
    Frank Dobie, 106, 109, 149
    Hally, 80, 81, 82, 89, 136 *(see also Wood, Hally)*
    Hamilton, 12, 14, 19, 25, 31–32, 53
Faulk, Henry: birth of, 1; death of, 53; described, 1–2, 27–28; education of, 2; on education, 103; marries Mattie, 4; as newspaper publisher, 5; political philosophy of, 6–7, 8, 9, 95–96; religion of, 15–16, 27; runs for public office, 7; supports racial equality, 8, 16, 27; as Travis County attorney, 3–4; as trial lawyer, 5–6, 9–10, 26
    Henry Lafayette, 1
    J. J., 2
    James Monroe, 13
Faulk, John Henry: as actor, 166–167, 172, 173, 174; affidavit signed by, 138–139; in American Red Cross, 69–70; and bird-watching, 94, 97; birth of, 10; on blacklisting, 111, 120, 131, 147, 158, 168–169; blacklisting of, 132, 135–149, 151, 158;

book written by, 166; boyhood of, 16–32, 152; boyhood home of, 13–14, 90; in California, 50; characters created by, 91–92, 95–96, 101, 102, 158–159, 172–174; children of, 82, 91, 93, 98, 106, 109–110, 149, 160, 167; in college, 40–55; on communism, 89, 177–178; death of, 174; defends First Amendment, xvi–xix, 28, 163, 171–172, 174–175, 183; described, 35, 100, 101–104, 105, 141, 161; fights AWARE, 137–149, 153–157, 159–164; fired by CBS, 149, 150–151; first job, 37; as folklorist, 42–45, 56–61, 70; honors/awards of, 139, 174; on hypocrisy, 18, 21–22, 63, 68, 69, 107; illness of, 109, 172; as instructor at U.T., 60–64; investigated by HUAC, 127–128, 155–157; marries Hally, 60 / Lynne, 84 / Liz, 167; master's thesis of, 52, 56–59; on McCarthy, 88, 93, 100, 111, 145; on the media, 118; in Merchant Marines, 64, 65–68; and Middle-of-the-Road slate, 131–132, 137–138, 143–147; as Pat the Rancher, 91; play written by, 159, 172–174; and politics, 67, 70–71, 82–84, 89–91, 93, 100–101, 108, 148, 164; and racial equality, 36–37, 46–47, 61–64, 69, 73, 83, 102, 109, 141, 181; radio career of, 78–82, 91–110, 148, 150–151, 153, 157–158, 159, 166–167; relationship with Dobie, Bedichek, Webb, 41–45, 48, 54, 96–97, 152, 165–166; relationship with father, 27–28, 33–34, 37, 50; sexual education of, 17–18, 35; as speaker, 33, 91, 110, 167–168; as storyteller, 20, 29, 33, 36, 54, 67, 72, 78, 92, 100, 103–104, 110, 131, 167; studies black religion/folklore, 26, 43–

44, 52–53, 55, 56–59, 61; television career of, 93, 98, 104–106, 110, 153, 157, 161, 166–167; on Texas, 151–152, 174; unemployment of, 153, 157–158, 159–160, 164; in U.S. Army, 71–73, 74; use of humor as a defense, 25–26, 29–30, 32–33, 36, 60, 78–79, 103, 109; as vice-president, Texas Broadcasting, 107–108; voice/accent of, 79, 95, 100, 102, 103; on women's issues, 101; with WPA, 51–52; as writer, 33, 45–46, 47, 49–50, 52, 58, 78-79, 109, 158–159
Johanna, 91, 94
Lucy Card, 1
Lynne, 84, 93–94, 95, 98, 109, 131, 147, 149, 159, 162, 167
Martha, 12, 19, 25 *(see also* Stansbury, Martha Faulk)
Faulk, Martha (Mattie): 11, 12, 13, 34, 35, 37, 50, 102–103; death of, 151; described, 4, 14–15; and discipline, 22, 23–26, 31; illness of, 106, 151; proclaimed "First Lady of South Austin," 15; religion of, 15–16; supports racial equality, 73–74; as teacher, 4
Mary, 12, 19, 25 *(see also* Koock, Mary Faulk)
Texana, 12, 19 *(see also* Conn, Texana Faulk)
Yohan, 167
Faulk vs. Aware, Inc., 119, 141–149, 153–157, 159–164
FBI, 85, 108–109, 117, 122, 127, 161, 178–179
Fear on Trial, 166
Fear On Trial (docu-drama), 167
Ferrer, Jose, 116
Fifth Amendment, 116, 128, 129, 164
Finnin, Annie Mae, 26
Fire Island, 129, 130
Firing Line, 112
Firm Foundation, 11

First Amendment, xv–xix, 111, 130, 171–172, 174, 178
"First Amendment Congress," 174
First Methodist Church, 12
Flamingo Dance Troupe, 109
Foch, Nina, 105
folk singers, 47, 80–82, 127–128
Fonda, Henry, 166
Forbis, Mrs., 25
Ford, Colonel Rip, 43
  Henry, 80
Fordham University, 115
Foreman, Clark, 63, 89, 98, 136, 139, 143
  Mairi, 98
Fourth Amendment, 178
Fowler, Barnes, 35
Fox, Matty, 147
Franco, Francisco, 49
Franklin, Reverend Tanner, 58, 79
Fred Allen Memorial Methodist Church, 15, 53
Freedom of Information Act, 108
Freedoms Foundation, 174
freedom of speech, 179, 182–183
Friday Mountain Ranch, 48, 96
Friedland, Eli, 72, 73
Friendly, Fred, 113
Friendly Will Baptist Church, 26
Frost, Robert, 162
Fulmore Elementary School, 21, 30, 31, 94

G
Gammell Bookstore, 11
Garcia, Alicia, 21
  Dr. John, 55
Gartman, Alvie, 43
  Willie, 35
Gartmans, 36
gays in the military, 181
Geer, Will, 135
Geller, Abraham, 119, 166
General Foods, 86
"George Skinner Show, The," 106
Georgetown, Texas, 42
"Gertrude Stein," 173
Gibson, "Hoot," 34
  Jackie, 81

Gilford, Jack, 123, 124, 134, 145, 162
    Madeline Lee, 114, 120, 123, 124, 126–127, 129, 134, 145, 163
Godfrey, Arthur, 150
Golden Girls, 180
Golden Horn, The, 51
Goodson, Mark, 104, 113–114, 120
Goodson-Todman Productions, 104
Goodwill Baptist Church, 26
Gould, Jack, 119, 166
Grace United Methodist Church of Austin, 16
Graham, Frank, 143
Grandpa Bible, 95, 96, 101, 102
Grant, Lee, 120, 122, 123, 126–127, 145, 146, 163
Grapes of Wrath, The, 87
Gray, Harold, 124
"graylist," 113
"Greater Tuna," 79
Green Pastures, 90
Greenpeace, 180
Greenwich Village, 80, 81
Grey Advertising, 139
Griffith, D. W., 7
Grumbles, 21
Guffaw, Congressman, 92, 100-101, 102
Guthrie, Woody, 47, 80, 81, 82, 128
Guy Town, 2, 8, 9, 10

H
Halberstam, David, 113
Hall, John, 180
Hancock Opera House, 6
Harburg, Yip, 106, 120
Hardin, John Wesley, 45
Harly Detective Agency, 117
Harriman, Averell, 108
Hartford, Connecticut, 119
Hartnett, Vincent, 115, 117–118, 119, 122–123, 124, 125–126, 127, 133–134, 135, 138, 139, 140, 141, 142, 145, 147, 154, 155, 161–162, 181
Harvard University, 43
Hayes, Lind, 159
Hays, Hull, 148

Lee, 81, 129, 136
Hayworth, Jean Owens, 121
    Vinton, 115, 121, 124
Head of the Class, 180
Headline Cabaret, 135, 142
Healy, Mary, 159
"Heaven in the Spring," 52
Hee Haw, 167
Heller, George, 134
Hellman, Lillian, 86, 116
Henderson County, Texas, 1
Herndon, Dr. E. W., 11
Herring, Mrs., 23
"Hi-Neighbor," 94
Hiss, Alger, 85, 111
Historical Records Survey, 51
Hitler, Adolf, 49–50, 62, 63, 66, 68, 70
Hoffman Beverage Company, 139
Hogg Memorial Auditorium, 52
Hogg Memorial Coliseum, 165
Hollenbeck, Don, 118
Holliday, Judy, 117, 134
Hollywood Anti-Nazi League, 114
Hollywood Ten, 84, 111, 118
Homer Hammity's Band of Bands, 45
Hoover, J. Edgar, 85, 108–109, 117, 178
Hornsby Bend, 4
Hottelet, Richard, 105
House Un-American Activities Committee (HUAC): changes in types of investigation of, 111–112; "clearinghouse" of, 116; cooperation with AWARE, 116, 123, 127, 135, 155–156, 161; investigates entertainment industry, 112, 127–132, 155; investigates federal employees, 84–85, 86; investigates Middle-of-the-Road, 136; jails "Hollywood Ten," 84, 111, 118; lists "communist-front" associations, 116–117, 127, 129, 137; media involvement with, 118; *(see also* Dies Committee)
Houston, Sam, 61

Hudson, Wilson, 96
Hulen, Reverend Chester, 58
Hunter, Kim, 116, 124
Huntington Library, 54

I
Ickes, Harold, 63, 143
Independent Citizens Committee of the Arts, Sciences and Professions, 136
INE (Information and Education) center, 73
INS (Immigration and Naturalization Service), 179
integration, 7, 27, 90
Internal Security Act *(see* McCarran Internal Security Act)
International Workers of the World, 7
Iron Head, 43
It's News to Me, 105, 120
Ives, Burl, 80
Ivins, Molly, ix, xv

J
Jackson, Aunt Molly, 47
Jaffe, Henry, 144
James Madison First Amendment Award, 174
Jefferson, Thomas, 28, 177
Jefferson School of Social Science, 125, 136, 143
Jester, Beauford, 82-83
Joan of Arc, 88
John Henry Faulk Conference on the First Amendment, 174
"John Henry Faulk Merchandising Plan," 101
"John Henry Faulk Show, The," 98-104, 139-140, 150
"John Henry Faulk Weeks," 101
"Johnny's Front Porch," 80, 82
Johnson, James, 61
    Lady Bird, 108
    Laurence, 133-135, 138-140, 142, 147, 164, 181
    Lyndon B., 67, 106, 107-109, 157
Julian, Joe, 119
Julius Rosenwald Foundation, 59

Jury Returns, The, 166

K
Kafka, Franz, 120
Katy Flyer, 13
Kaye, Danny, 117
Kazan, Elia, 116
"Keep 'Em Smiling," 94
Keith, Richard, 121
Kellam, Jack, 13, 24, 31, 33, 37, 45-46, 47
    Mrs., 24-25
Kellogg's Pet Milk Show, 134
Kennedy, John F., 164
Kenyon and Eckhardt, 144
KFRC Radio, 153
Kilgallen, Dorothy, 105
Kitchens, Lester, 14, 30
Klein, Harvey, 122
Knots Landing, 180
KNOW Radio, 94, 159
Koock, Mary Faulk, 7, 8, 23, 24, 26, 28, 90 *(see also* Faulk, Mary)
Korea, 178
Kraft Foods, 133
KTBC Radio, 78, 107
KTBC TV, 108
Ku Klux Klan, 8

L
labor rights, 112
labor strikes, 50, 67, 68, 85
labor unions, 68, 71, 74, 85
La Follette, Robert F., 47
Lake Austin, 160
Lally, Howard, 139
Lampell, Millard, 81, 163
Landau, Eli, 147
Lardner, Ring, 118
"Lark, The," 88
Lawrence, D. H., 181
Lawson, John Howard, 118
Leadbelly, 43, 47
League for Industrial Democracy, 48
Lear, Norman, 166
Leave It To the Girls, 105
Ledbetter, Huddie "Leadbelly," 47

Leder, Robert, 153
Lee, Anna, 120
left-wing, 81, 82, 90, 180
Lennen & Mitchell, 134
Leonard, Mark, 173
Leopard's Spots, The, 7
Lerner, Harry, 73
Lester, Mariel, 47
Let's Take Sides, 106
Libby's Canned Vegetables, 138
Libby's Frozen Foods, 138
libraries, 87, 88, 165, 181
Library of Congress, 43, 59
Lie, Trygve, 143
"Life and Literature of the South-
    west," 42
Limbaugh, Rush, 182
Live Oak County, Texas, 42, 44
Loeb, Phil, 134, 145
Lomax, Alan, 43, 47, 53, 56, 57, 58,
    59, 60, 61, 78–79, 80, 158–159
    Elizabeth, 80
    John, 43, 48
LOOK magazine, 162–163
Los Angeles Superior Court, 119
Louis, Joe, 143
Loy, Myrna, 147
loyalty oath, 85, 87, 100, 112, 137,
    138
Lubbock, Texas, 66

M
MacArthur, Douglas, 99
McCarran Internal Security Act, 86
McCarthy, Joseph P., xviii, 76, 86,
    87–88, 93, 100, 108, 110, 113,
    118, 145, 182
McCullough, Hester, 119
MacElhone, Eloise, 105
McGinnis, John H., 42
McKeller, Elsie, 18–19
McNamara, Frank, 114–115
McNeil, Brownie, 45, 51–52
McNellis, Maggie, 105
McWilliams, Michael, 180
Madison, James, xviii, 28, 172, 174
Madison Square Garden, 91
Madonna, 181
"Maggie Haye's Show," 106

Magness, Eloise, 95
Malone, Ted, 105
Mandingo, 47
Manhattan, 79
"Man of La Mancha, The," 172
Manlove, Mrs. Robert, 37–38
    Robert, 37-38
Manoff, Arnold, 145
Manson, Alan, 162
Marcantonio, Vito, 63
Marre, Albert, 172
Mars, Inc., 180
Marshall, Rex, 128
Martin, Marty, 173
Martinson, Paul, 163, 164
Mart, Texas, 83
Maverick, Maury, 63, 67
May Day Parade, 136, 143
Mayehoff, Eddie, 142
Mayne, Clyde, 11
Media Research Center, 180
Merchant Marines, 64, 65–66, 71
Methodist Federation for Social
    Action, 84
Mid-Century Conference for Peace,
    137
Middle-of-the-Road slate, 131–132,
    135, 138, 141, 143–147
Miller, Tom, 15, 34
Milton, Paul, 115, 135
Miner, Ashford, 4, 13, 24
    Lee, 102
    Martha "Mattie" *(see* Faulk,
        Martha "Mattie")
    Medora Murrell Jones, 4
minimum wage, 90
"Minnesota" Dairy Princess, 102
Missouri, Kansas, and Texas rail-
    road, 13
Mitchell, Fred, 157
Mix, Tom, 34
monopolies, 3
Montgomery, Bob, 48
Montopolis Bridge, 15
Moody, Dan, 35
Moon Car Agency, 11
Mooney, Tom, 7
Moore, Garry, 120, 132, 161

Mormon Church, 179
Morning Show, The, 106
Mossner, Ernest, 165
Mostel, Zero, 145
Mostellar, Annie Lee, 18
    Frank, 18
    Old Man, 102
Mostellar family, 18, 93
Motion Picture Alliance for the
    Preservation of Ideals, 112
Muir, Jean, 86
Murray, Tom, 139-140
Murrow, Edward R., 87, 103, 107,
    113, 127, 141, 147–148
Mussolini, Benito, 49

N
Nagel, Conrad, 128
Name's The Same, The, 106, 134
Nation, The, 118, 181
National Association for the
    Advancement of Colored
    People, 62
National Association of Retail
    Grocers, 133, 135
National Civil Rights Legislative
    Conference, 129
National Committee for the Defense
    of Political Prisoners, 67
National Council of the Arts,
    Sciences, and Professions, 125
National General, 167
National Negro Congress, 67, 114
National Prayer Breakfast, 180
National Press Club, 106, 139, 174
National Public Radio, 167
National Wage Earner, 114
Navarro Refining Company, 5
Navasky, Victor, 116
NBC, 106, 117
NBC Radio, 106, 110
NBC TV, 104
New Deal, 40, 47, 48, 51, 71, 74, 112
"New North Jersey Datebook," 94
New Republic, The, 181
Newspaper Guild, 80
New York Herald-Tribune, 125
New York Police Department, 141
New York Supreme Court, 119, 164,

166
New York Times, The, 119, 126, 162,
    166
New York World-Telegram & Sun,
    118–119
Nielson ratings, 110
Nightline, 180
Nixon, Richard, 84, 106, 178
Nizer, Louis, 141–142, 145, 147,
    154, 155, 160, 166, 167
North Haledon, New Jersey, 93
Norton, Cliff, 144
nuclear weapons, 89, 90, 99, 112
Nyack, New York, 84

O
Oak Hill, 15, 40-41
O'Daniel, W. Lee (Pappy), 67, 74
Of Mice and Men, 181
Old Jules, 109
Old Knick Music Hall, 142
Olsen, Culbert, 8
Onondaga County American
    Legion, 140–141
Orson Bean Show, The, 144
Orum, Anthony M., 75
O'Shea, Daniel T., 113
Ostroff, Anthony, 72, 91
Overton family, 17
Owens, William A., 60

P
Paap, Joseph, viii
Paar, Jack, 106, 131
Paisano Ranch, 54
Parks, Larry, 116
Paterson, New Jersey, 91
"Pat the Rancher," 91–92
Patrick, Dennis, 138
Patterson, Elizabeth, 180–181
    J. M., 6
Paul, Lonnie, 24–25
Pear Orchard Methodist Church, 59
"Pear Orchard Texas," 159, 172–174
Pearson, Drew, 110
Pegler, Westbrook, 141, 145
People for the American Way, 181
People's Artists agency, 81
People's Drama, 145

People's Songs, 81, 127–128, 136, 143, 163, 181
People's World, 161
Pepper, Claude, 63
Phillips, Nizer, Benjamin and Krim, 141
Pickford, Mary, 34
Pine, Philip, 121, 124
Plato, 16, 165
"Plumber's" (Special Investigations) Unit, 178
Pollack, Nancy, 124
poll tax, 62, 63, 90, 114
Pope Pious XI, 49
Poppleton, Cliff, 141
Prager, Stanley, 129
Preparedness Day Parade, 7
Priest, George, 32
Progressive Citizens of America, 127, 135–136, 163
Progressive Party, 47, 84, 89
Prohibition, 8, 31
"pro-life" organizations, 182
Pryor, Cactus, 102, 107, 108, 167
PULSE rating, 104, 148
Pyburn, Brother, 26

Q
Quakers, 99
Quayle, Dan, 179
Queen Plaza, 51

R
racism, 7, 27, 37, 48, 62–64, 69
Rainey, Homer P., 63, 74–77, 82–83
Randall, Tony, 122, 131
Randolph, John, 123, 129, 145, 162
Ranger, The, 47
Rankin, John, 85
Rayburn, Sam, 108, 156, 157
RCA Corporation, 117
Reagan, Ronald, 178-179
Red Channels, 86, 114, 119, 121, 122, 180
Red Scare, 76
Redwood City, California, 50
Reedy, George, 108
Reese, Reverend A. A., 44, 79
Reiner, Carl, 130

Republican Party, 100–101
Revere, Anne, 119
Reynolds, Quentin, 105, 141, 145
Riggs family, 21
right-wing, 112, 113, 115, 147
"Road Back (to self-clearance)," 115
Robertson, Pat, 181
Robeson, Paul, 181
Robinson, Earl, 136, 143
    Jackie, 114
Rockefeller, John D., 3
Rogers, Will, 103
Rollins, Fanny, 95, 173
Roosevelt, Eleanor, 64, 143, 147
    Franklin D., 33, 40, 67, 68, 70, 73, 74–75, 82, 84, 89, 93, 112, 143
Rosebud, Texas, 59
Rosenwald Fund, 63
Ross, Lanny, 149, 150
Royal Navy, 66
Rule, Janice, 131
Rusk Literary Society, 2
Russian War Relief, 114
Ryan, Clendenin, 110

S
Salinger, J. D., 181
San Antonio, Texas, 51–52, 56
Sandoz, Mari, 109
San Francisco, California, 7
Saturday Evening Post, The, 42
Saturday Evening Report, 106
Sayers, Joseph, 4
Saypol, Irving, 119
Schary, Dore, 147
Scherer, Rep., 130
Schlitz Playhouse of the Stars, 134
Schmidt, Godfrey, 115, 121, 125, 126, 144, 155
Scott, George C., 167
Scoundrel Time, 86
Screen Actors' Guild, 178
Screen Writer's Guild, 121
Security Oil Company, 5
Seeger, Pete, 80–81, 127–128, 129, 130, 136, 163
See It Now, 87, 113
Segall, Alex, 166
segregation, 27, 37, 62, 69, 73, 114

Sellers, Grover, 82-83
Sevareid, Eric, 174
Sex, 181
Shaffner, Franklin, 166
Shaw, George Bernard, 88
Shein, G. David, 88
Sherman, Max, 30
Sherman Anti-Trust Act, 3
Shivers, Allan, 105
Shor, Toots, 151
"Showtime for Henry Wallace," 135, 142
Sign, The, 117
Simpson, Buck, 92, 93
Sinatra, Frank, 143
Siringo, Charlie, 43
Skinner, Cornelia Otis, 103
Skinny's Theater, 34
Slate, Sam, 138, 139, 148, 150, 163
Slater, Bill, 105
Slaughterhouse Five, 181
Smith, Henry Nash, 54, 76
    J. L., 82-83
    John Lee, 67
    Lynne *(see* Faulk, Lynne)
    Tucker B., 47
Smolens, Jolly, 81
Snodgrass, Ed, 92, 102, 182
Social-Democratic Herald, The, 6
Social Problems Council, 47
Social Questions Bulletin, The, 84
Soffer, Helen, 162
Sondergaard, Gale, 119
South Austin Methodist Episcopal Church, 15
Southern Association of Colleges and Secondary Schools, 76
Southern Conference for Human Welfare, 63-64, 127, 128, 136, 143
Southern Methodist University, 42
Southwestern University, 42
Spanish Civil War, 49
Spanish Loyalists, 49
Spanish Refugee Relief Campaign, 117
Spanish Relief Fund, 80
Spanish War Relief, 181

"Speaking of the People," 91-92
Spencer, Kenneth, 136
Sperber, A. M., 148
Spotlight, 122, 140
Stage for Action, 135
Standard Oil, 3, 5-6
STANDBY!, 146
Stansbury, Martha Faulk, 10, 24, 53
    (see also Faulk, Martha)
Stark, Dick, 144
State Department, 88
Steinman, Anne, 147
    Herb, 147
Stephens, Dr. David, 68-69, 70
Stettinius, Ed, 143
Steve Allen Show, The, 125
Stevenson, Adlai, 148, 182
    Coke, 71, 74, 83
Stone, I. F., 120-121
Strickland, D. F., 82
"Stud's Place," 103
Subversion Activities Control Board, 86
Sullivan, Ed, 144
    Elliott, 129, 130, 162
Susskind, David, 147, 161
    Evelyn, 147
Sutherland, Alice, 33
Swanson & Co., C. A., 134
Swanson & Sons, 133
Sweetish Hill Bakery, 11
Syracuse, New York, 133

T
Taft-Hartley Act, 85
Talley, John, 38, 45
Talleys, 39
Tavenner, Frank, 129-130
Taylor, Davidson, 79
"Ten Negro Sermons," 56
Tenney Commission, 117
Terkel, Studs, 103-104
Texas Broadcasting Corporation, 107
Texas Capitol, 2
Texas Cowboy, A, 43
Texas Folklore Society, 42, 43, 48, 59
Texas Legislature, 142
Texas Regulars, 75

Texas Senate Committee on Education, 76
Texas State Historical Association, 61
Thomas, Norman, 47–48
Thoreau, Henry David, 16, 28, 48, 100
Thornberry, Homer, 108, 156–157
Thurmond, Strom, 91, 110
Tinkle, Lon, 68, 74, 165
Todman, Jerry, 104
Tom Sawyer, 21
Town Lake, 15
Townsin, Effie Lou, 173
Travis County Courthouse, 37
Travis County, Texas, 3, 56
Trial, The, 120
Truesdale, Reverend, 101
Truman, Harry S., 84, 85, 86, 87, 89, 90, 99, 100, 108
Truman Doctrine, 89
Trumbo, Dalton, 118
TV, etc., 180
Twain, Mark, 54, 79, 88, 100, 103, 159, 181
24th Amendment, 63
Tyne, George, 129, 130

U
U.S.A., 75
U.S. Department of Justice, 125
U.S. International Information Agency, 88
Union Tank Line Company, 5
United Nations, 73, 90, 143
United States Supreme Court, 164
University Folk Festival Center, 60
University Interscholastic League, 48
University Light Opera Company, 52–53
University Methodist Church, 53
University of North Carolina, 143
University Press Club, 59
University of Texas, 2, 36, 40, 42, 47, 63, 72, 73, 74–77, 179
University of Texas at Austin General Libraries, 174
University of Texas at Austin's

Center for American History, 174
University of Texas Board of Regents, 74–77

V
Van Dyke, Dick, 106, 167
Van Horne, Harriet, 104
Van Rooten, Louis, 132
Vaquero of the Brush Country, A, 42
Variety, 105, 128, 129
Vern, Jack, 110
Veterans of the Abraham Lincoln Brigade, 117
Veterans Action Committee of Syracuse Supermarkets, 133
Veterans of Foreign Wars, 115
Vidal, Gore, 166
Vietnam War, 178
Volenburg, J. L., 134
Von Horne, Harriet, 141
voting age, 90

W
Wage Earners Committee, 114, 116
Waldorf Peace Conference, 125
"Walk a Mile," 106
Wallace, Henry, 84, 89, 90–91, 103, 135–136, 164
Walters, Francis, 129–130, 156–157
Ward, Carl, 138, 163
Wardlaw, Frank, 96, 165, 166
Washington Committee for Democratic Action, 67
Waters, Mrs., 172
Waterson, Winnie, 95
Waters-Pierce Oil Company, 3–4, 5–6
WBAI-FM, 158
WCBS Radio, 98, 104, 110, 138, 140
WCCO Radio, 153
Weaver, Mark, xv
  Ned, 121
Webb, Walter Prescott, 48, 54, 96–97
Webber, Palmer, 139
Webberville, Texas, 4
Well, Herbert, 52
"Wendy Barrow's Show," 106
We Take Your Word, 104
What's My Line, 106

Wheeling, West Virginia, 86
"whitelist," 113
Whitman, Walt, 48, 93, 100
Wilkes, Donald, 142
Willard, Dr. Rudolph, 53, 56–57, 60
Williams, Arleatha Overton, 17
  Jaston, 79
  John Herman, 17
  Robert, 121
Willis, Judge Tom, 171
Winn School, 12
Wirtz, Alvin, 71
Wobblies, 82
Wolfson, Martin, 129
Woltman, Frederick, 118–119
Women's Methodist Missionary
  Society, 25
Women's Quilting Circle, 16
Women's Republican Club, 86

Wood, Hally, 60 *(see also* Faulk,
  Hally)
Works Progress Administration, 51
World War I, 16
World War II, 64, 65–66
WOR Radio, 153
WOV Radio, 82, 91
WPA, 70
WPAT Radio, 91, 92, 94
Wren, Jack, 114
Wright, Martha, 148
Wukasch, Mr., 8

Y
Yarborough, Ralph, 157
YMCA, 143
You Are There, 105
Young Democrats League, 47
Youngstein, Max, 147